AUS:TIN

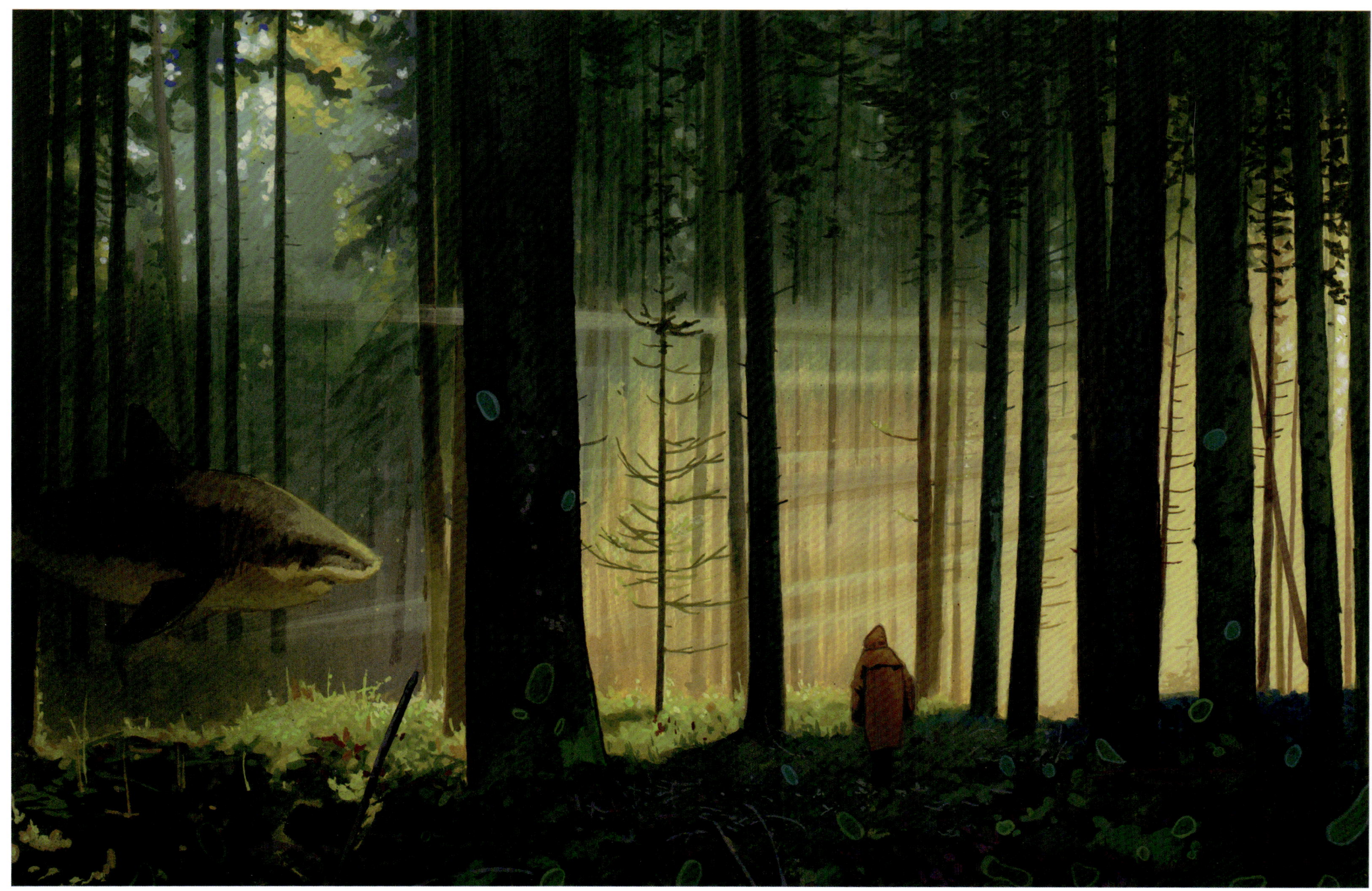

Greet The Morning (study) l 8" x 10" l gouache on paper l 2024

CONTRASTS THE ART OF CHRIS AUSTIN

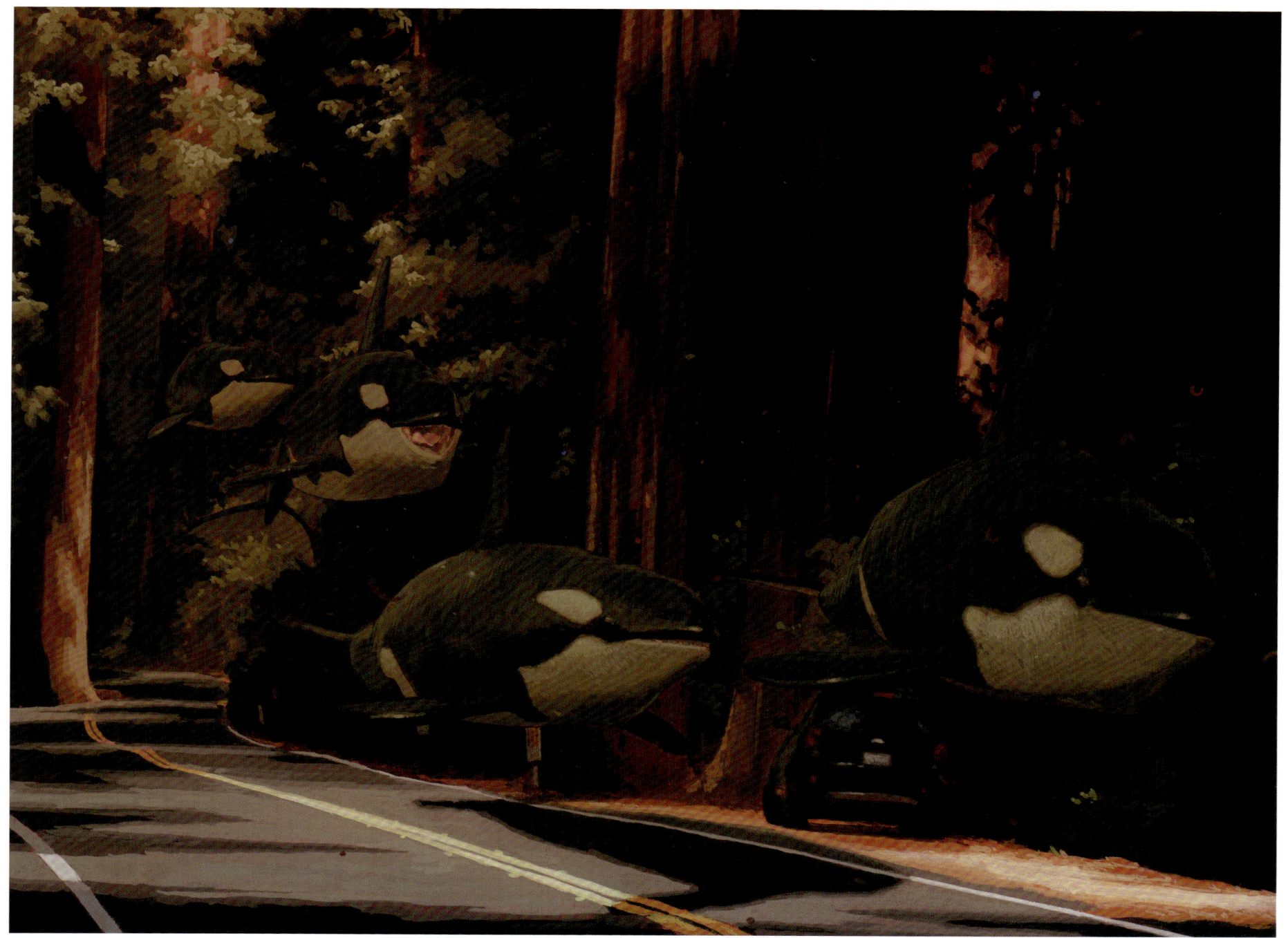

Highway 101 | 12" x 16" | gouche on wood | 2022

CONTENTS

I grew up in Kitchener, Ontario, a vibrant yet close-knit city just outside Toronto. From an early age, I was captivated by bold colours, pop culture, and the dynamic energy of Saturday morning cartoons and skateboarding culture. My artistic journey is self-taught, fuelled by a desire to push my limits. Watching older kids create in art class inspired me to challenge myself, constantly striving to elevate my own work. Alongside my love for art, I've always had an adventurous spirit, finding joy in exploring the outdoors and drawing inspiration from the world around me.

As I grew older, my connection to art deepened, evolving beyond simple inspiration from the things I loved. Art became a way to express the contrasts and dualities I experienced, both in the world and within myself. While pop culture and skateboarding fuelled my rebellious, energetic side, my time spent outdoors brought me a sense of calm and reflection. This balance between chaos and peace shaped the way I approach creativity. Every piece I create is a reflection of that journey—a blend of vibrant, playful elements, juxtaposed with moments of introspection.

Though I didn't follow a formal path in art education, I thrived on self-discovery and experimentation, always pushing boundaries and learning from my own experiences. My work is both personal and exploratory, representing not just what I see in the world, but how I interpret the tension and harmony between conflicting influences. Art, for me, is more than just expression—it's a way of navigating the complexity of life.

Growing up, I often found myself turning to my friends for support rather than my family. My friends became my anchor, providing a sense of understanding and acceptance that I didn't always find at home. They were the ones who fueled my creative energy, encouraged my wild ideas, and stood by me during difficult times. In many ways, they became my chosen family, shaping not only my art but the person I grew to be. Their influence runs deep in my work, where themes of connection, trust, and loyalty often emerge.

This reliance on my friends helped me build a sense of community and belonging, and it continues to inspire how I approach collaboration and creativity. In my art, I often explore the dynamics of friendship, using symbols and contrasting imagery to represent the ways my friends helped me navigate life's challenges, providing guidance when I needed it most.

One person in particular, Samara Lovell, played a pivotal role in shaping me into who I am today. Her presence in my life was transformative—she challenged me to think deeper, to question my assumptions, and to embrace the parts of myself that I once kept hidden. Samara wasn't just a friend; she became a mentor, pushing me creatively and personally. Her influence is evident in much of my work, where themes of growth, self-discovery, and resilience often surface. Samara taught me to embrace both the light and dark aspects of life, encouraging me to channel everything I felt into my art, which gave me the freedom to express who I truly am.

I dedicate this book to you Samara.

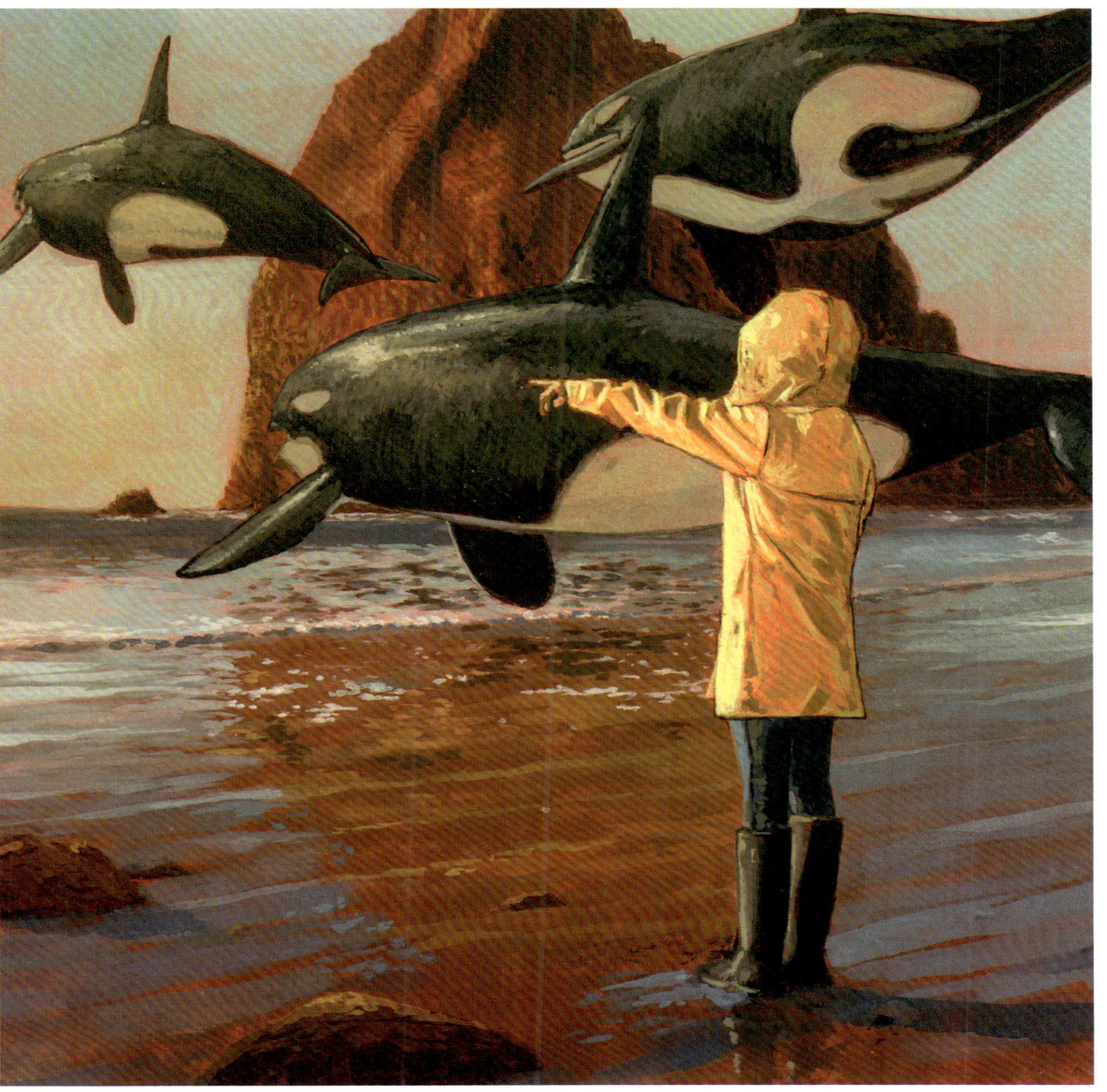

There's so many times I've come back to writing this. Not because it's hard, it's easy, and that's the problem. I could go on and on about Chris' drive, passion, talent and my undefinable love for him. How do I condense all of the thoughts and feelings about one of the most important people in my life, into a few paragraphs? How do I articulate the love and admiration I and others feel for him in such a short space? It seems impossible. But I will try.

You know how when you're a kid, every class has that one kid who's good at sports? One who gets straight A's? The class clown? The one who's good at art? That was Chris, the one who was good at art.

I met him when I moved to a new school in 4th grade, and immediately was drawn to him. It seems like this was who he was destined to be from the beginning, an artist. Now that's not to say he had it easy, I would say his talent was the only thing that was easy in his life and a reliable constant—his safe space, amidst a hidden internal chaos.

Some of my favorite memories with him are when we were struggling through life together. Laughing at our suffering. Dreaming about a time when we could pay our bills and have jobs we loved. Not realizing that the time would eventually come and we would be filled with nostalgia for our past together, when things seemed simpler.

Chris' path to being a full time artist seemed inevitable to me, it wasn't an if, but when. For him, it seemed like a pipe dream. He was used to obstacles and this didn't seem any different, why would it be?

His last full time job before he began to sell his paintings seriously was at a bread factory in our hometown. We were roommates at the time, I rented an old house with my partner and Chris was living in the cramped upstairs spare bedroom.

I remember falling asleep on the couch watching TV as Chris left for his overnight shifts and then being woken up by him walking through the front door. We would laugh about something he messed up that night at work and then he would head up to his room to start his second shift, as an artist.

On garbage day we would scour the neighborhood for "wood trash" that he could break apart and paint his next piece on, laughing hysterically as we dragged home a wagon filled with other people's junk. This was the routine for a while, until I finally convinced him to do an art show. And I use the term "art show" loosely. It was put on at a vegan cafe that I worked at downtown. When the cafe's doors closed for the day, it turned into a mini gallery at night to share his work. His paintings hung strategically above the tables and chairs, hoping daytime patrons would also get a glimpse of his work.

And that's all it took.

All of the people who had seen Chris' talent throughout the years showed up to support him along with new people. Instagram was just making its way in popularity, and it was an exciting new tool for artists to share their work. He started to consistently post, his sales began to increase and the rest is history. A world outside of our hometown was exposed to his art, finally.

When you meet Chris, there is immediately "something" about him. You feel it as soon as he enters a room. Now it doesn't help that he's 6'5" and towers over everyone, but he has this presence. Like when you meet a performer who has charisma, but with Chris it's different. There's this unseen depth that you can feel, but just can't reach. I think his art allows others to reach that piece of him.

This isn't to say his art isn't striking in beauty and his talent unmatched. But I truly believe it's him. I may be biased—let's be honest—I am. But even so, he's in his art. His life, his struggles, his pain, his happiness, him.

And whether they realize it or not, others feel that and are drawn to his work time and time again.

Stepping into Chris Austin's world for the first time can be a disorienting experience, as you find yourself in territory that is at once both familiar and strange. Paintings of distinct and recognizable environments provide the setting for unusual events to unfold, encouraging the viewer to suspend preconceptions. The works invite us to consider how times of flux may transform places we feel we know well into potent sites for the unknowable and unexpected. The appearance of an anonymous observer in multiple works, most often a child in a yellow rain slicker with the hood up, affords us the opportunity to place ourselves within the scene, a further provocation to interrogate and assess what we see.

A beautifully rendered west coast forest, distinguishable by its giant redwoods and majestic firs, is recontextualized by the Orca floating through it. A street in New York City where pedestrians negotiate the streets with distinctive yellow taxis is subjected to a narrative shift via the looming presence of a great white shark. These colossal beasts, unmoored and luxated, shift our perspective and force us to ask new questions about places for which we thought we already had all the answers.

Depictions of manatee in a snowy clearing or turtles ascending above a mountain peak find real-world analogues in elevated, inland mountain towns experiencing the impacts of hurricanes, or in large swathes of urban Los Angeles engulfed by the flames of a wildfire. We don't expect these things to happen in those places, yet increasingly they do. In some of the works, reference to those actual events is more overt, as non-human subjects encounter forests on fire or city streets filled with riot police.

Chris' body of work explores a rapid shortening of the distance between humanity and the wild environment, both physically and through metaphor. In **Long Winter's Night** (p.166-167) a family of polar bears walks down a frozen city street, something which is becoming increasingly common. A combination of habitat encroachment by humans and the bears expanding their range in search of food due to depleted resources creates the conditions for increased confrontations. As the culminating effect of societal choices increasingly manifest identifiable and devastating consequences we are faced with a more philosophical confrontation.

We are at a point in our societal journey at which the power and influence required to shift focus from a desire for profit at all costs to a project which seeks to create an equitable and livable world seems entirely captured by people who don't share a willingness to do so. With each passing destructive event hope fades that such devastation will lead to an urgently required awakening. As an artist, Chris seeks to provoke a re-evaluation of our relationship with the natural world we have inherited and our stewardship of it.

Chris has described the ocean animals in his work as being representatives of moments of introspection and deeper understanding amid chaos. With this in mind, I see them as a punctuation mark, instructing me to pause and reflect on what he is trying to communicate. Rather than a critique or indictment of how things are, they invite all of us to contemplate what we see with our own eyes and assess if it feels logical or inevitable.

How much longer will we continue to refuse to learn the lessons that would lead us toward a better future? For how long will we unthinkingly move forward as though there is no alternative? Will there come a time where we can no longer ignore the shark gliding through an inferno?

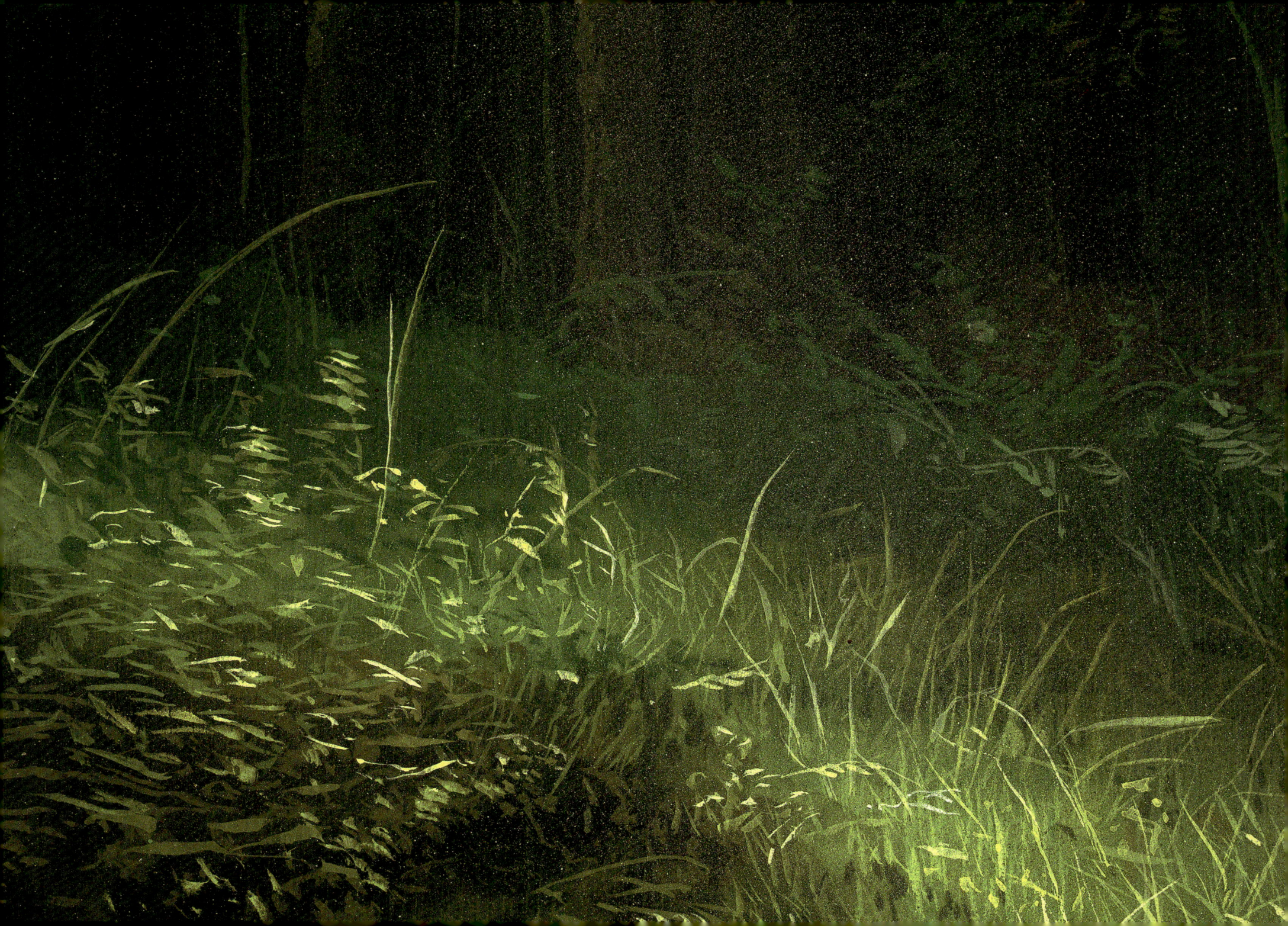

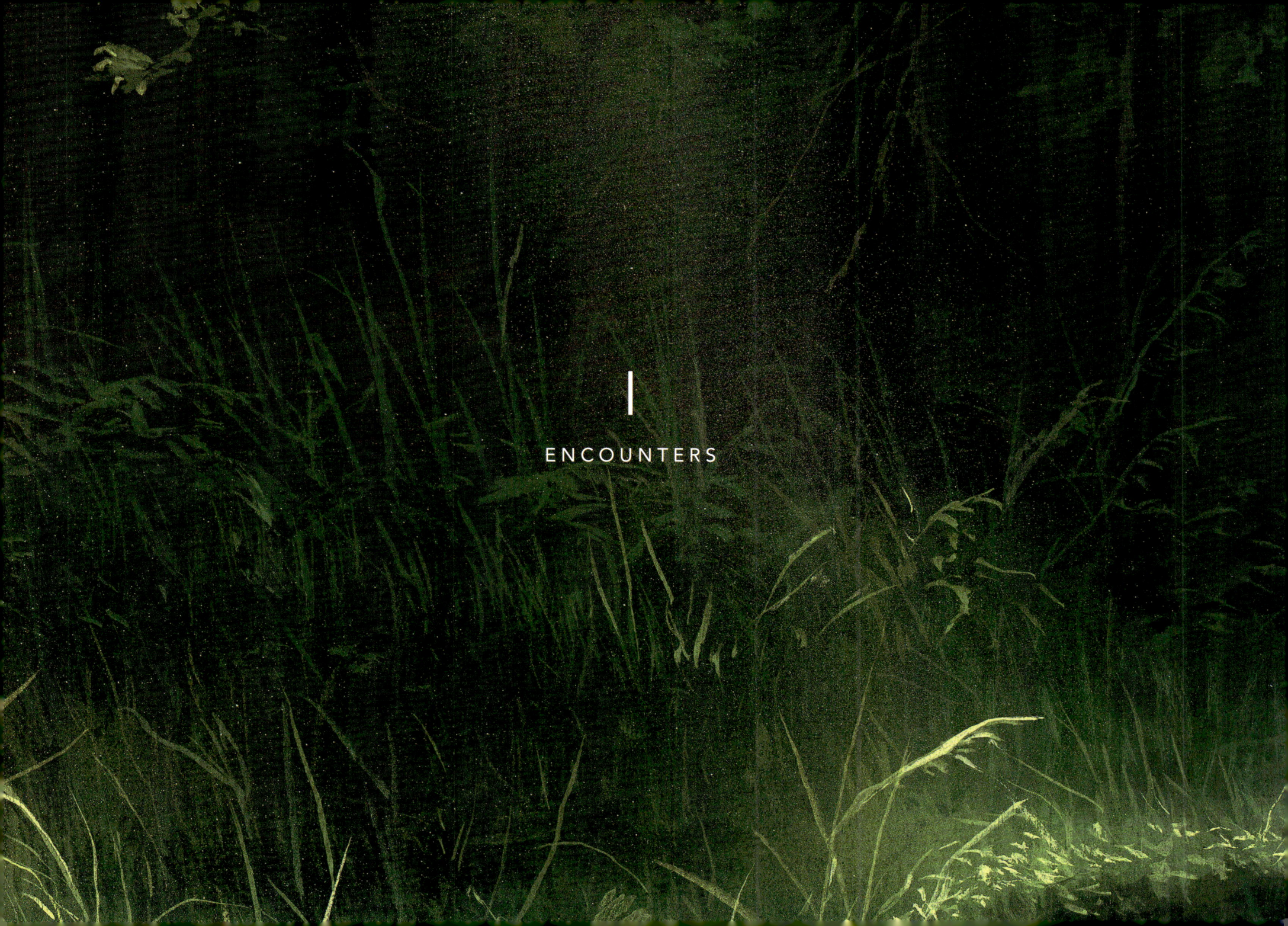

I

ENCOUNTERS

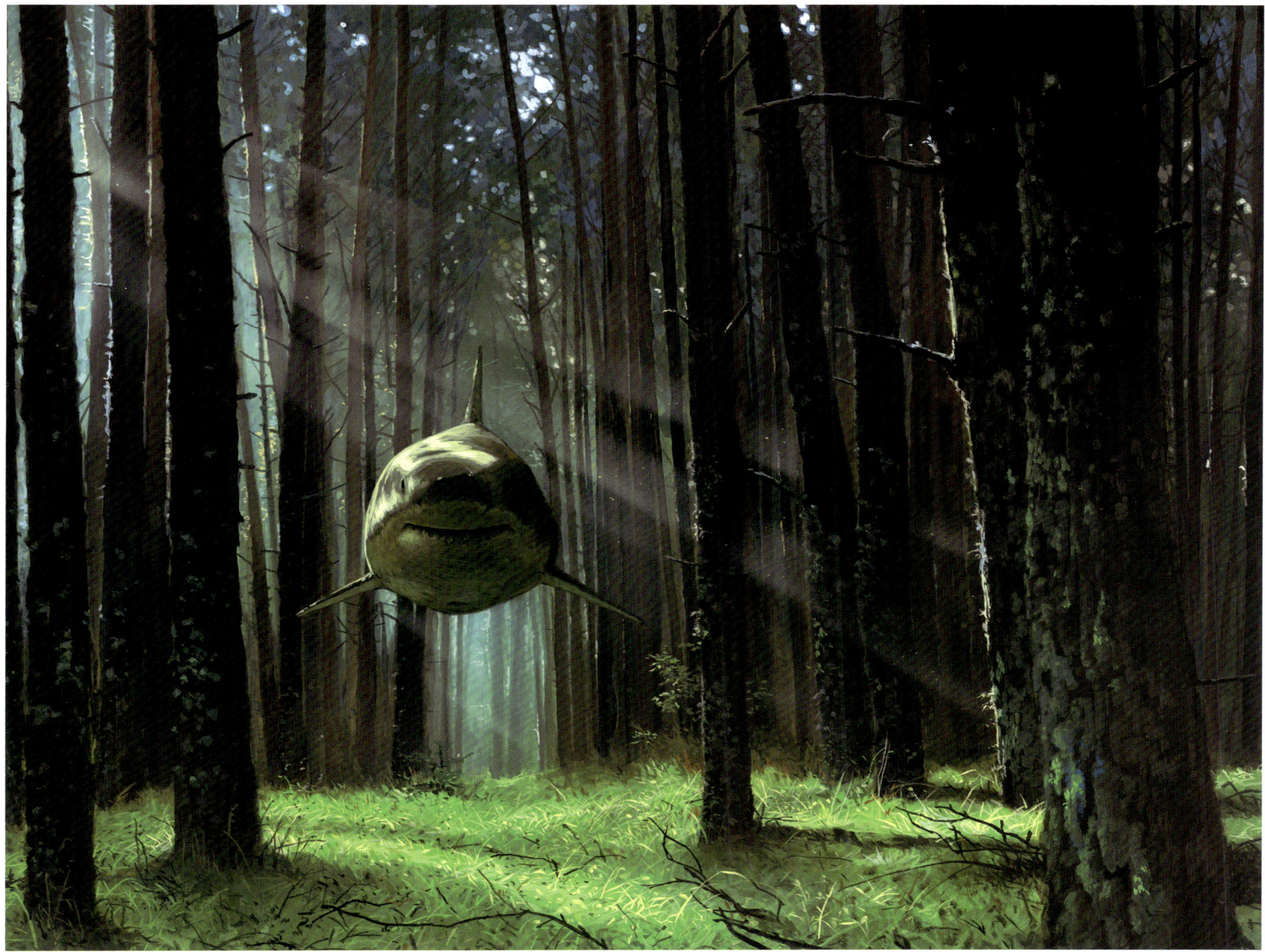

Always Searching For Your Ghost | 16" x 12" | gouache on wood | 2019

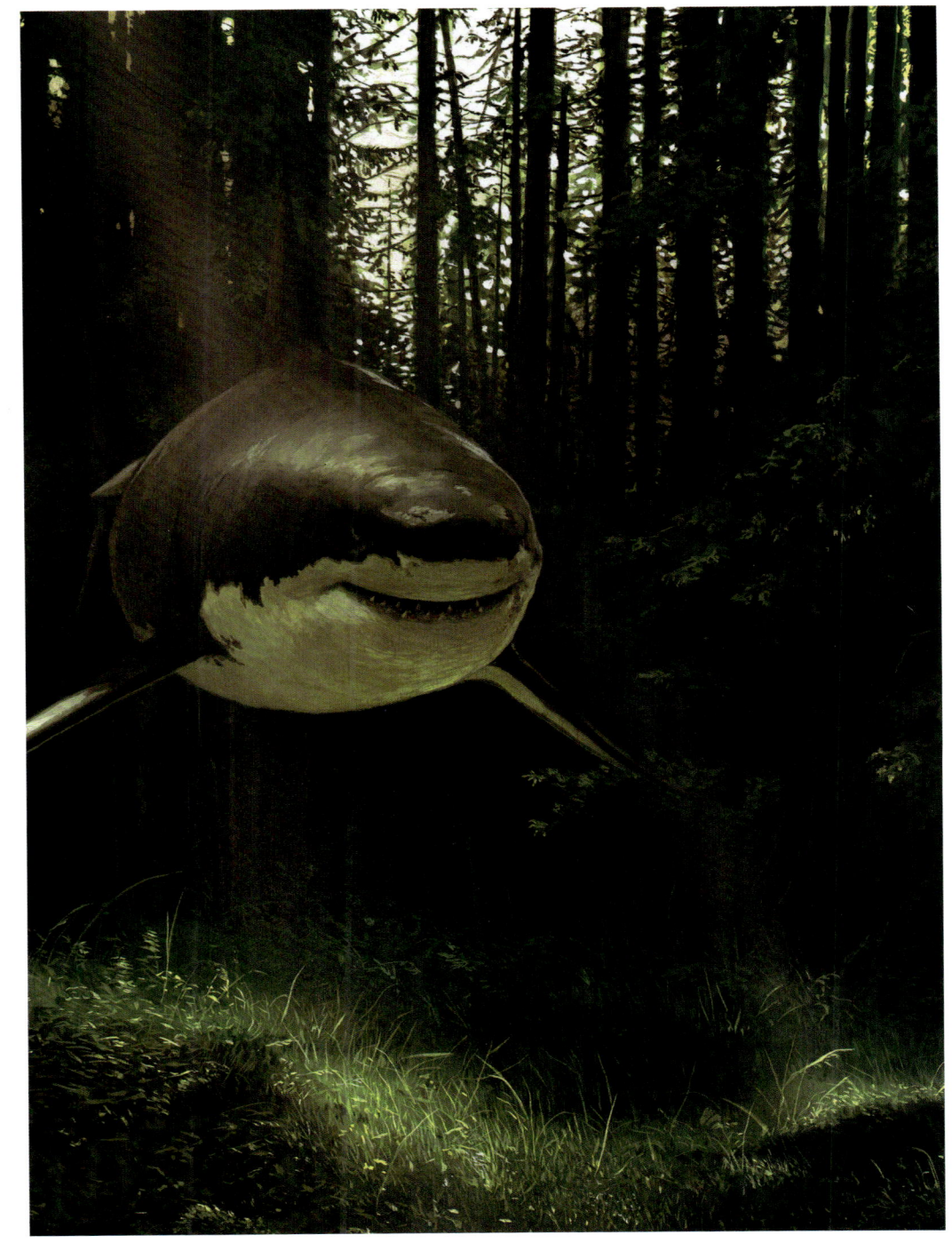

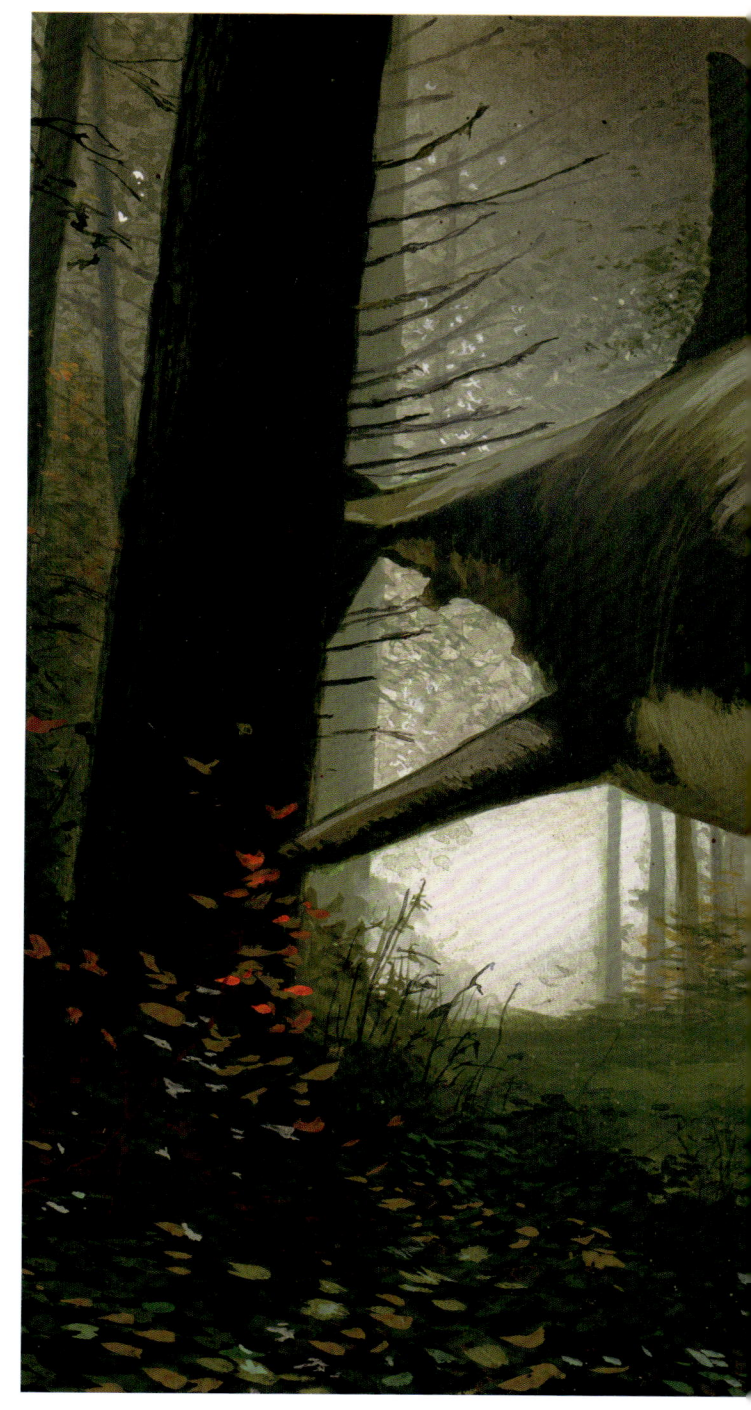

A Joy Made Double | 8″ x 17″ | gouache on wood | 2020

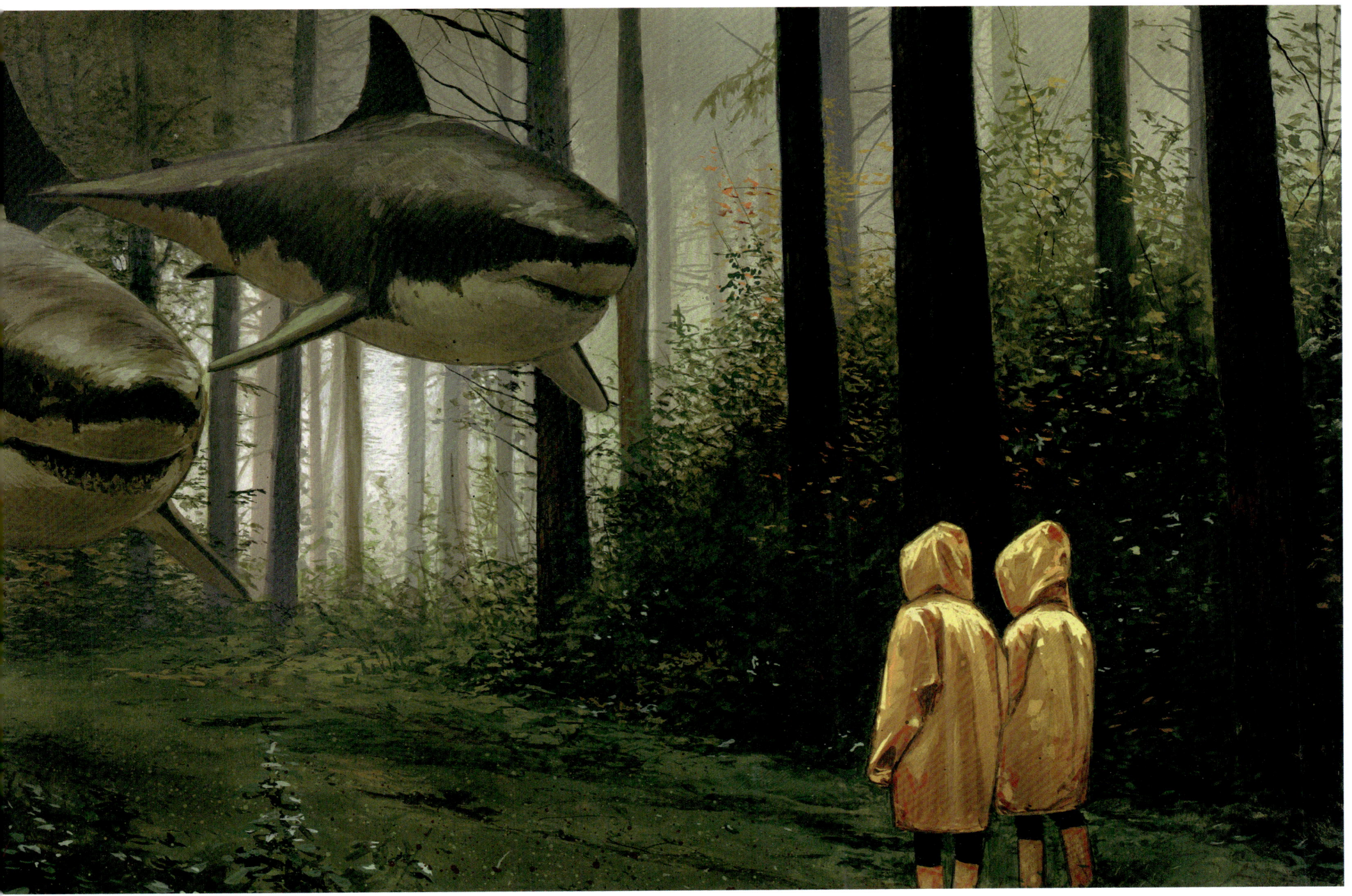

Tangled In My Heart | 15" x 11" | gouache on paper mounted to wood | 2023

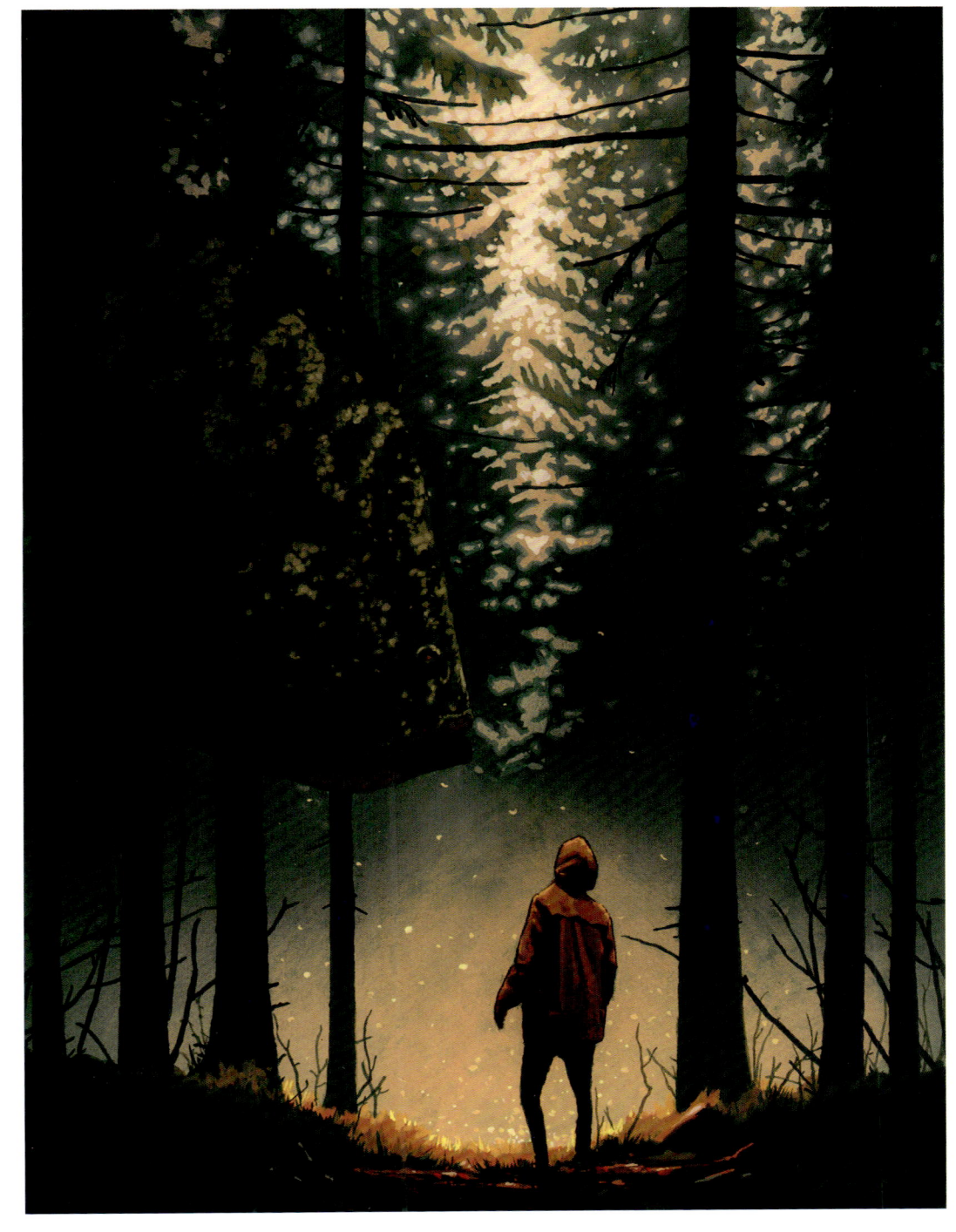

The imagery is both surreal and intimate,
where nature becomes unnatural, challenging
the viewer to question the boundaries between
instinct and reason, the familiar and the
unknown. The creatures I depict are more than
mere animals; they are manifestations of our
internal struggles, triumphs, and moments of
enlightenment. By merging different worlds
and environments, I hope to inspire others to
face their own fears and discover that often,
the things we fear the most are the things we
should fear the least.

It's You I'm Dreaming Of | 18" x 18" | gouche on wood | 2022

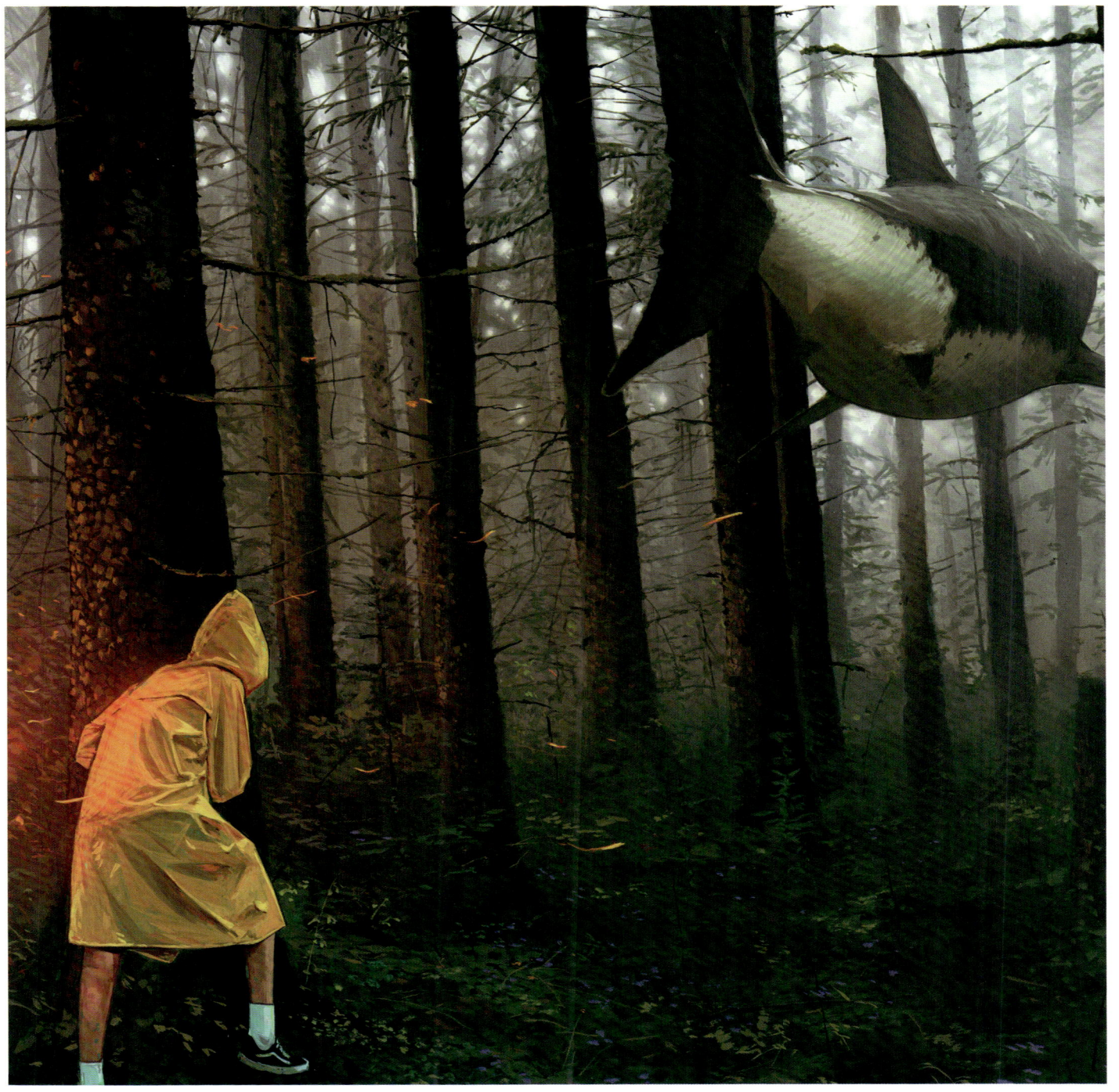

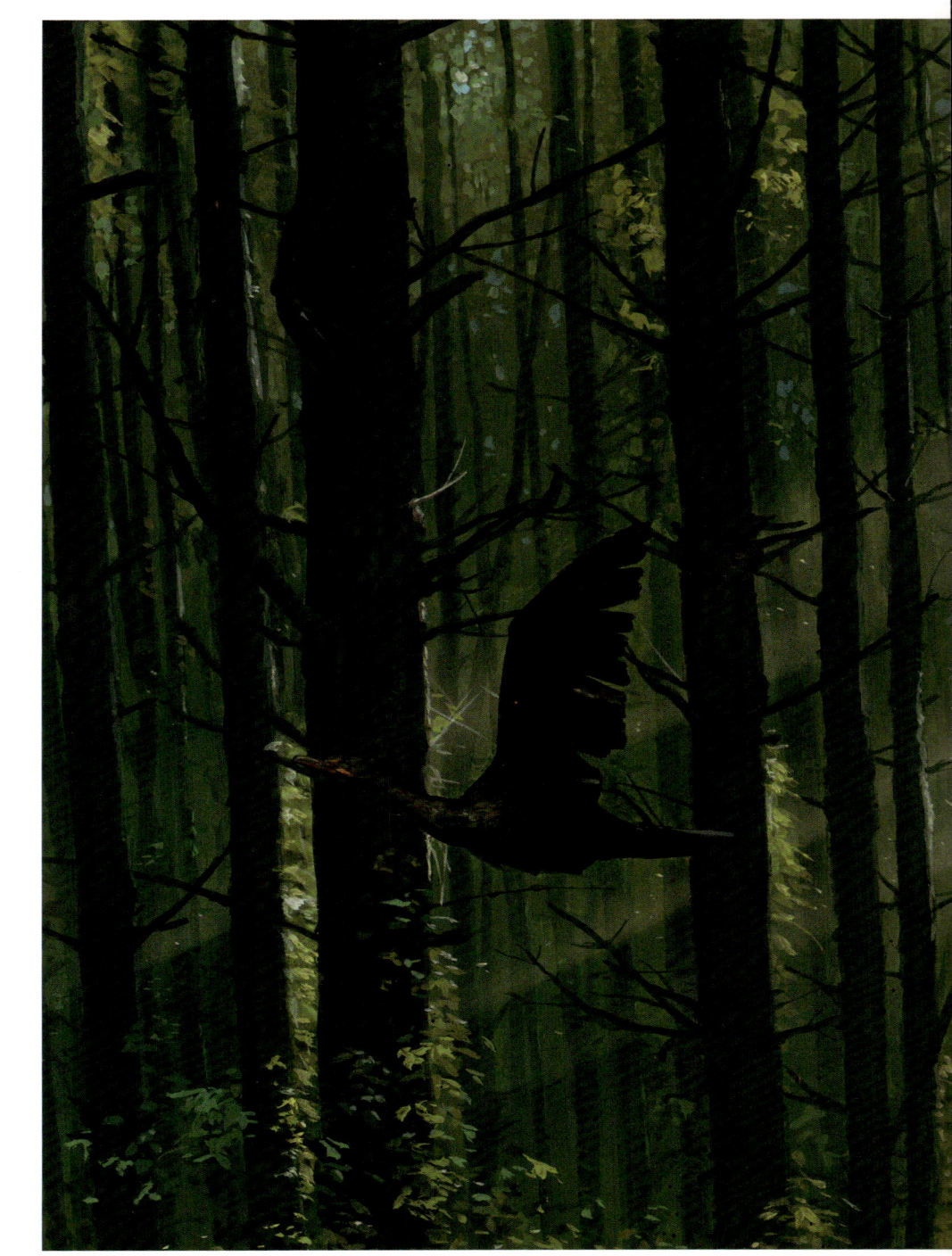

Back To The Other Place Where I Cannot Go | 10" x 20" | gouache on wood | 2021

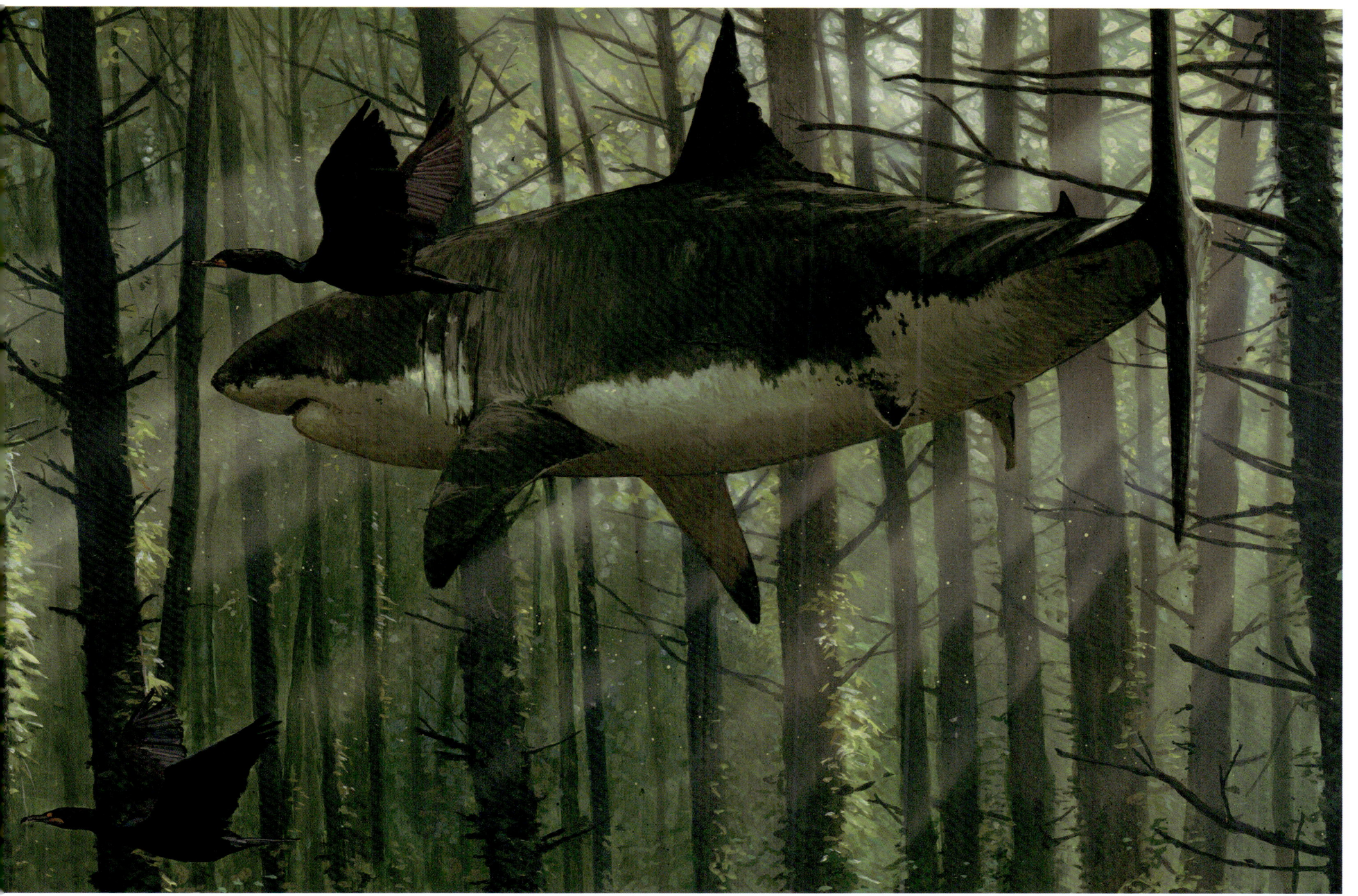

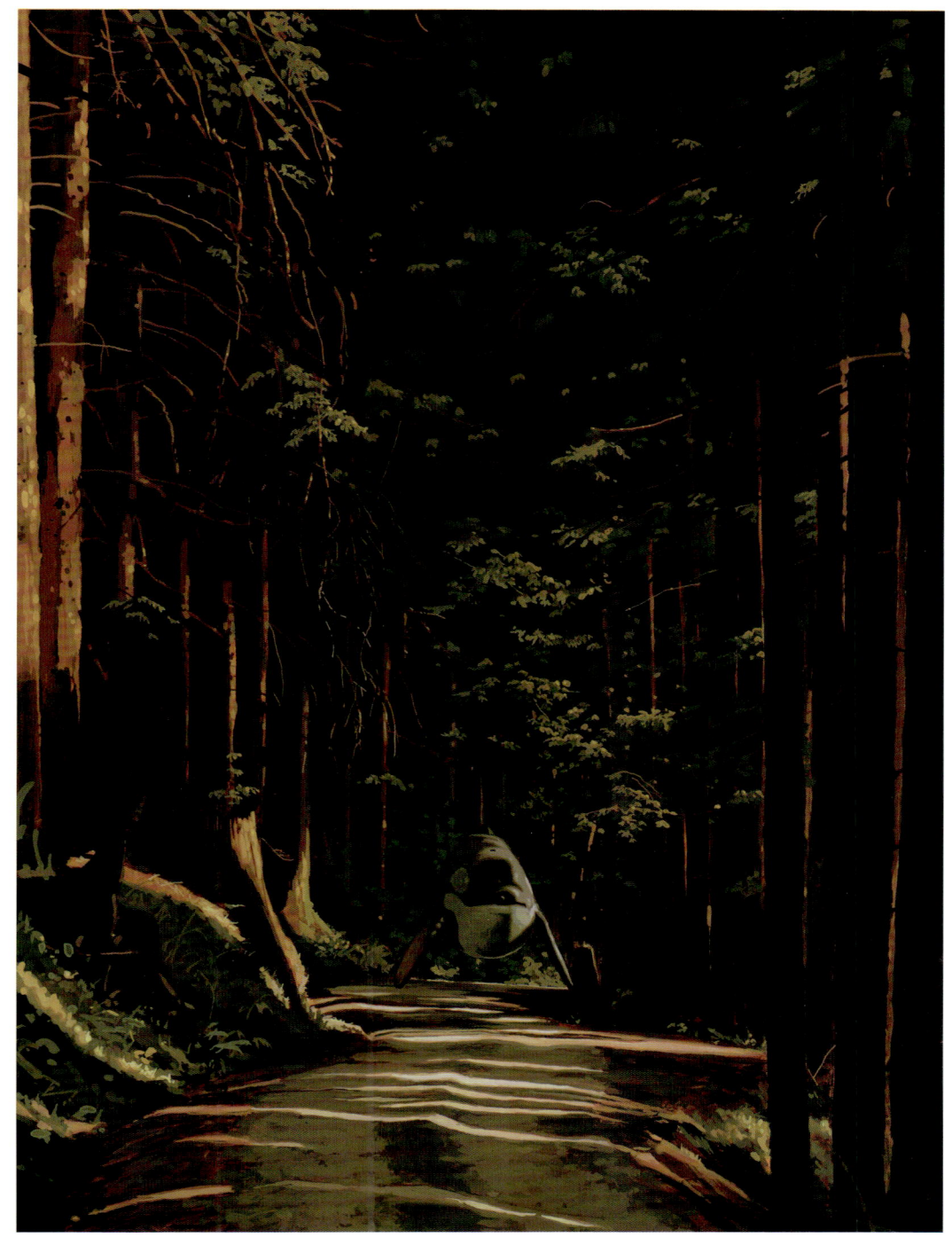

My artwork serves as a visual metaphor for my internal struggles, where the chaotic mingling of wildlife from different ecosystems mirrors the disjointed path of my upbringing. Each piece I create seems to embody a moment from my life—moments when I was in environments that didn't suit me, among influences that didn't align with my true self, yet somehow managing to find escape or guidance.

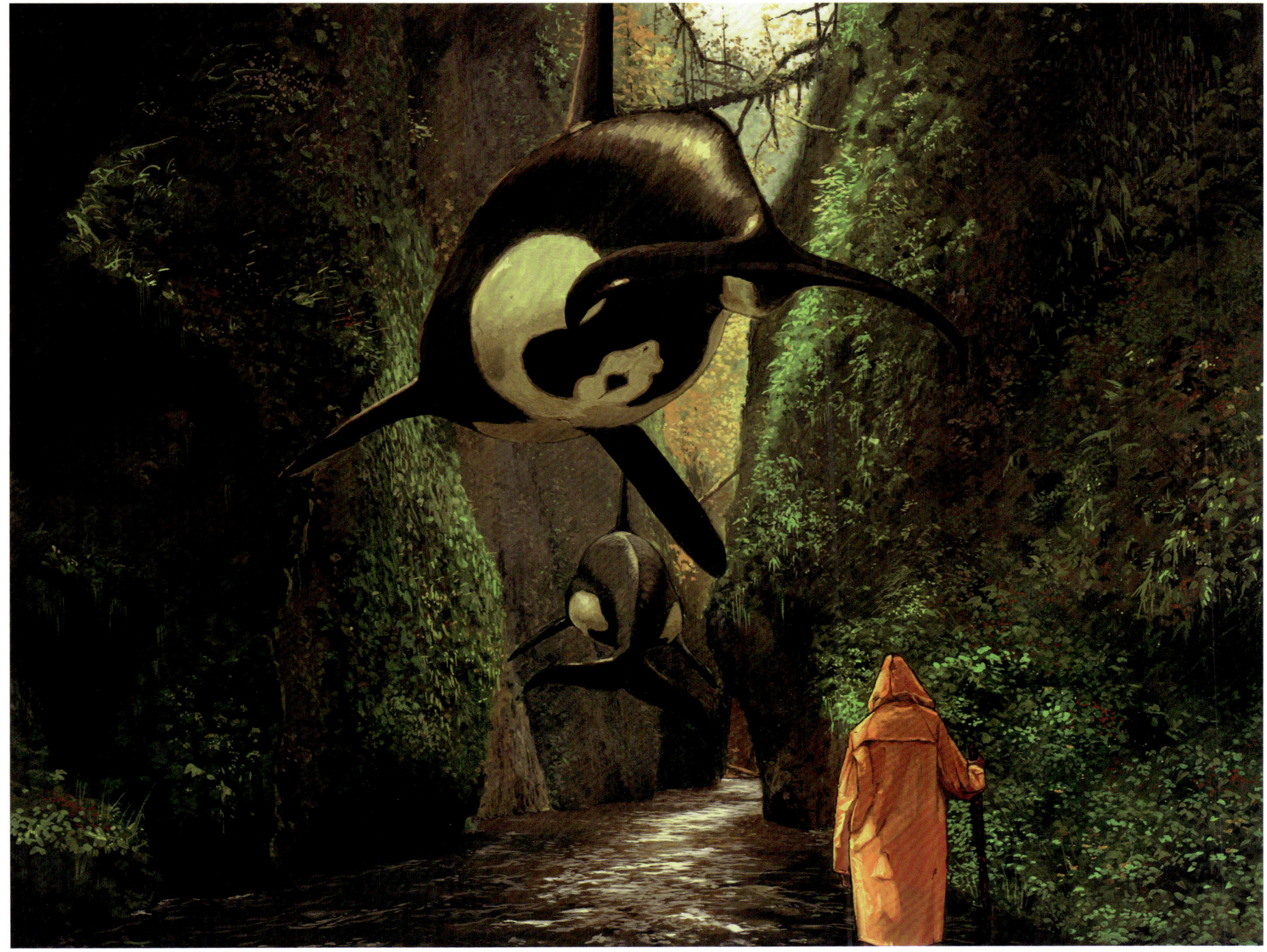

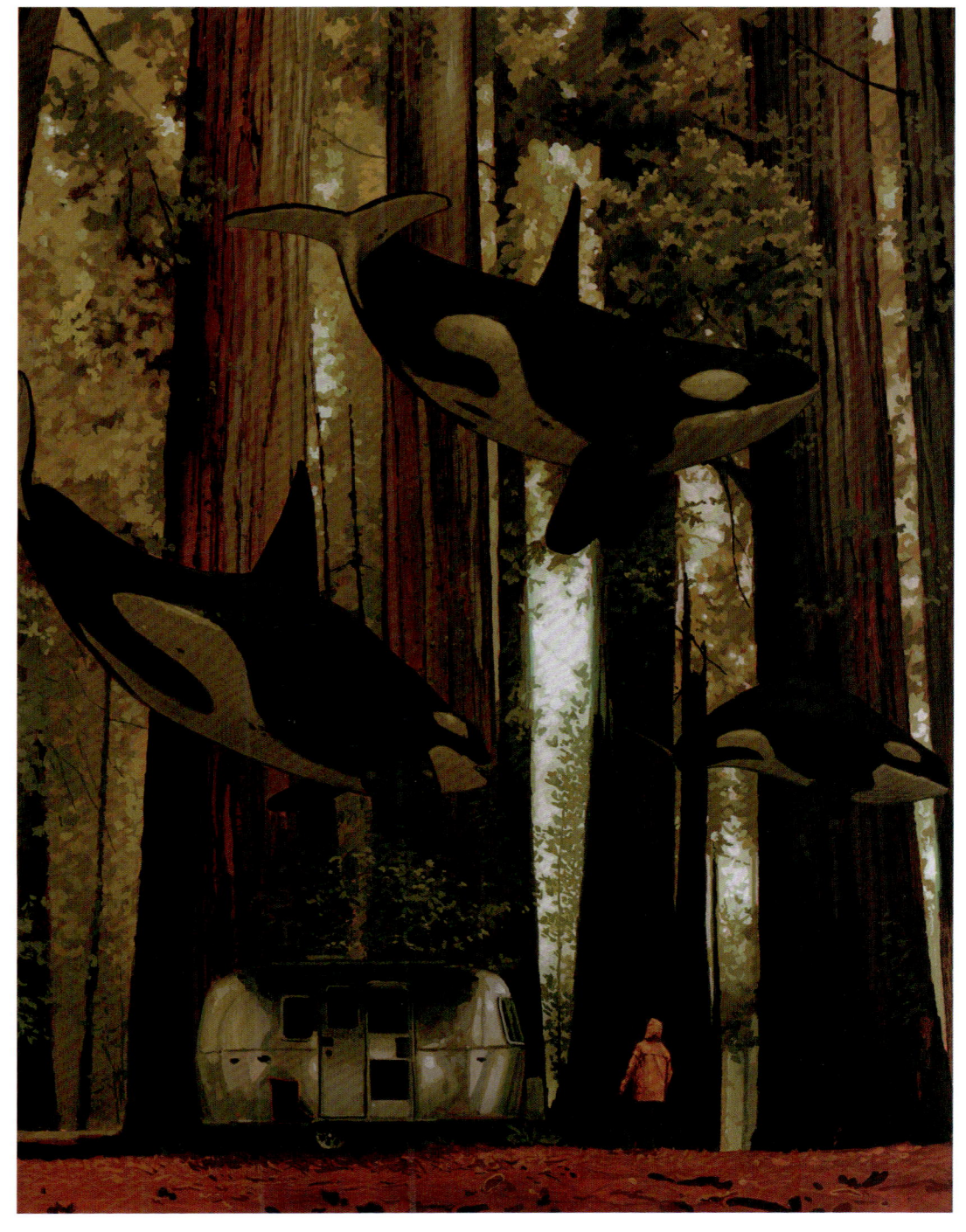

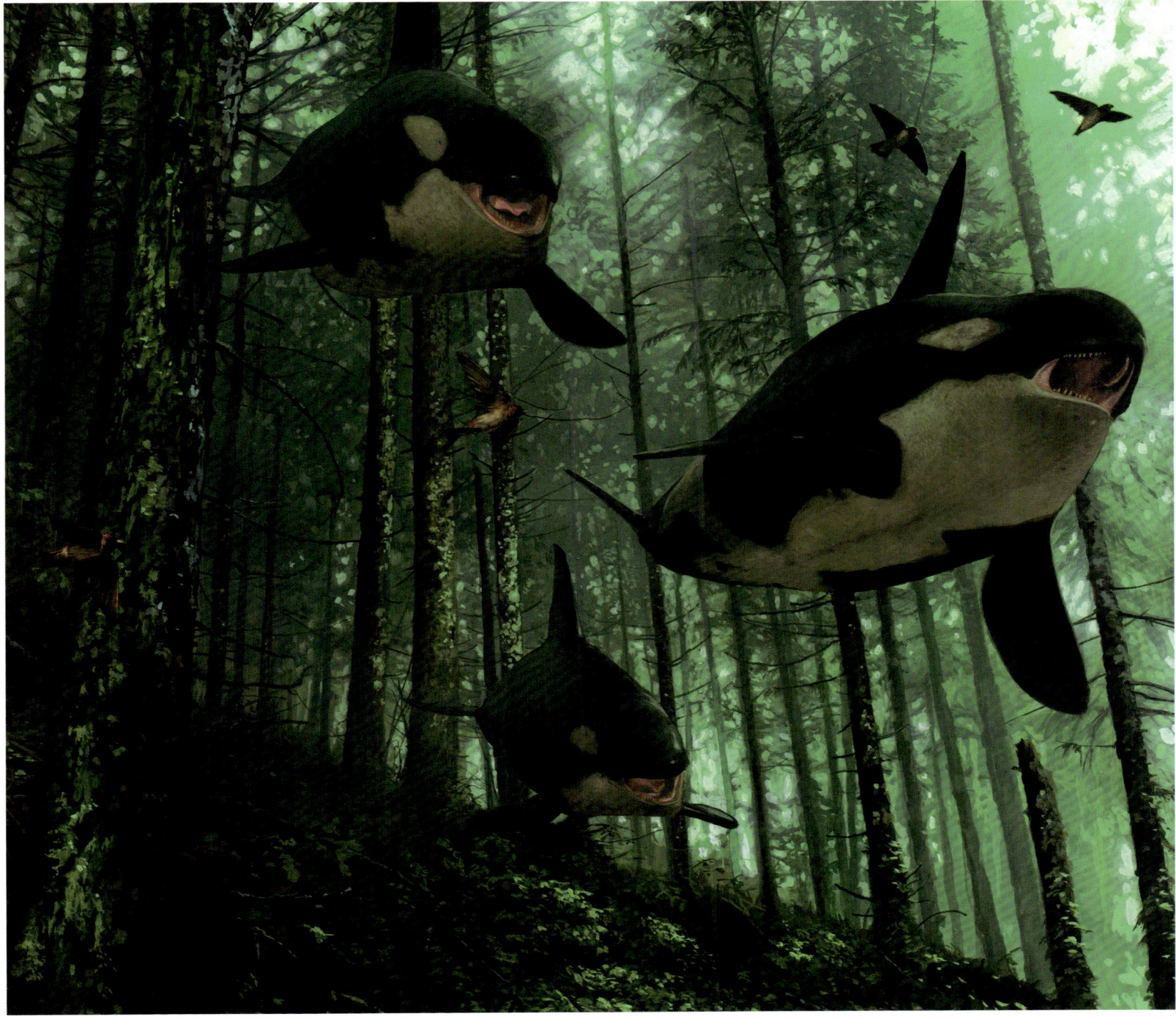

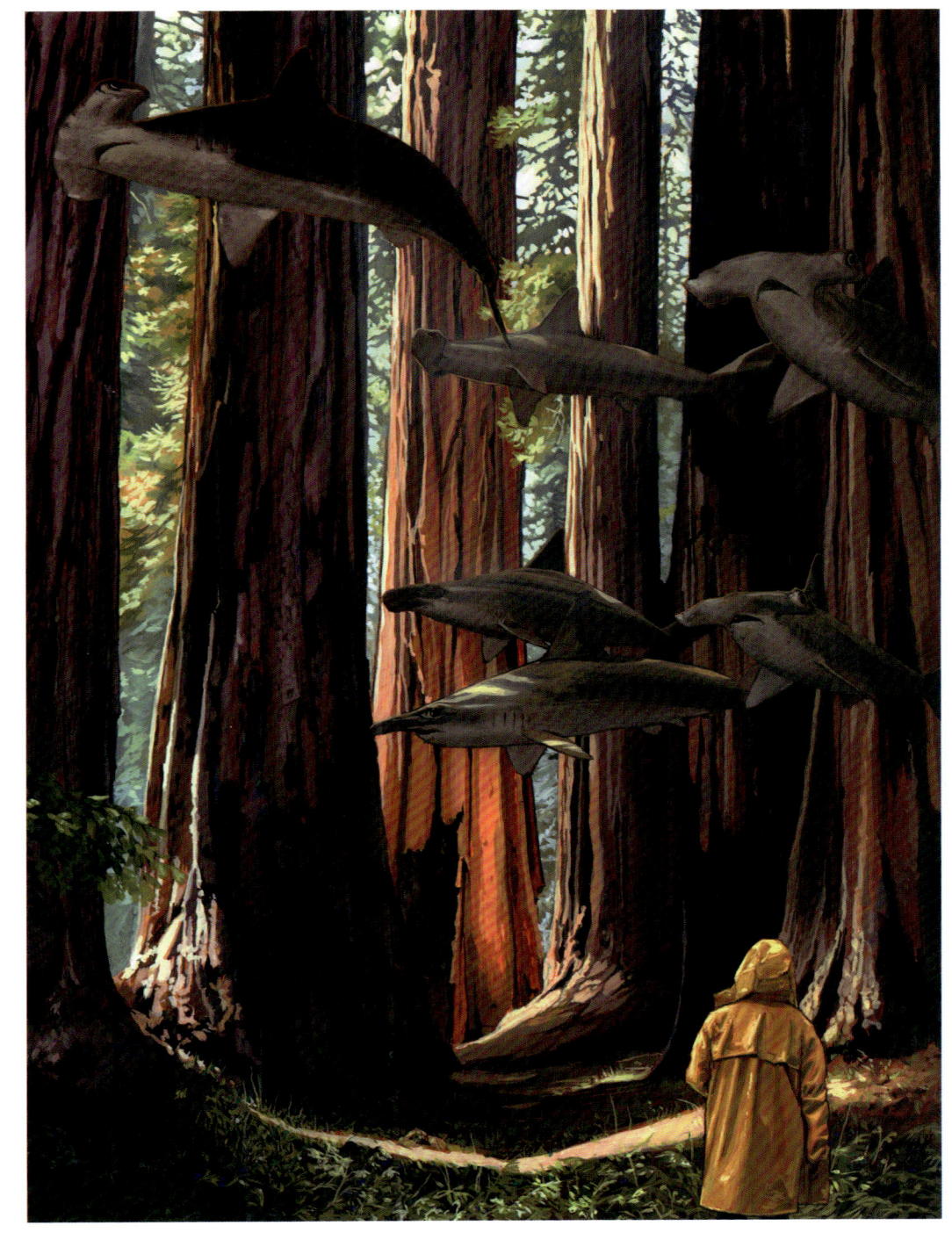

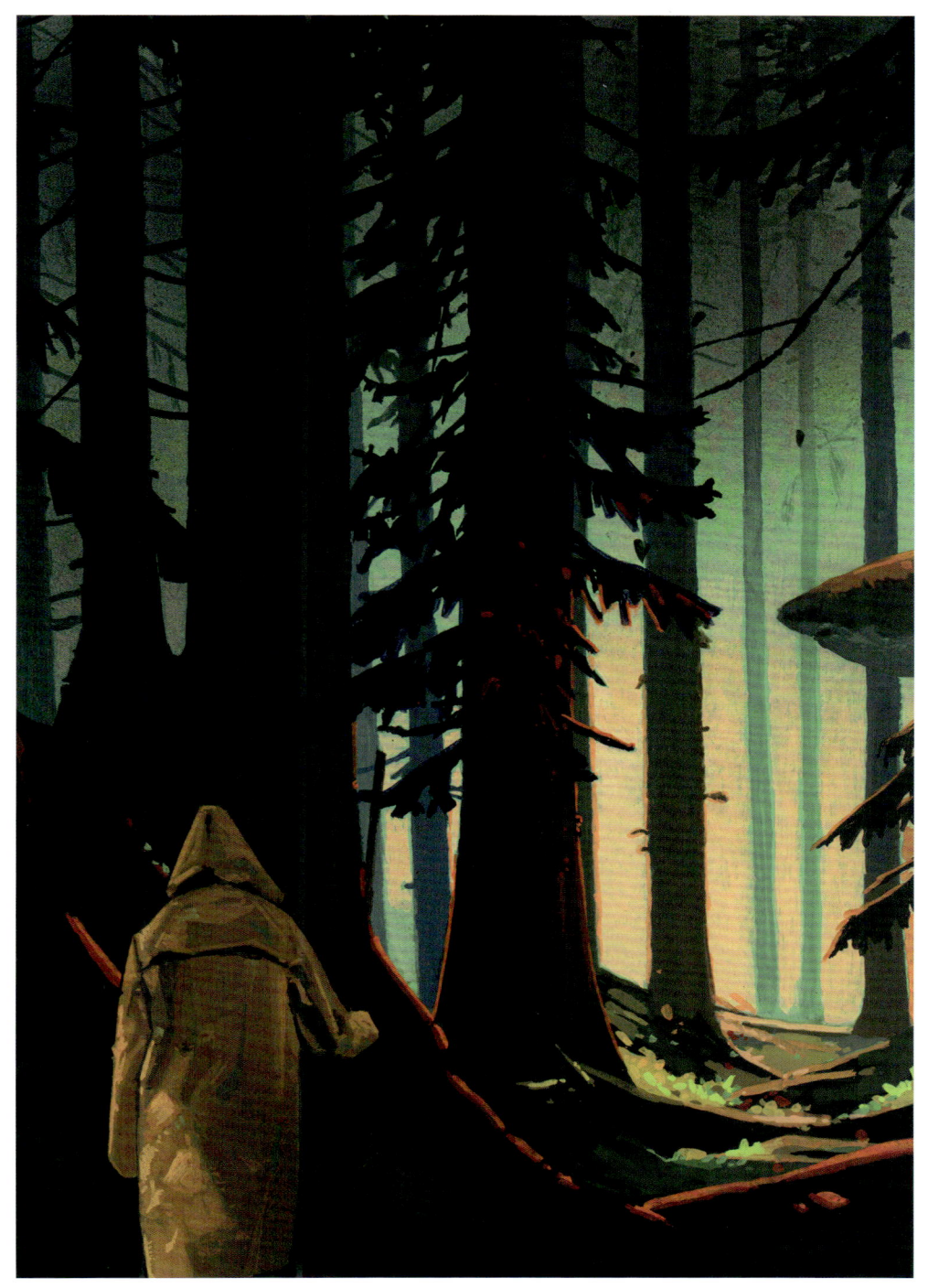

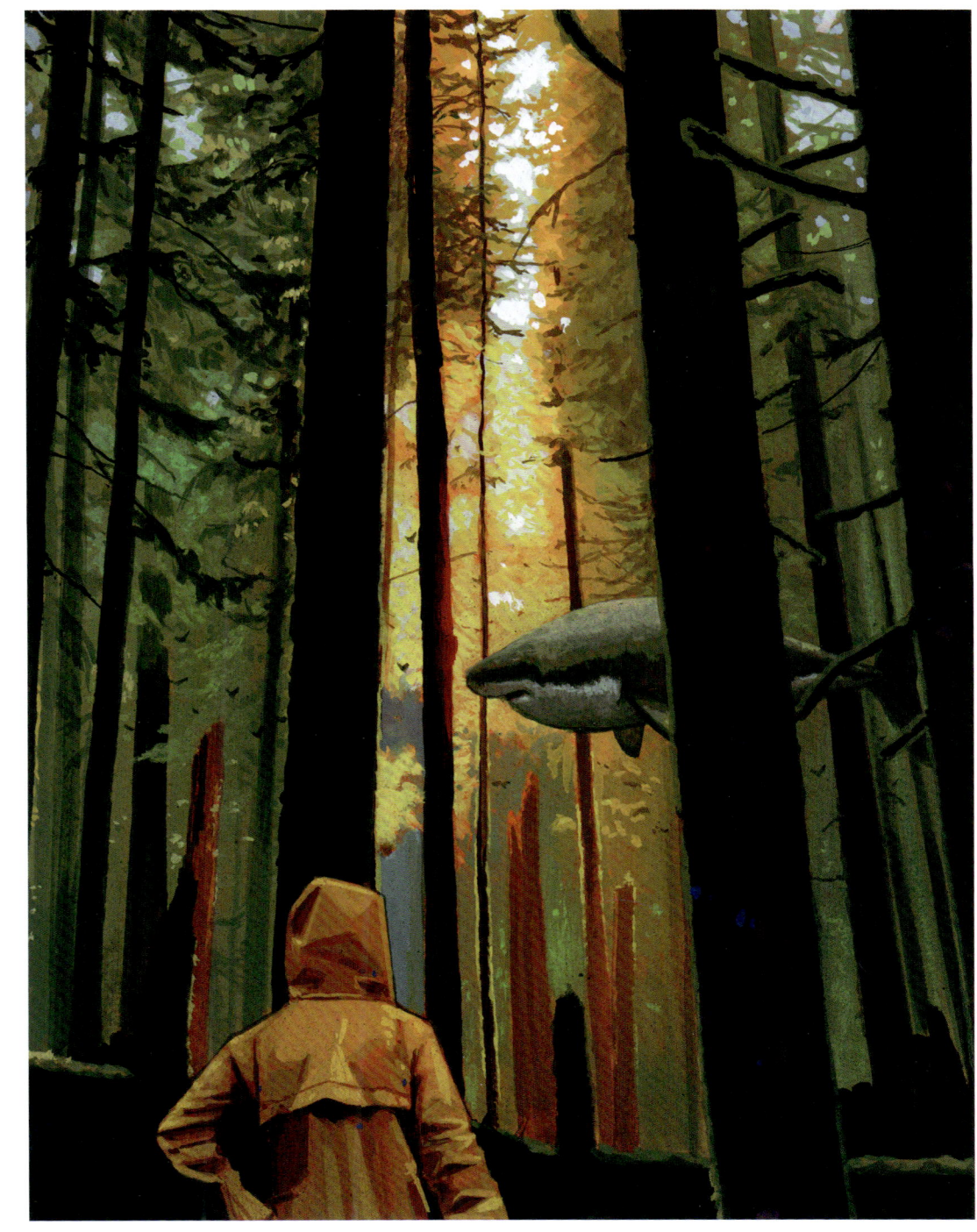

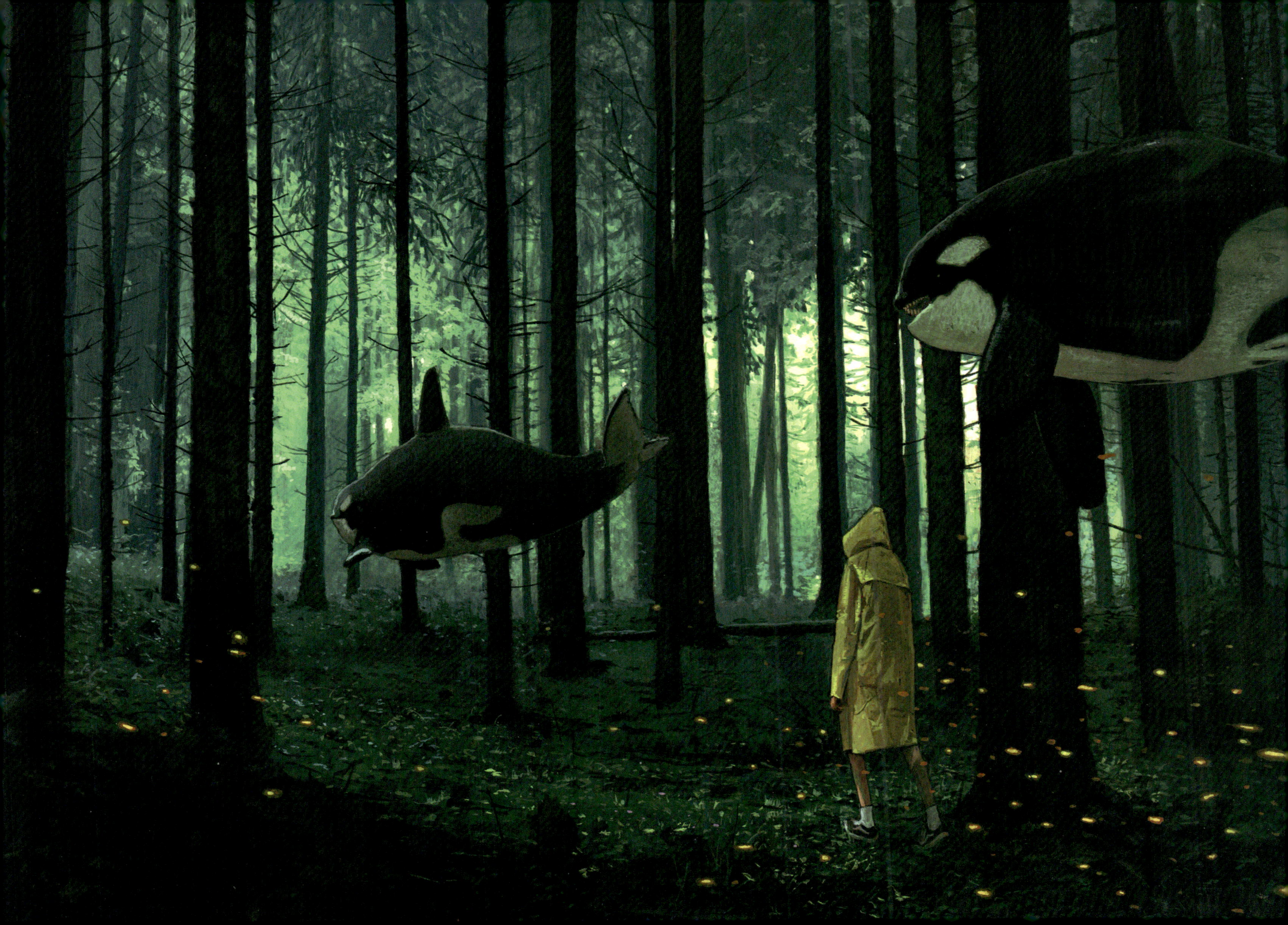

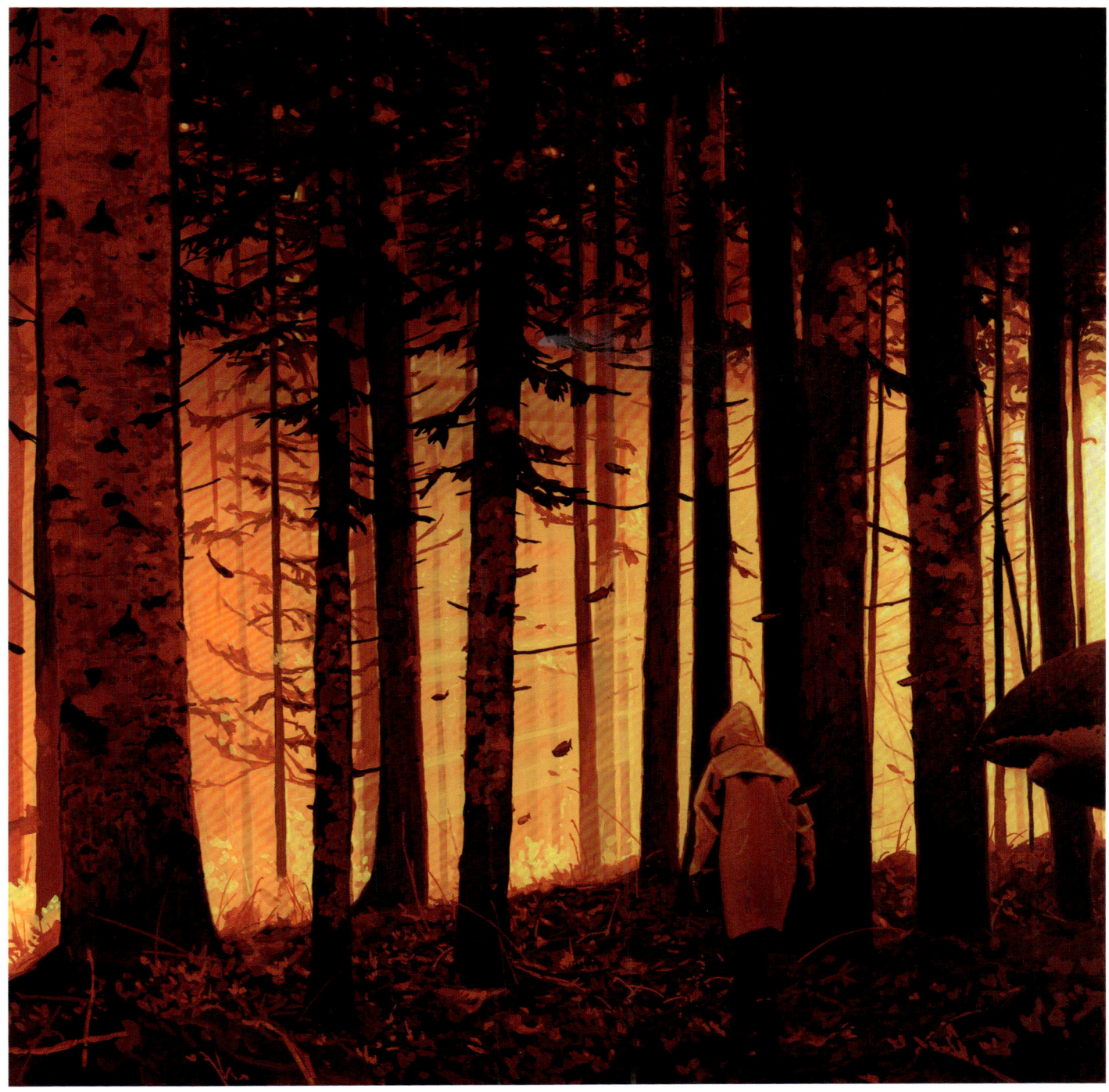

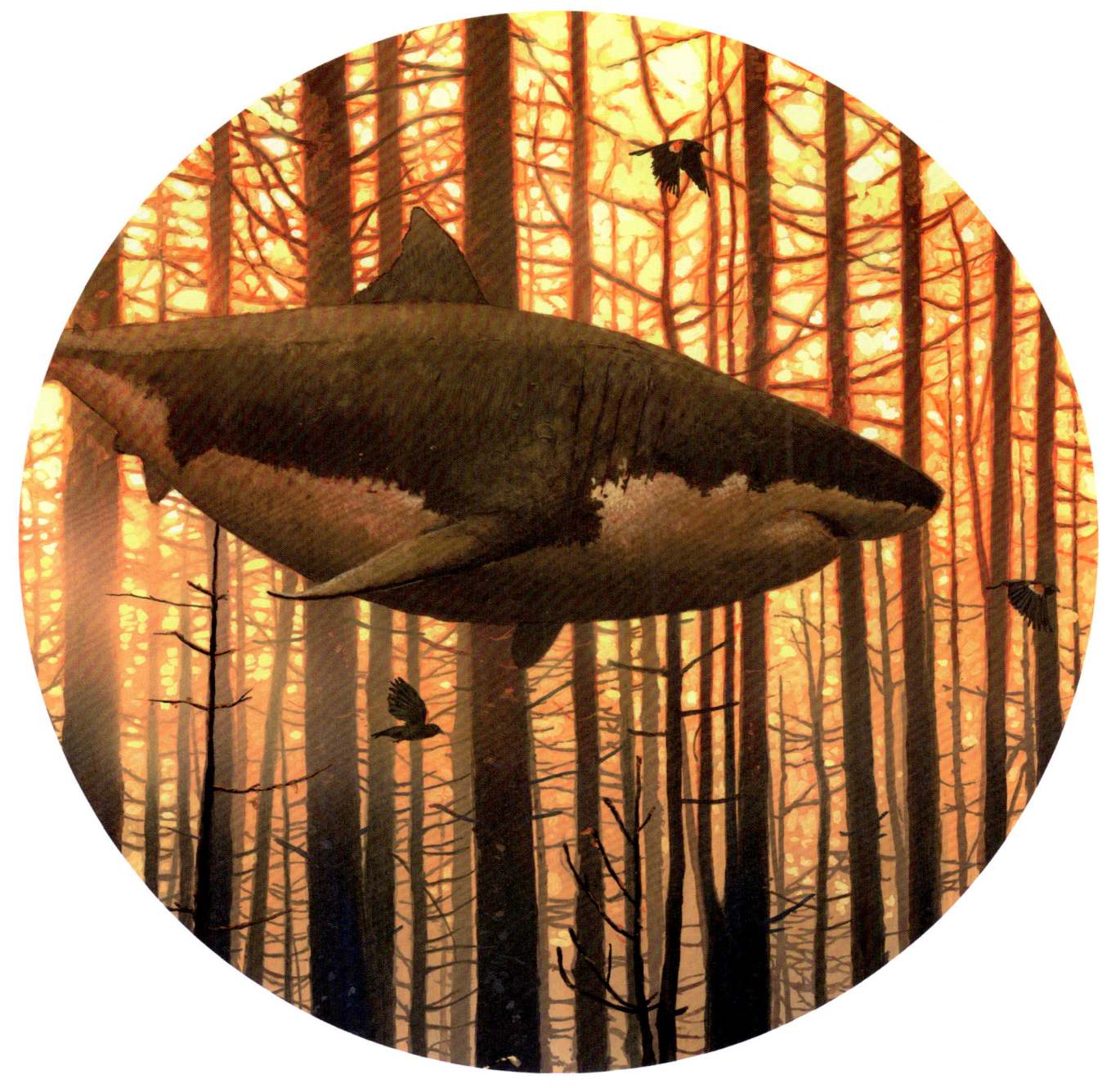

I enjoy playing with contrasts and opposites, particularly through the lens of wildlife and nature. This approach allows me to challenge expectations and norms, drawing the viewer into a surreal world where the natural becomes unnatural. By placing animals from different habitats together—such as a shark interacting with a deer—I create a space that challenges the boundaries of environment and companionship.

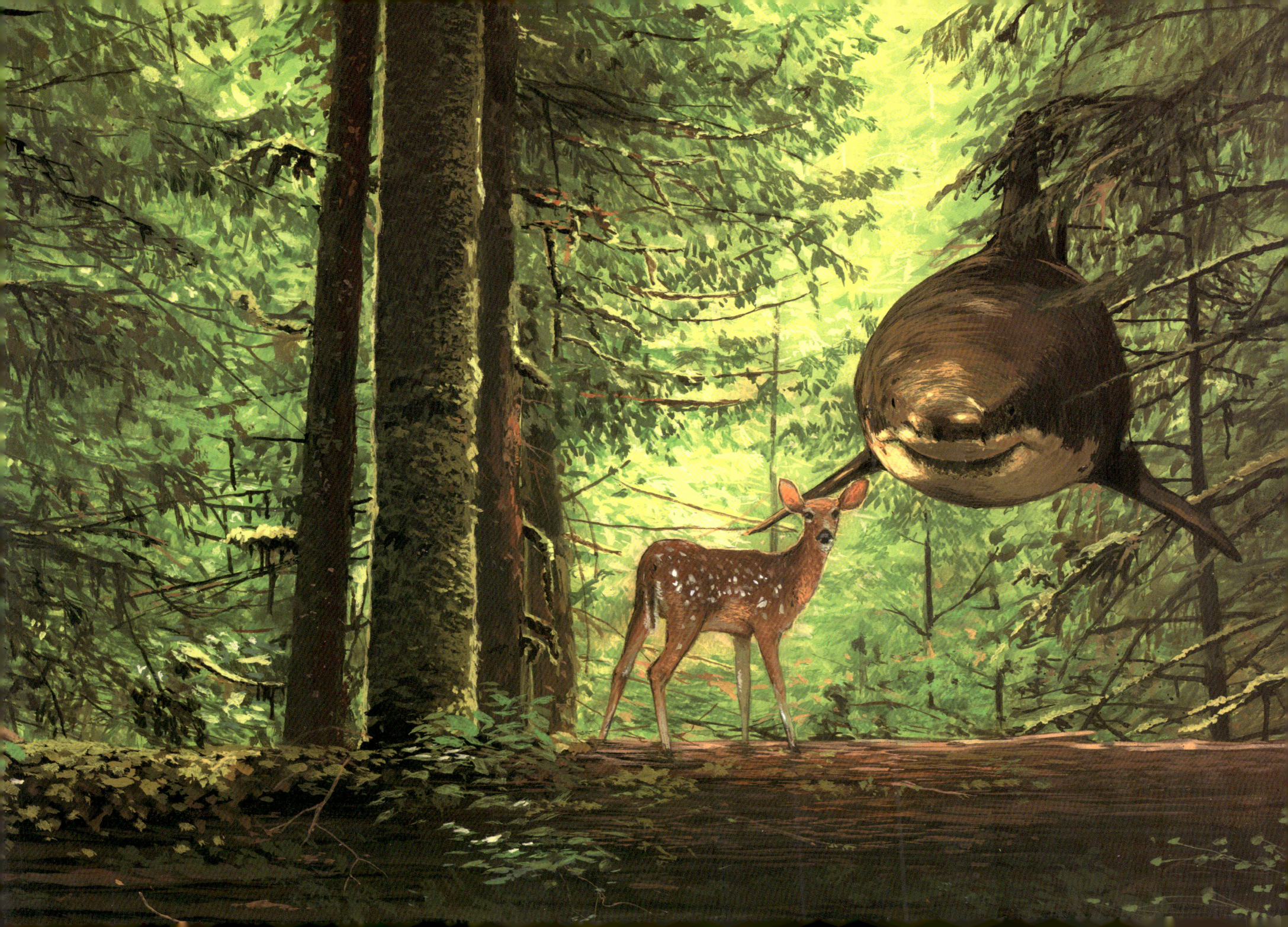

In a deeply personal reflection on my life's journey, I explore the contrasting forces that have shaped me, using wildlife as symbolic characters. The interplay of different species represents the influences that either led me astray or guided me back. Central to this narrative, marine life embodies a higher consciousness—moments of clarity and peace that I sought amid the chaos of my youth. Through this work, I confront fears, embrace contradictions, and reflect on the human experience.

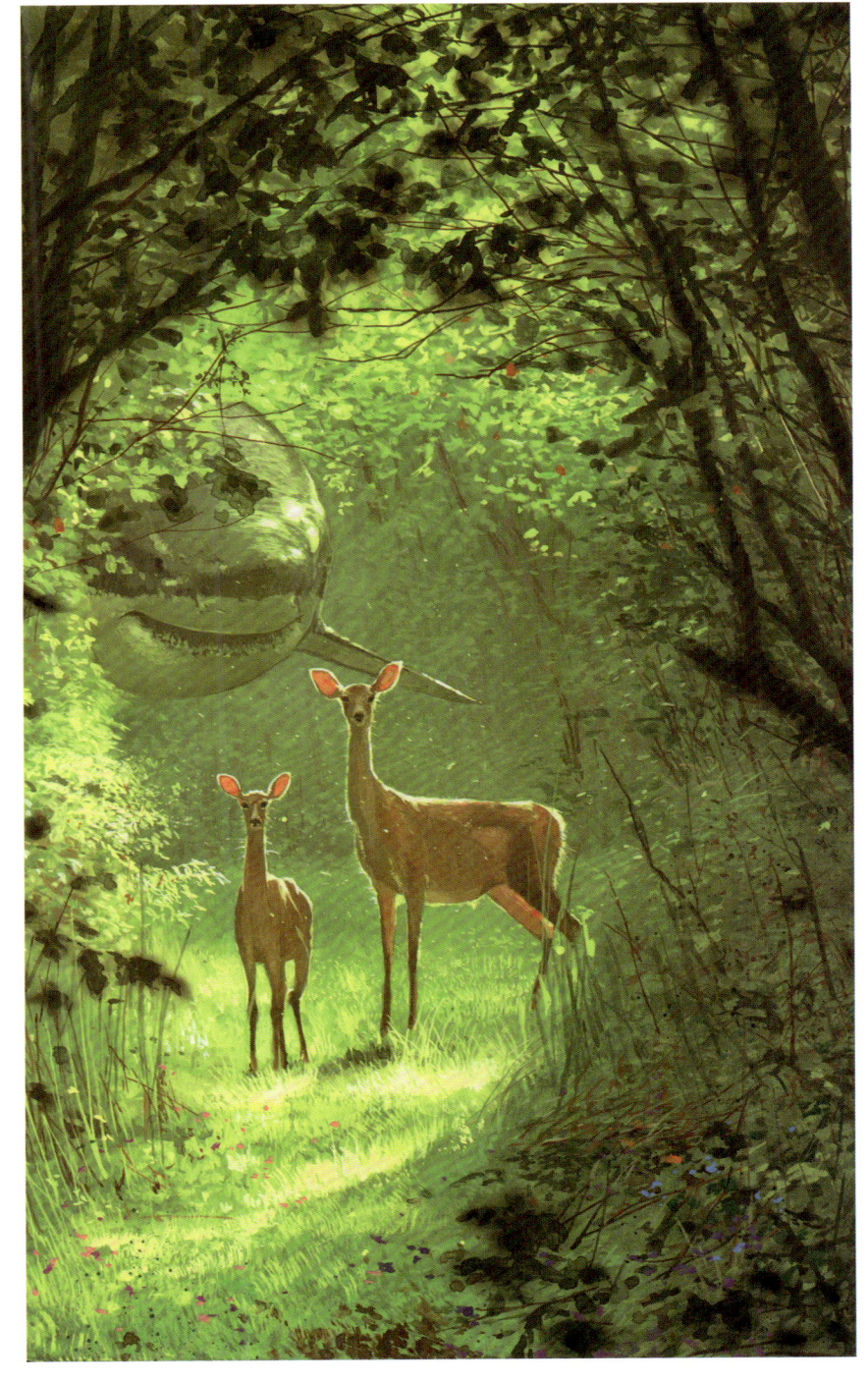

Marine life, with its fluid and often mysterious existence, takes on a more ethereal role in my narrative. It's not just about survival but about a higher consciousness—a deeper, more spiritual sense of awareness that I tapped into as a child. The underwater world, in its vastness and stillness, represents a place where I could retreat, reflect, and gain insight. It stands in contrast to the chaotic, mismatched land creatures, offering a space of clarity and peace, much like the moments when I found understanding in my confusing reality.

Perhaps the ocean, with its depth and expansiveness, symbolizes my ability to transcend the limitations of my immediate surroundings and connect with something larger and more meaningful. This layering of contrasting environments, improbable animal friendships, and symbolic marine life adds depth to my work, creating a rich narrative of my personal growth. It's as if the unnatural becomes a pathway to self-realization—a way for me to explore and reconcile the fragmented parts of my life.

Each piece of art I create feels like an act of healing, inviting the viewer into my surreal world and encouraging them to question not just the boundaries of nature, but also the boundaries of their own experiences—and how they too might find harmony in chaos.

Imprisoned By A Faded Memory | 16" x 12" | gouache on wood | 2019

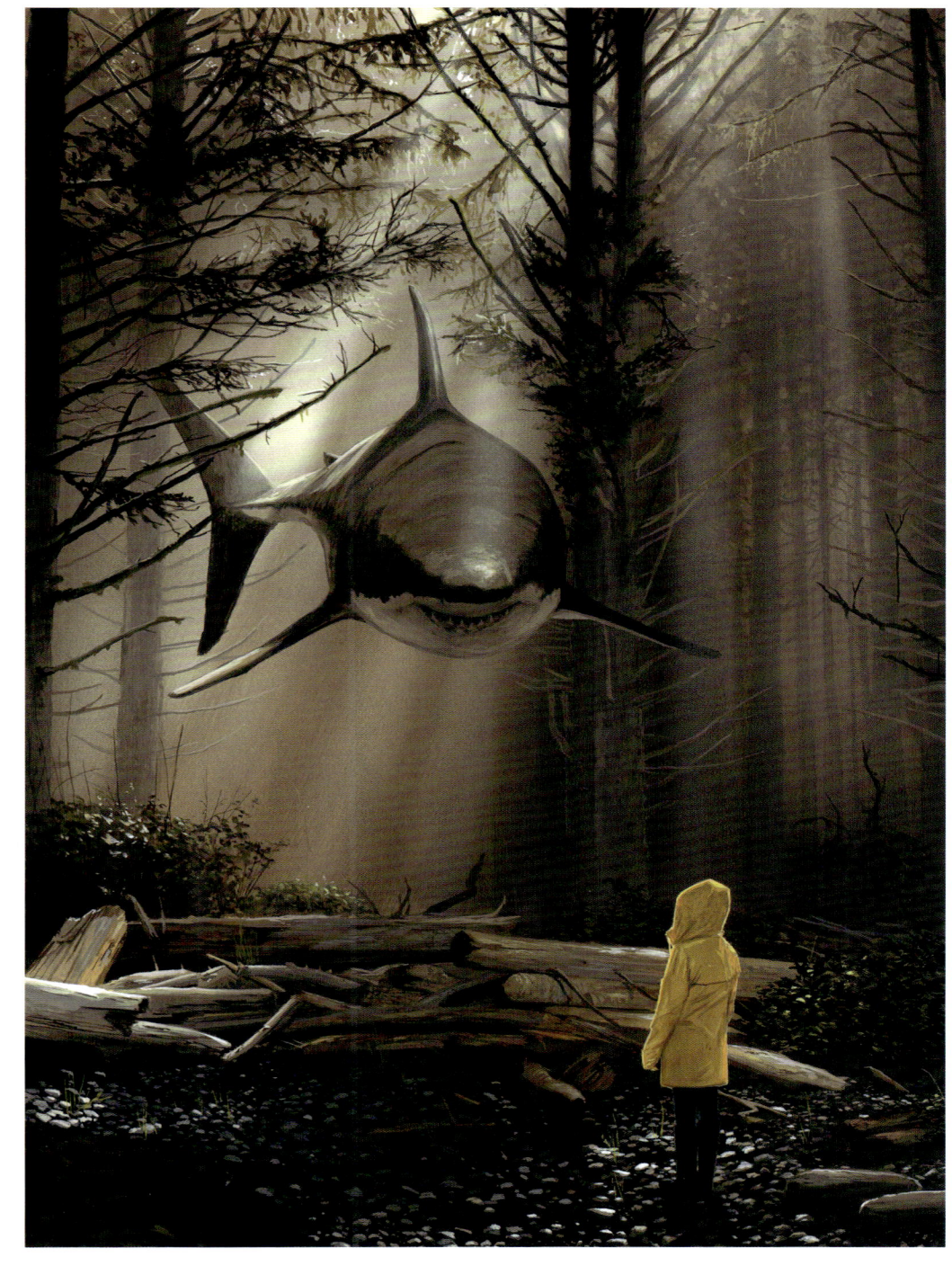

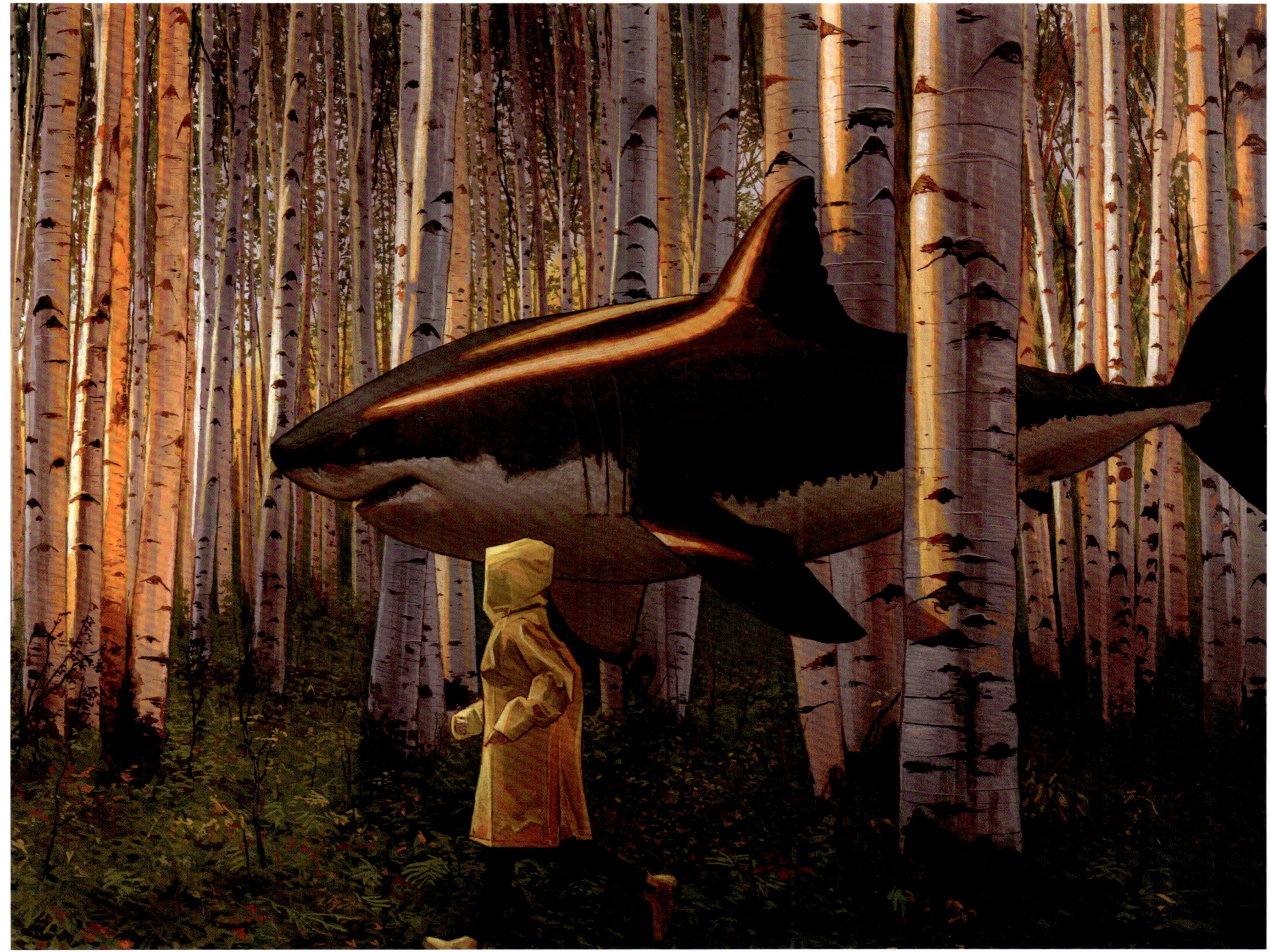

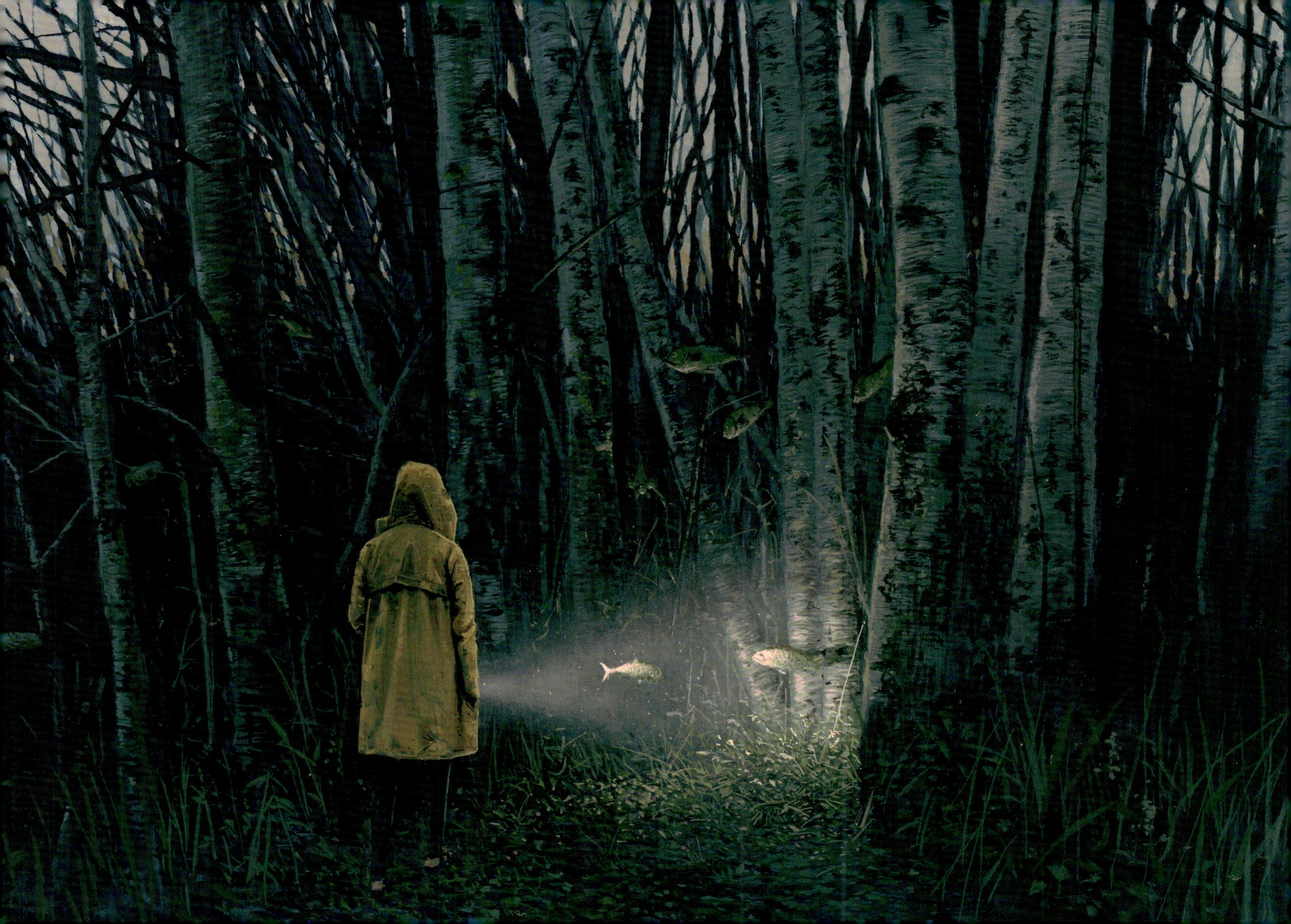

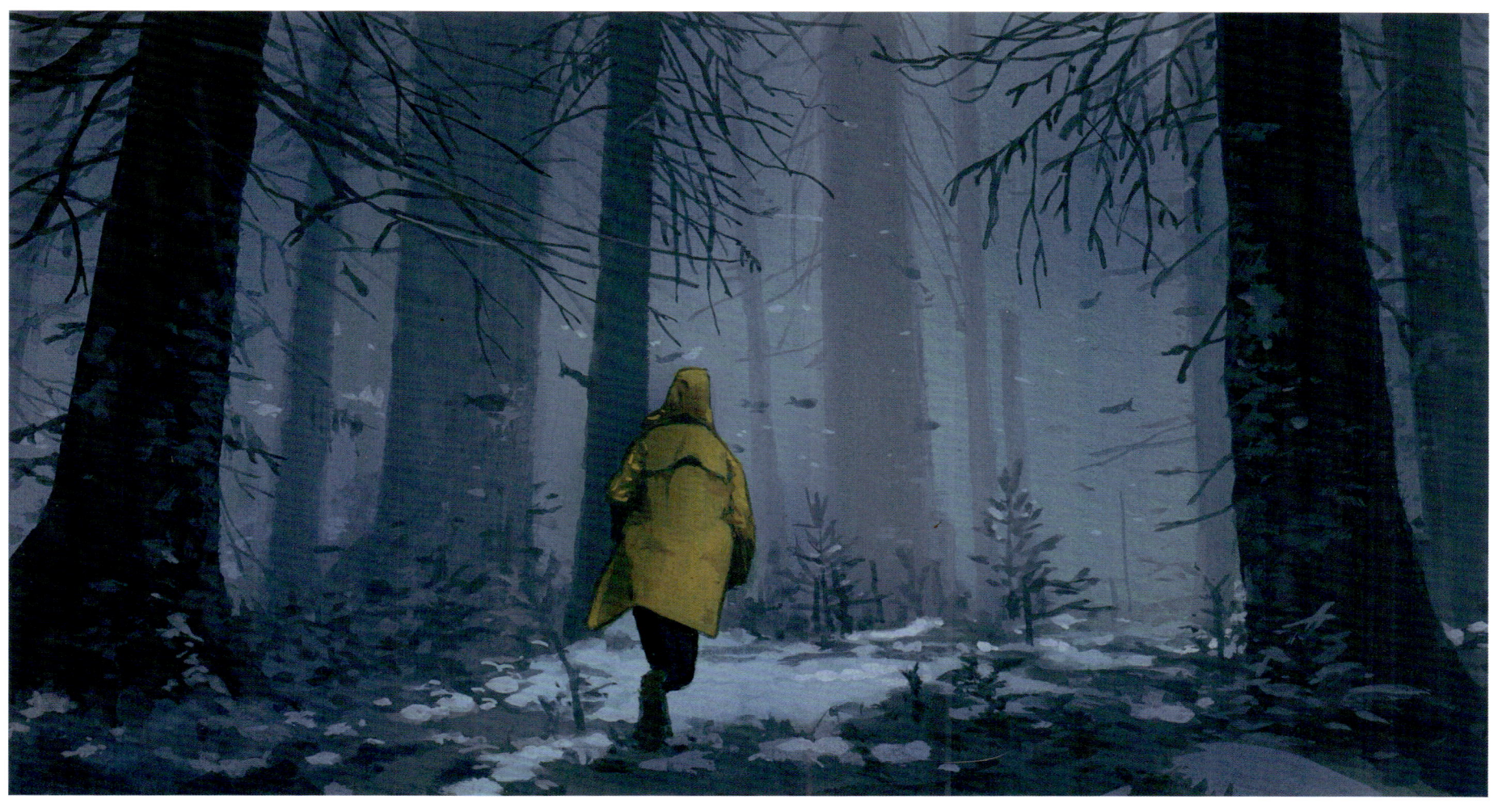

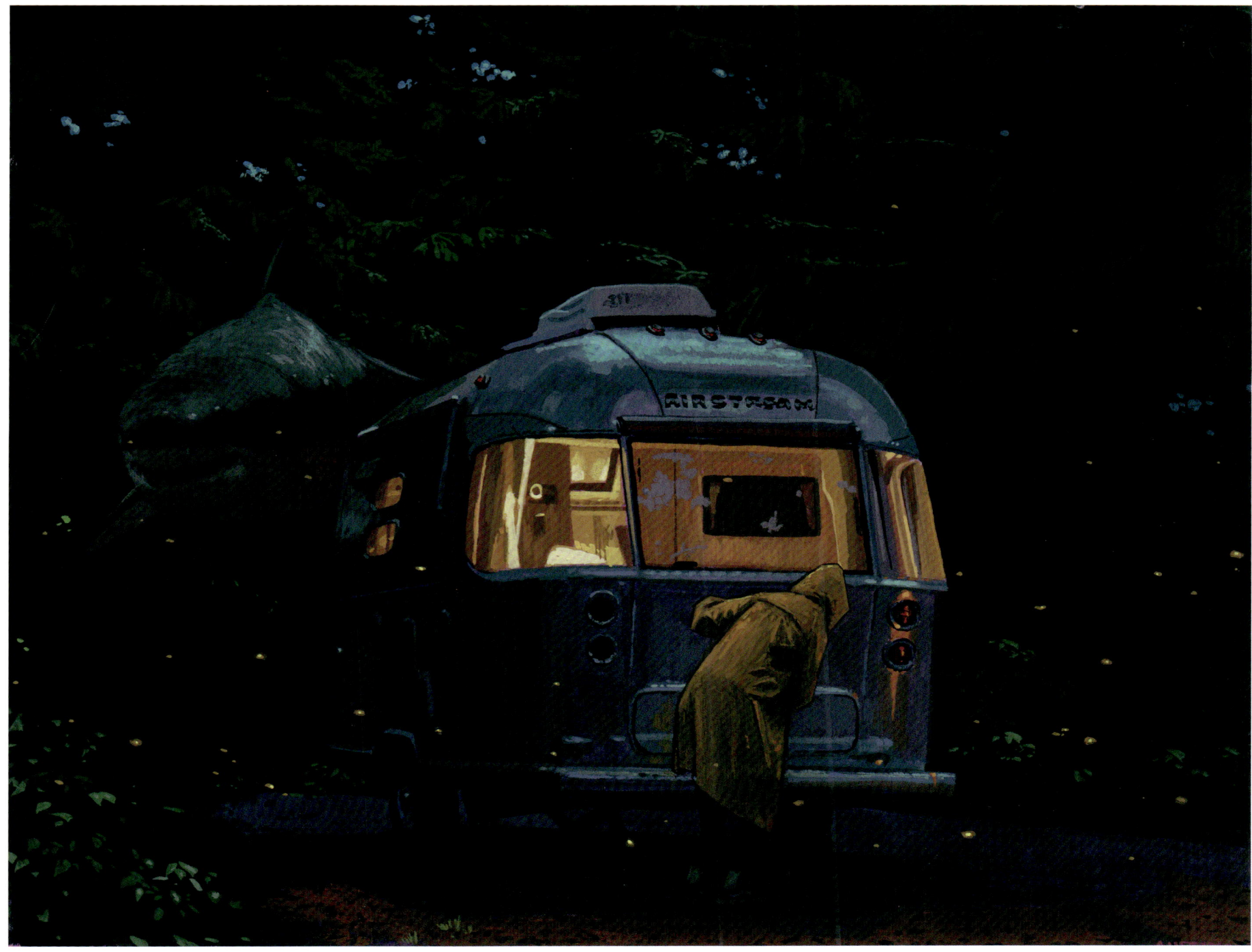

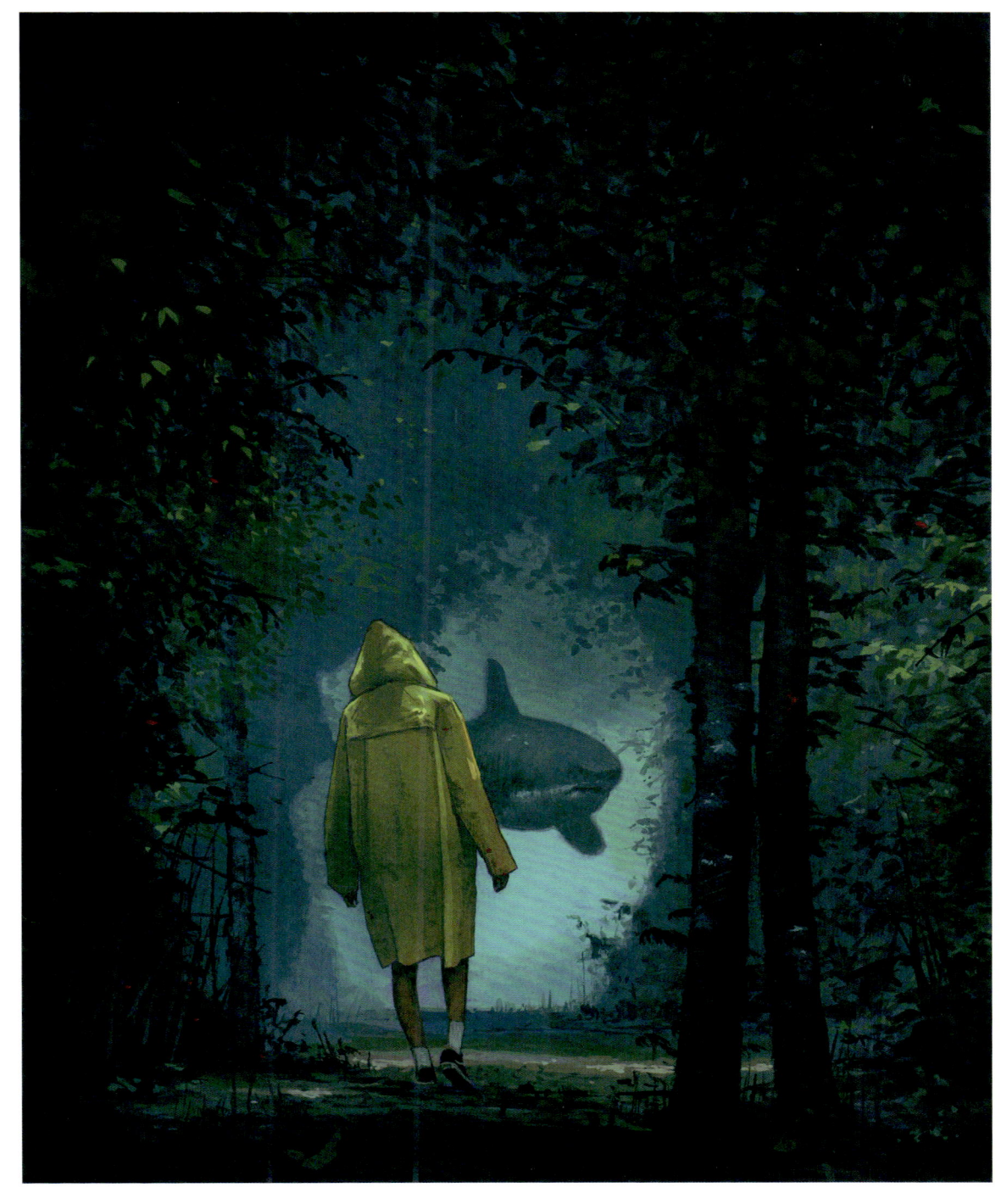

Her Happiness Was The Journey | 6" x 8" | gouache on paper | 2018

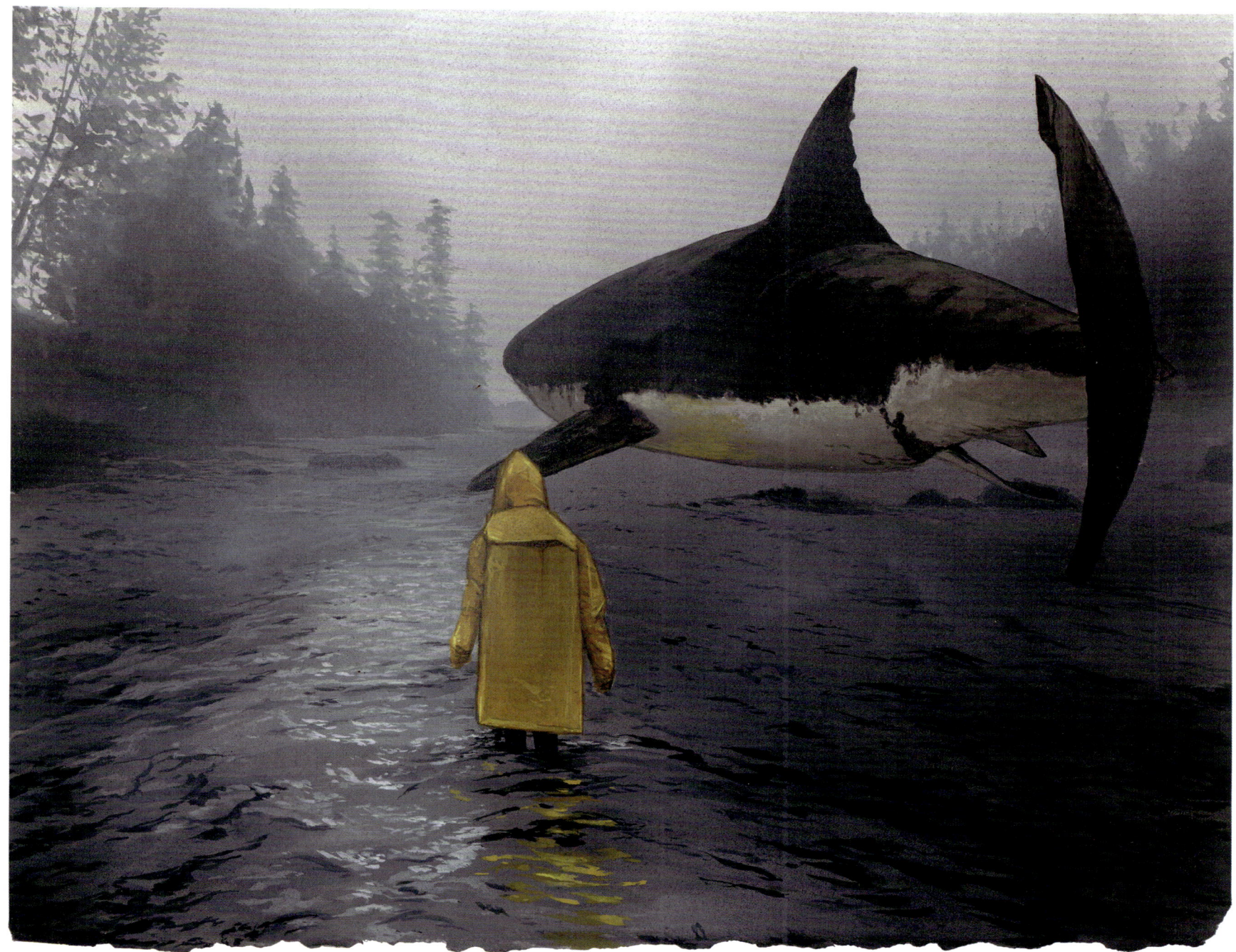

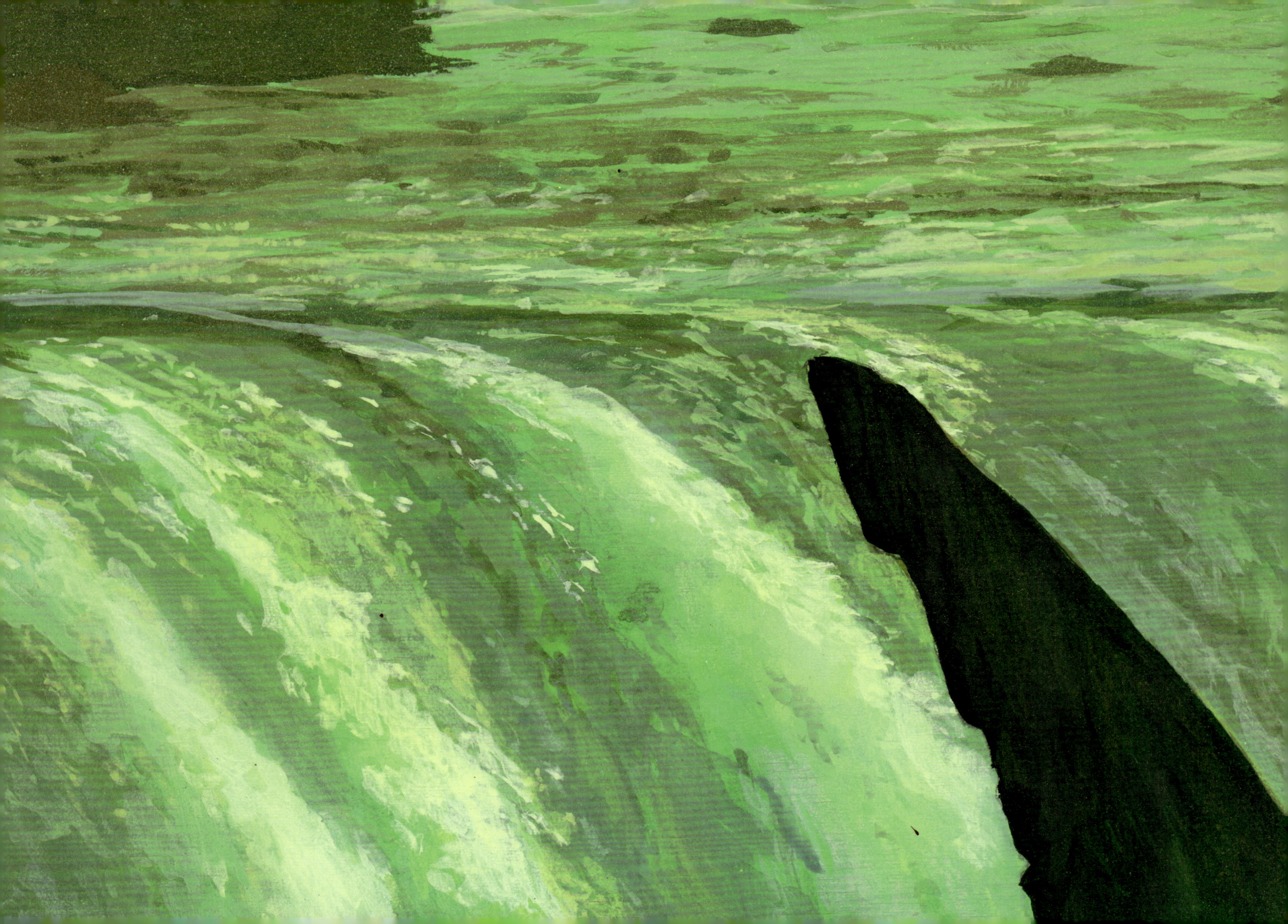

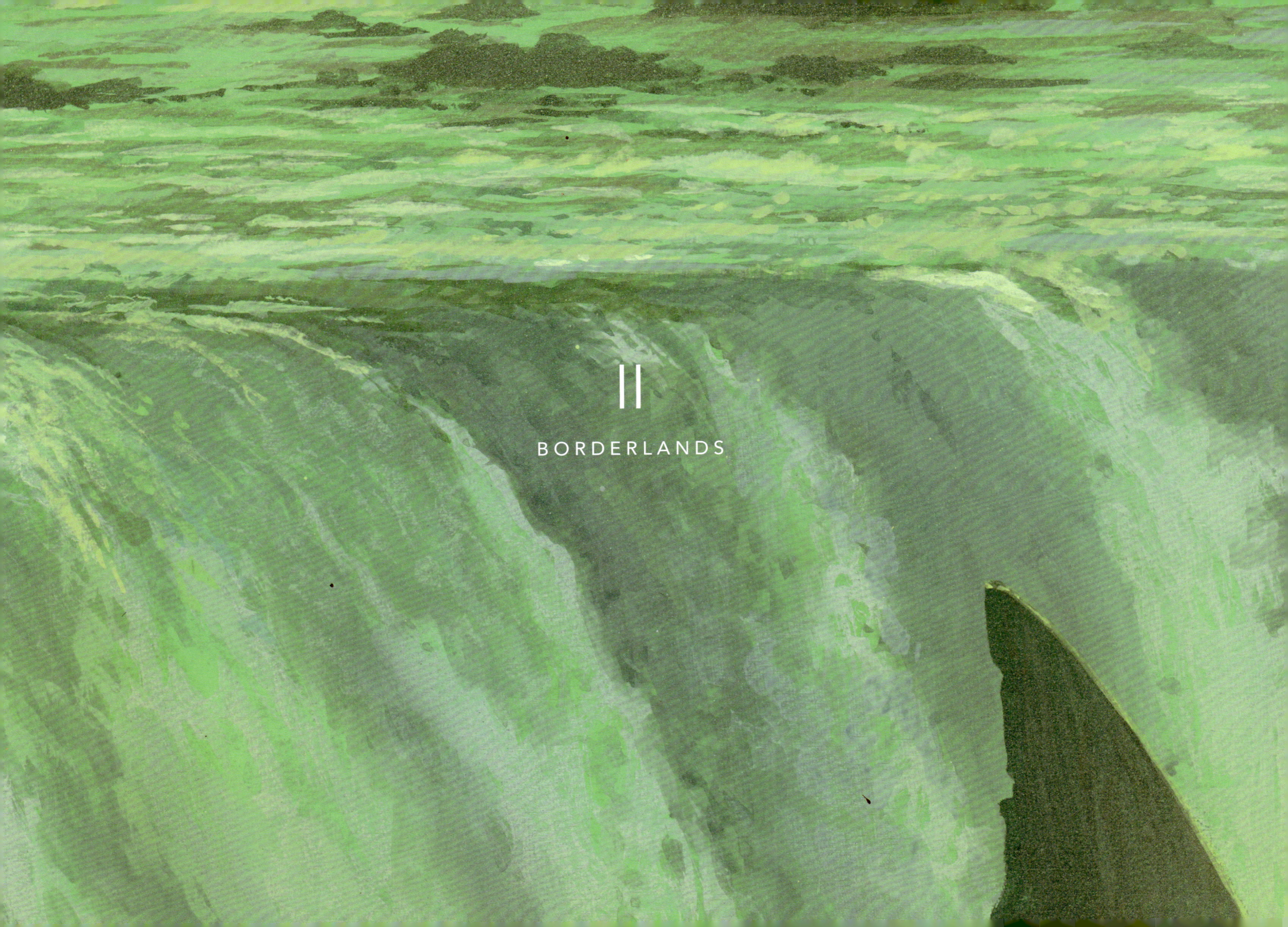

BORDERLANDS

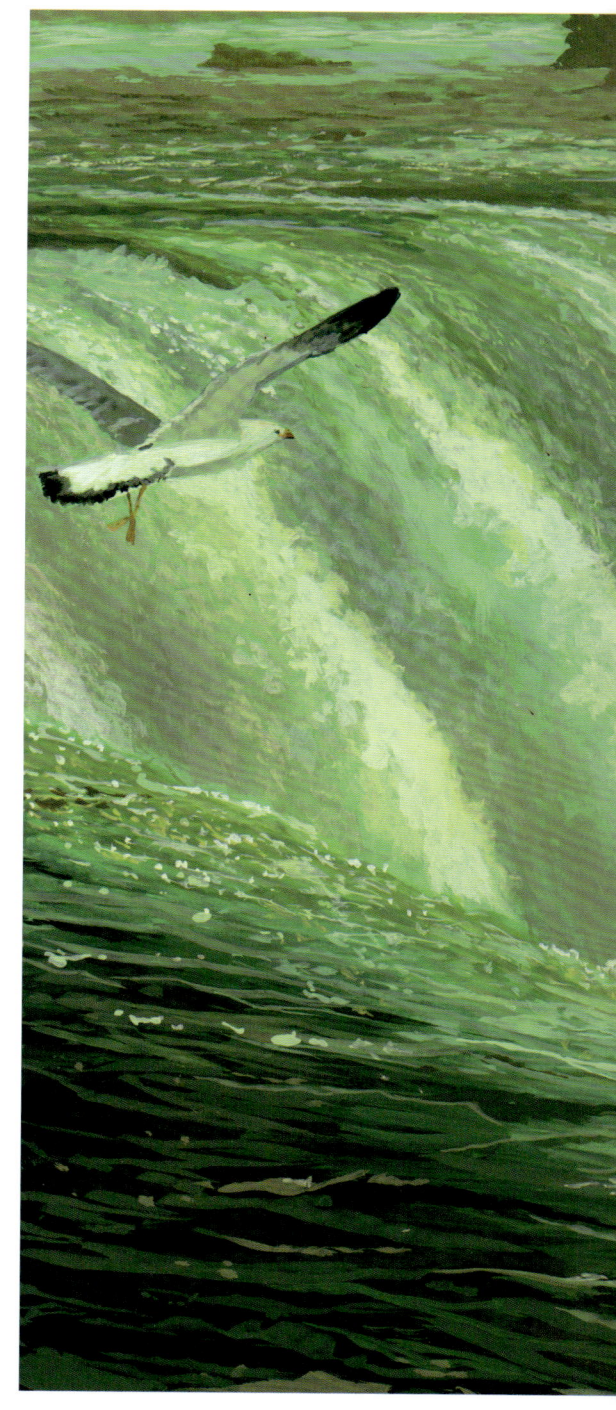

Where It Falls | 12" x 24" | gouche on wood | 2022

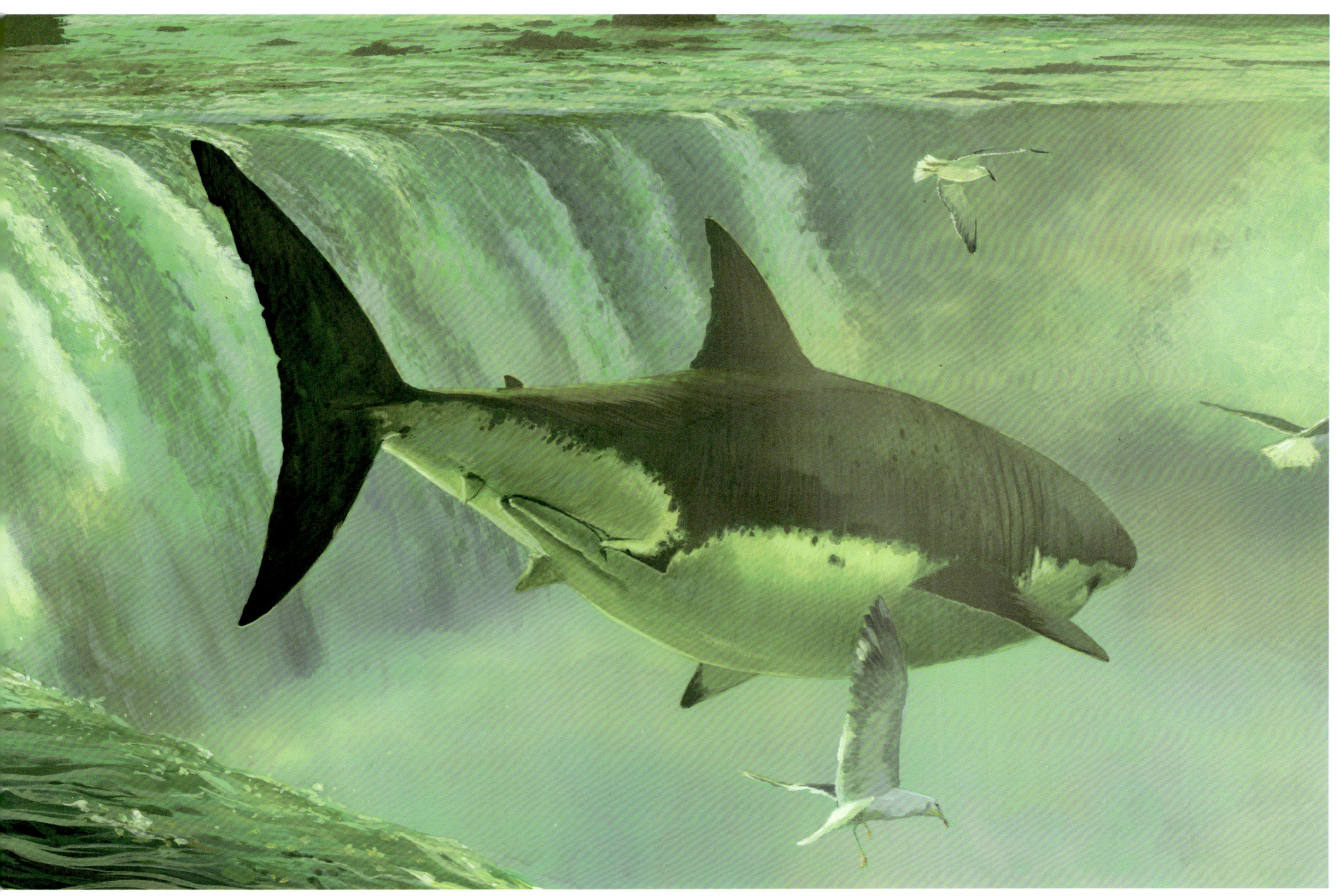

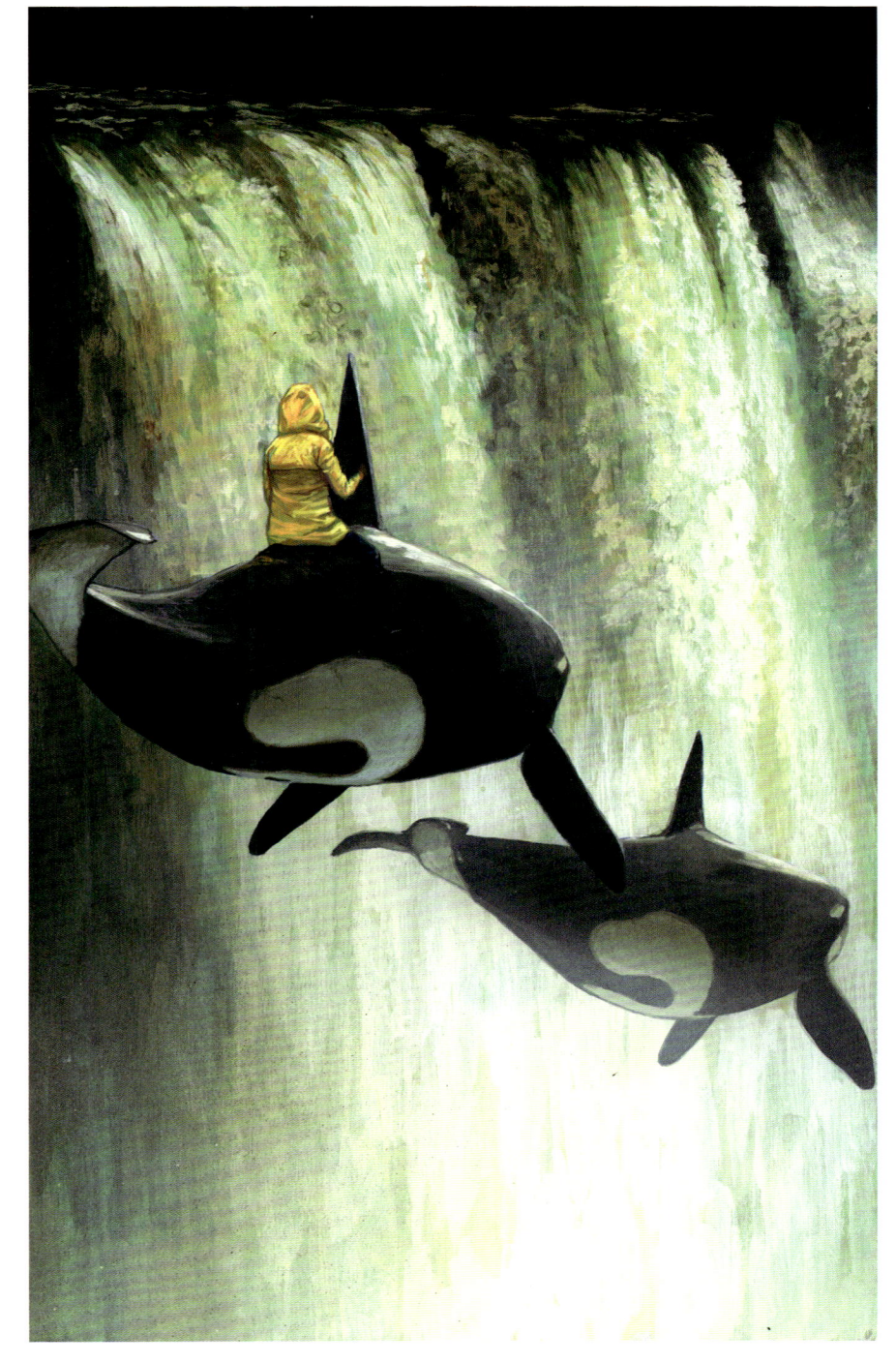

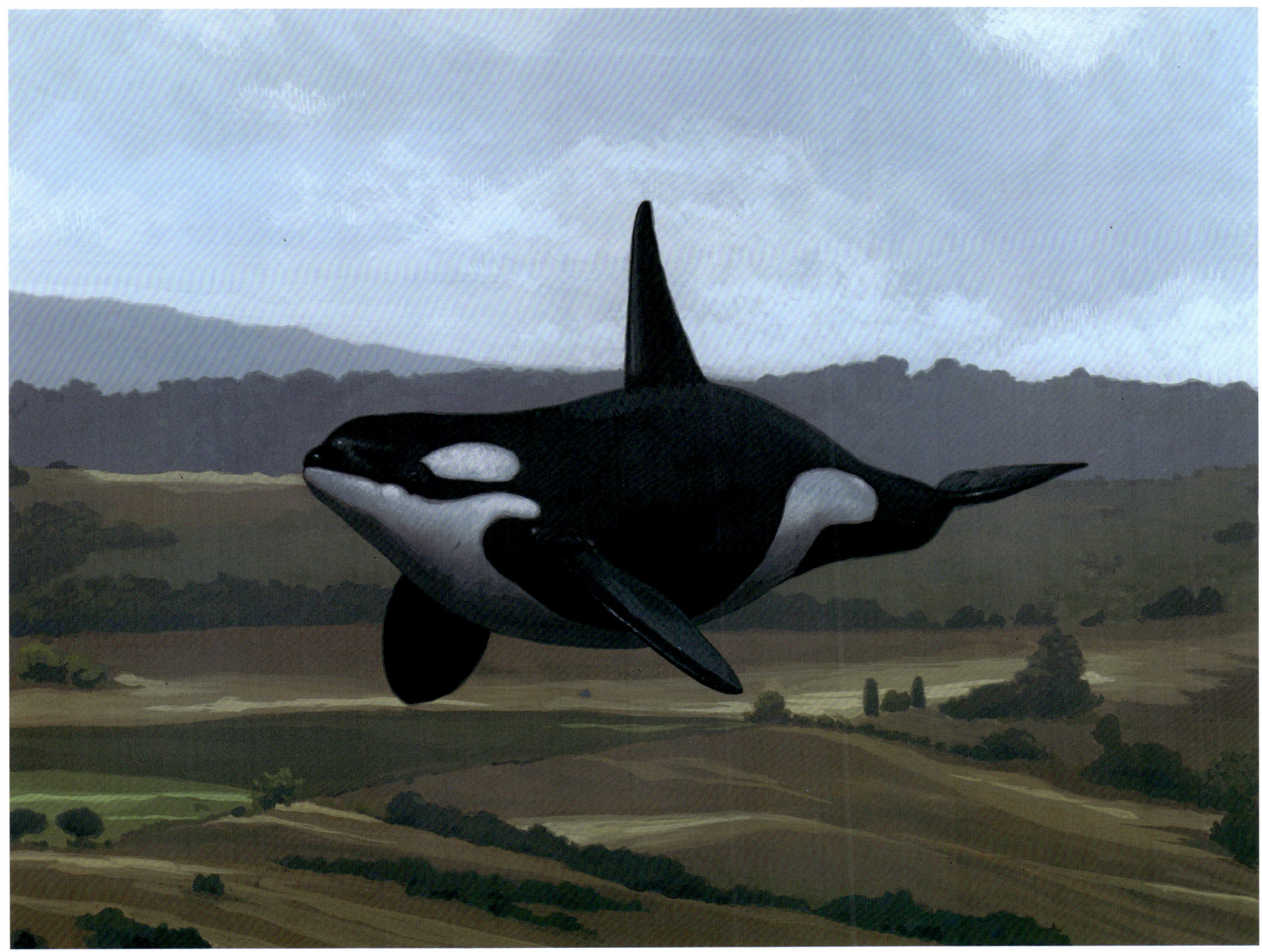

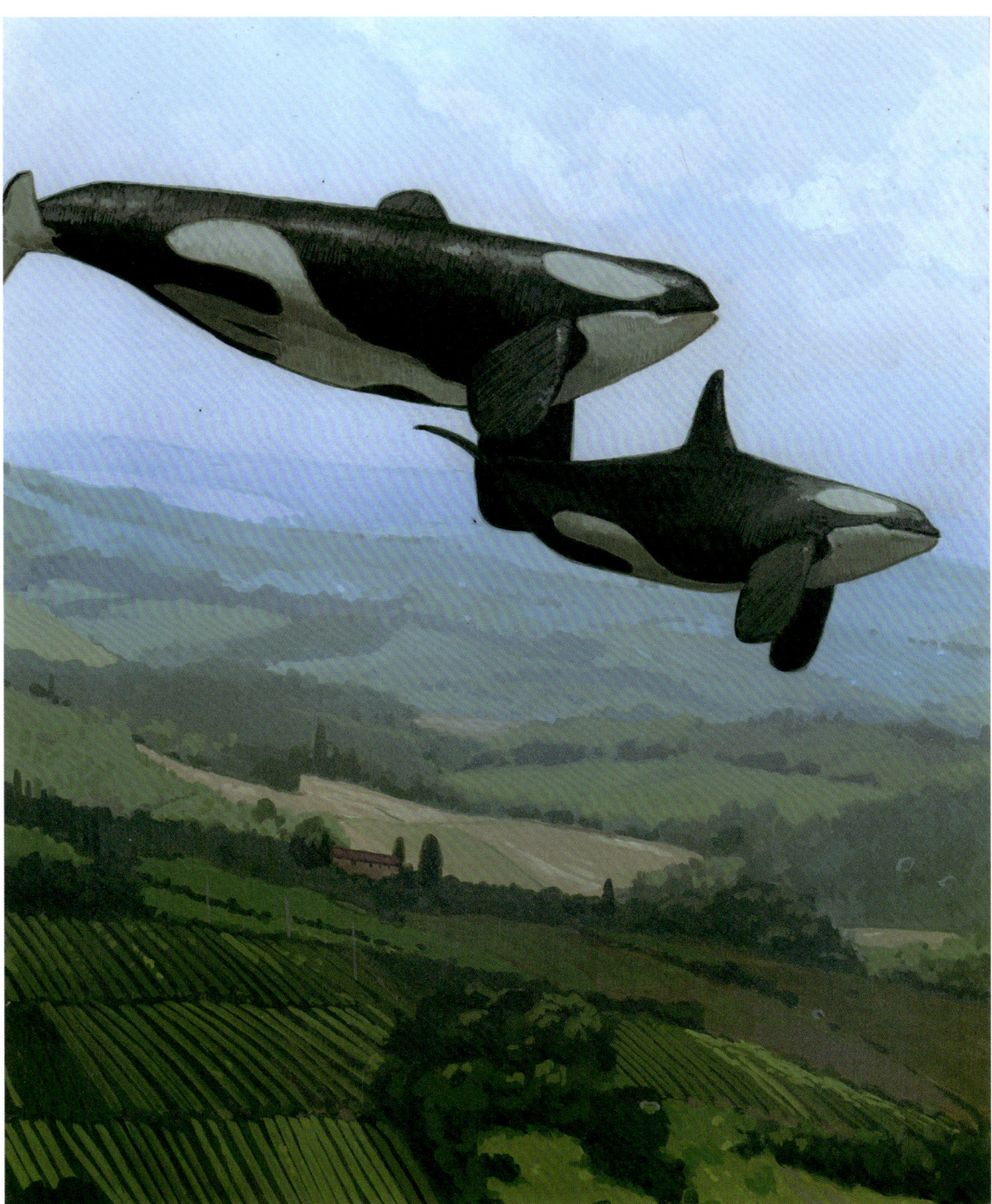

Trains Don't Go There (study)
9.5" x 7"
gouache on paper
2024

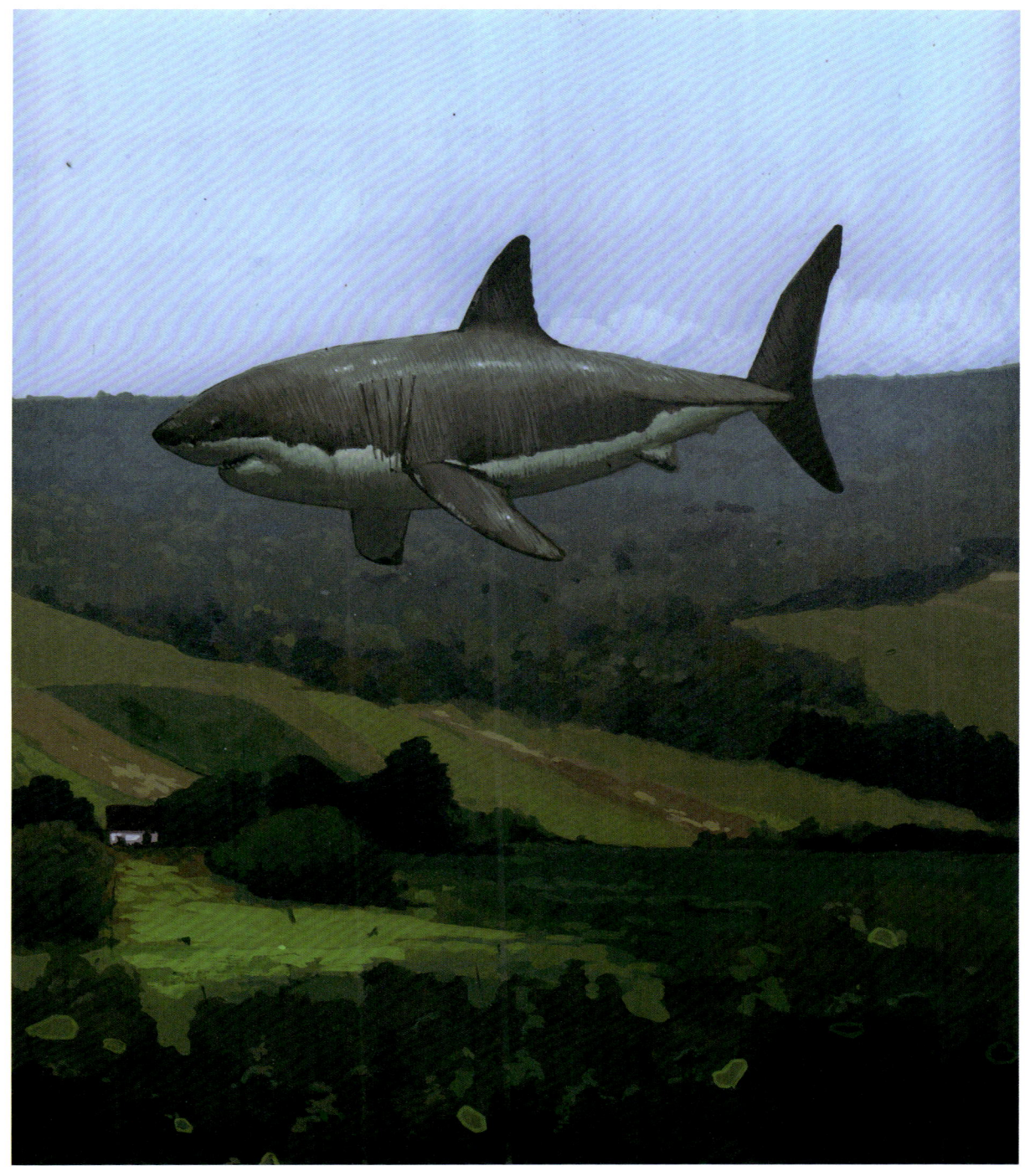

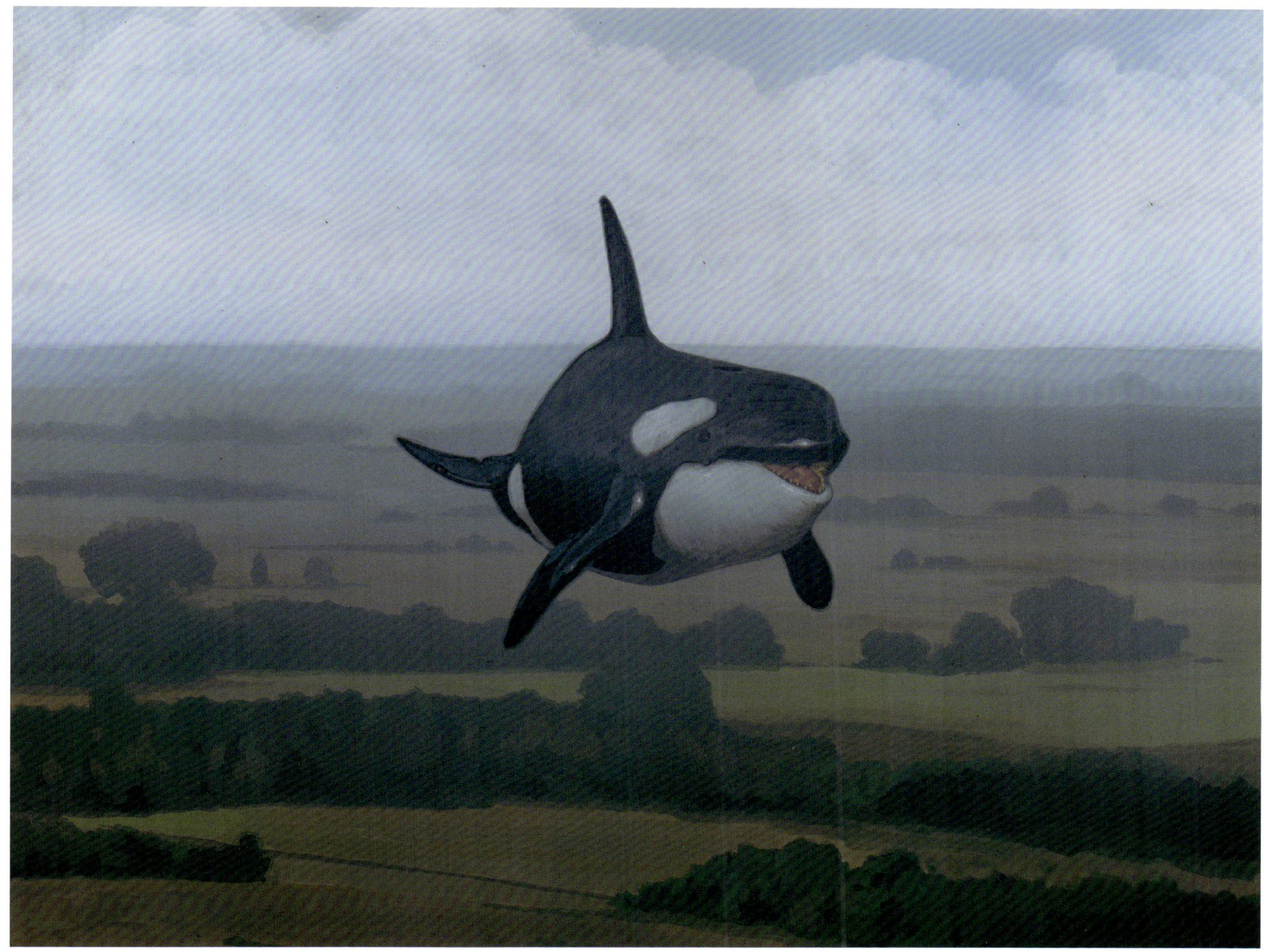

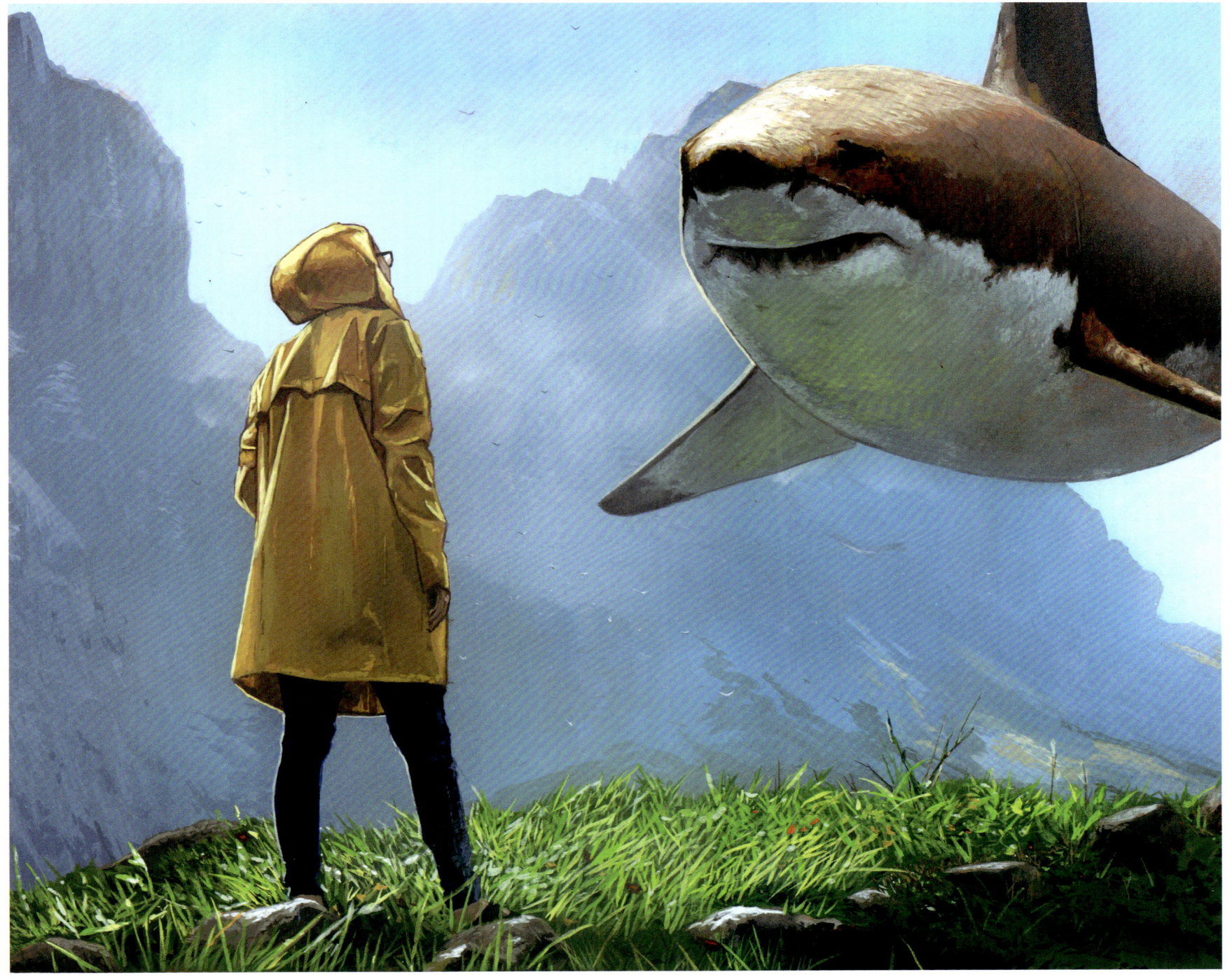

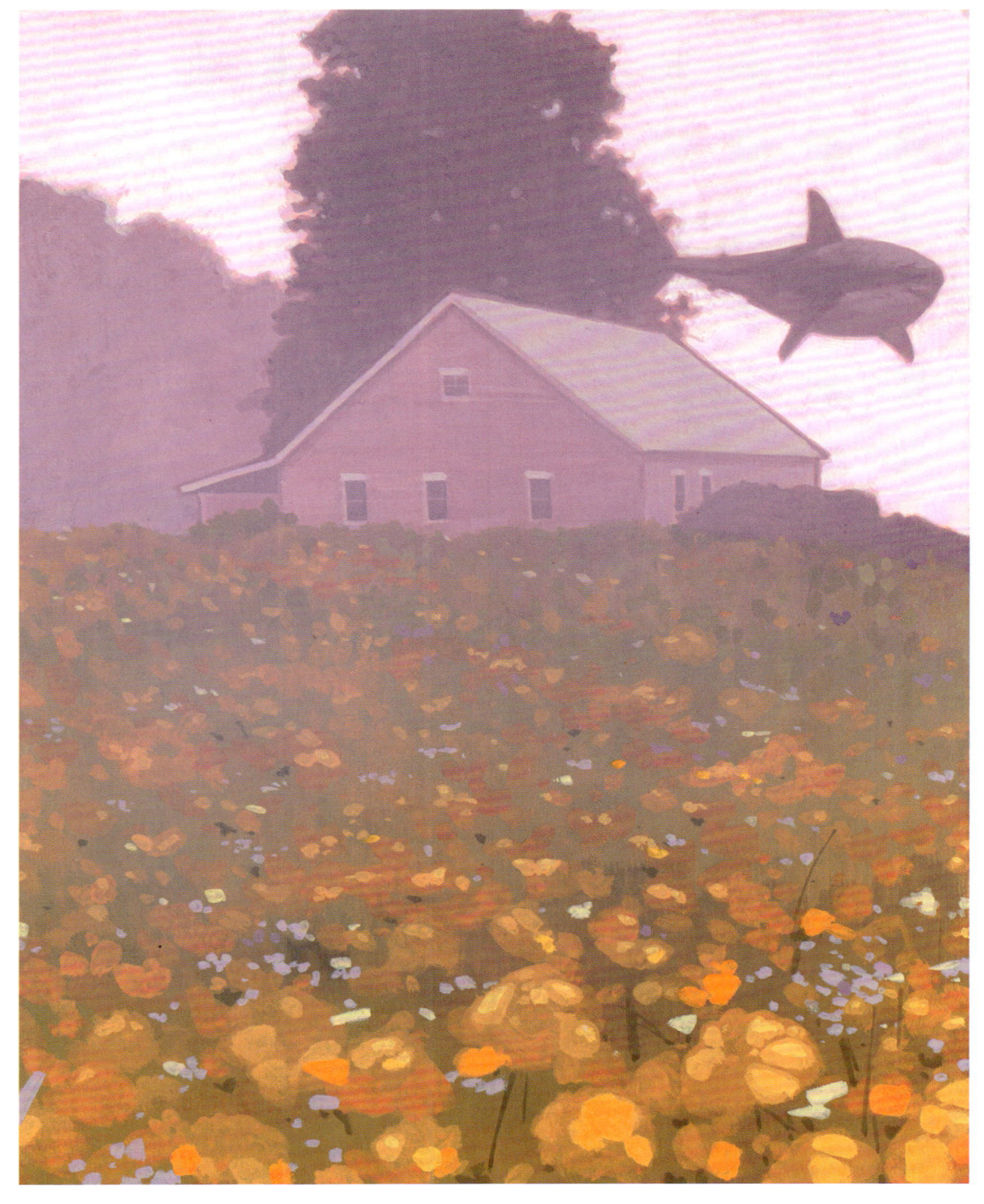

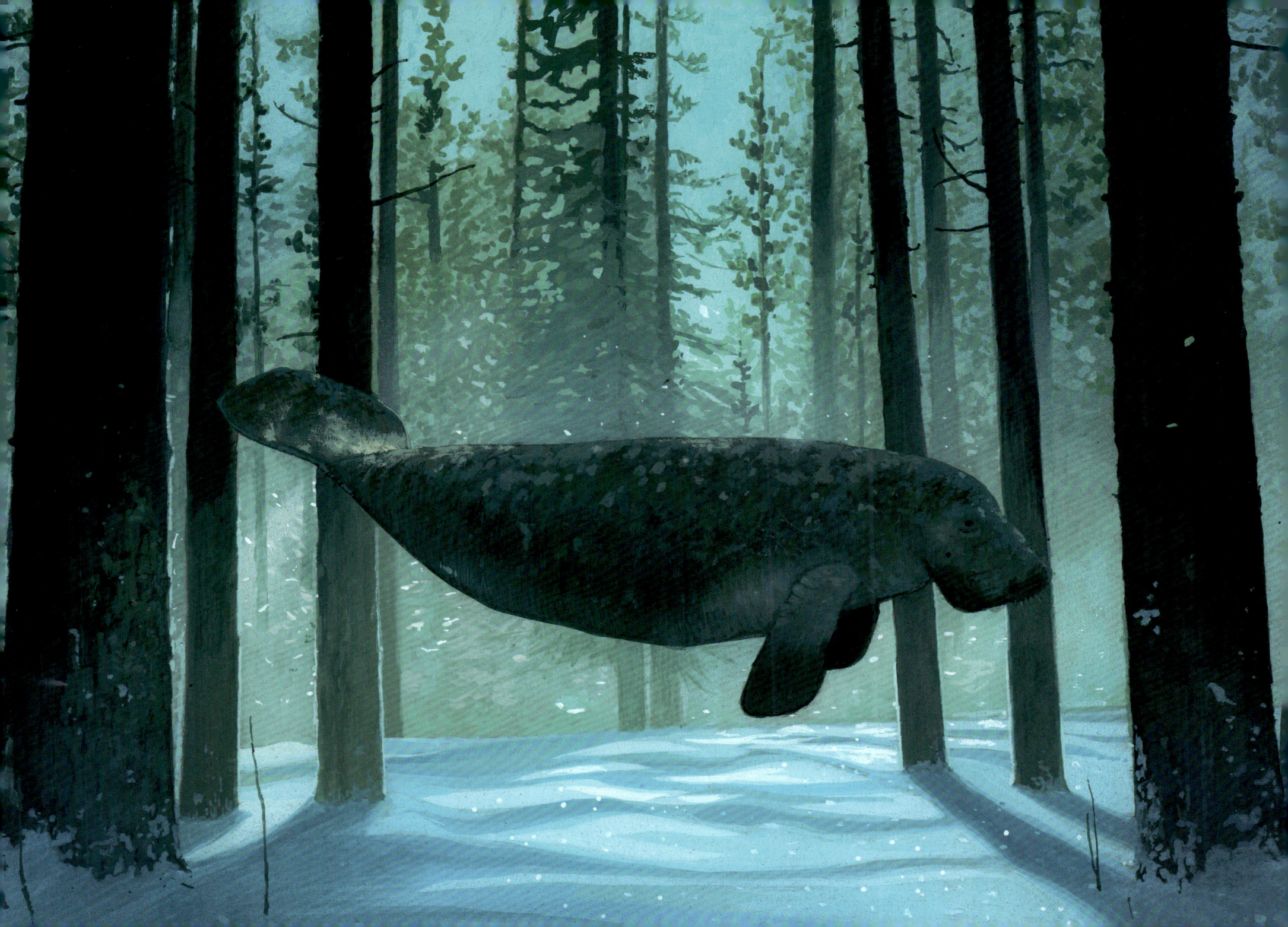

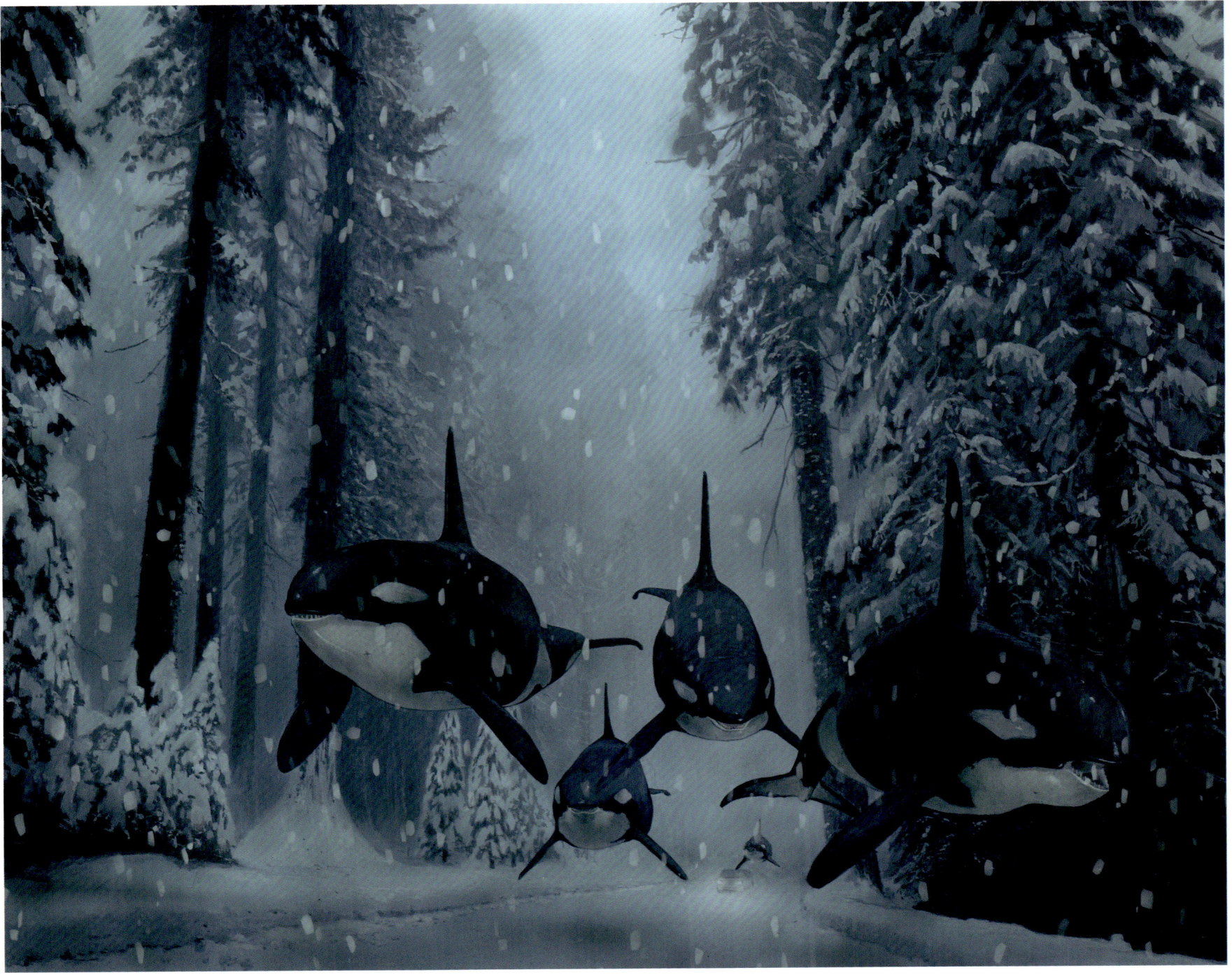

In The Teeth Of A Crashing Gale | 8″ x 9.5″ | gouache on paper | 2020

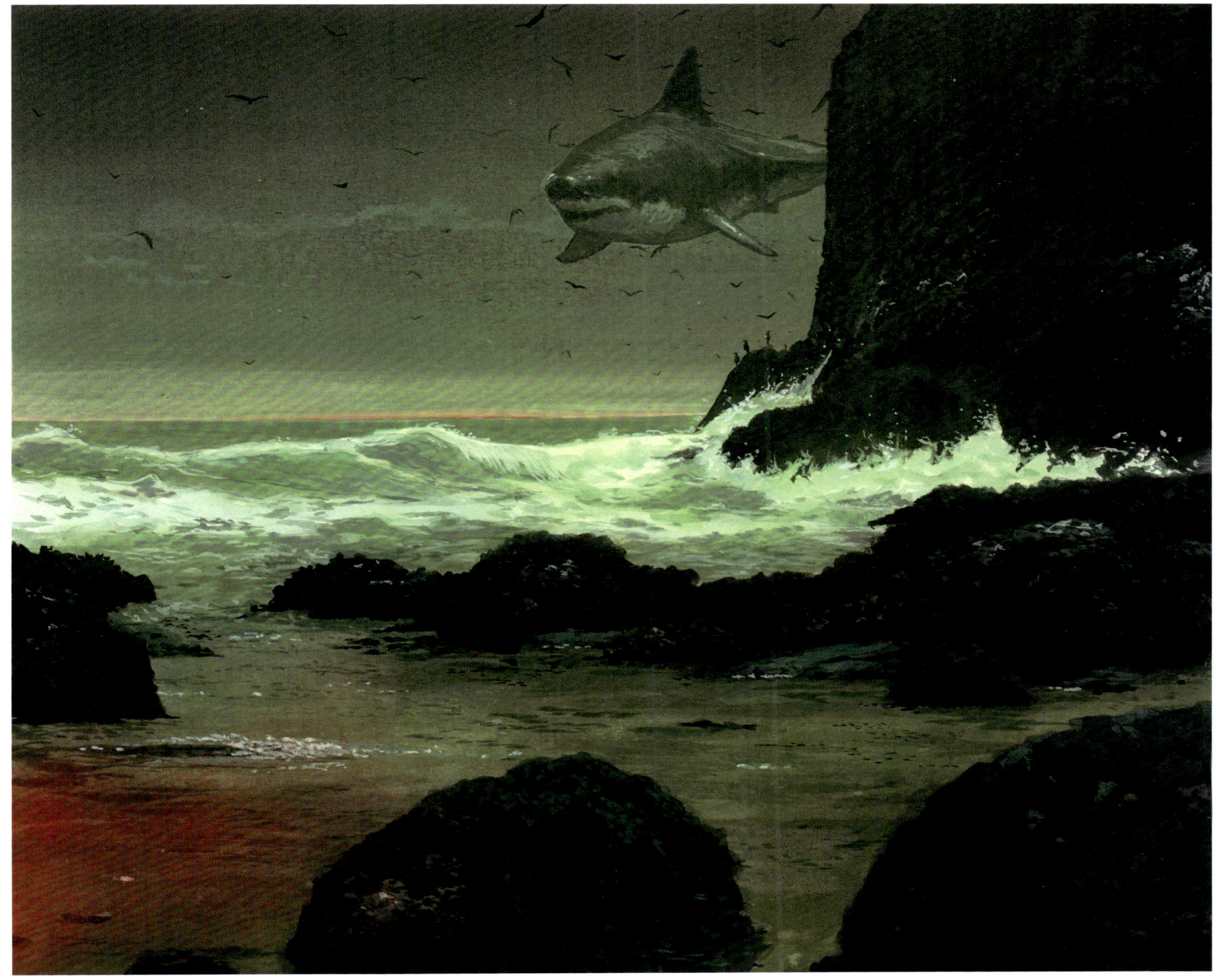

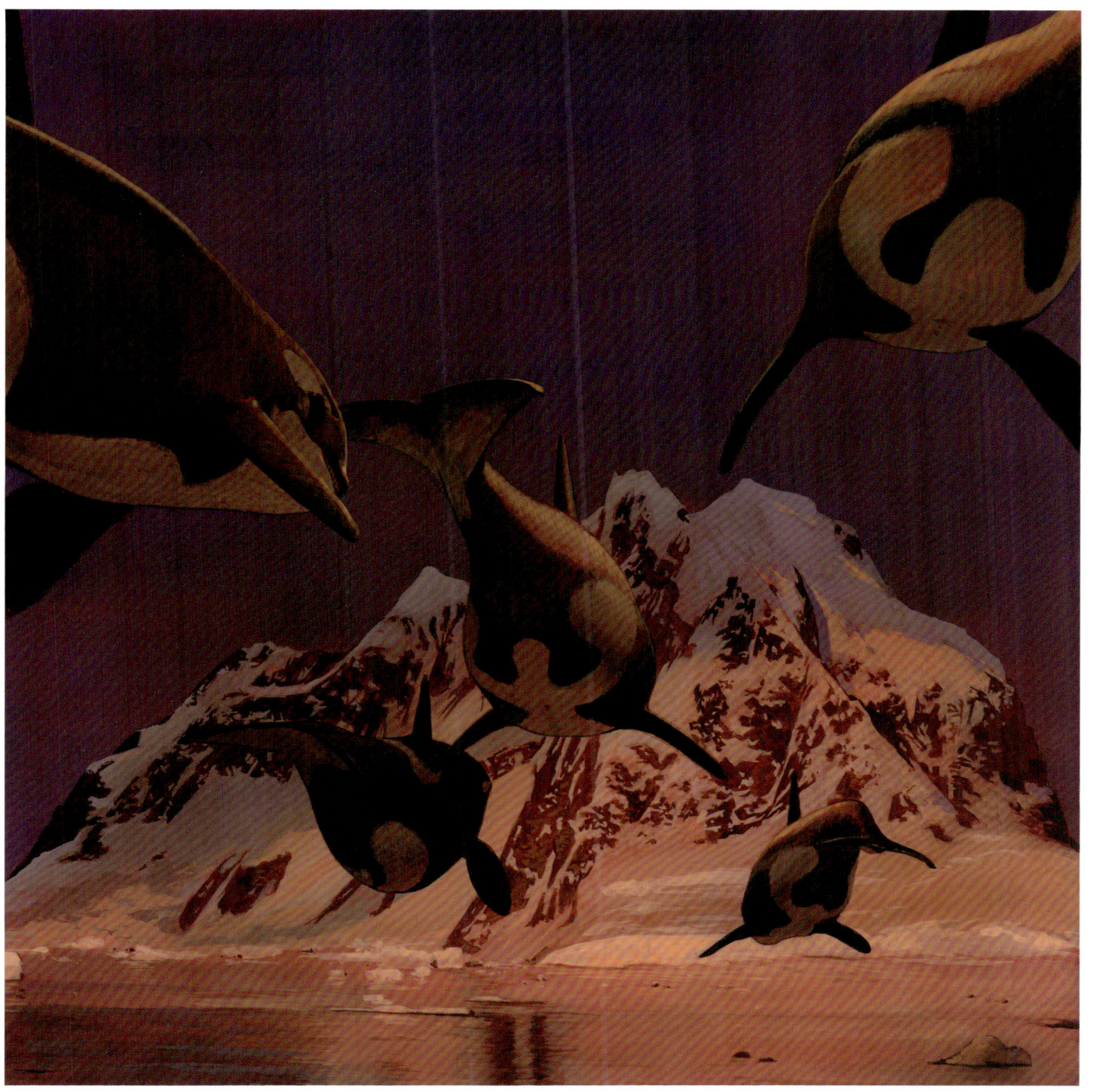

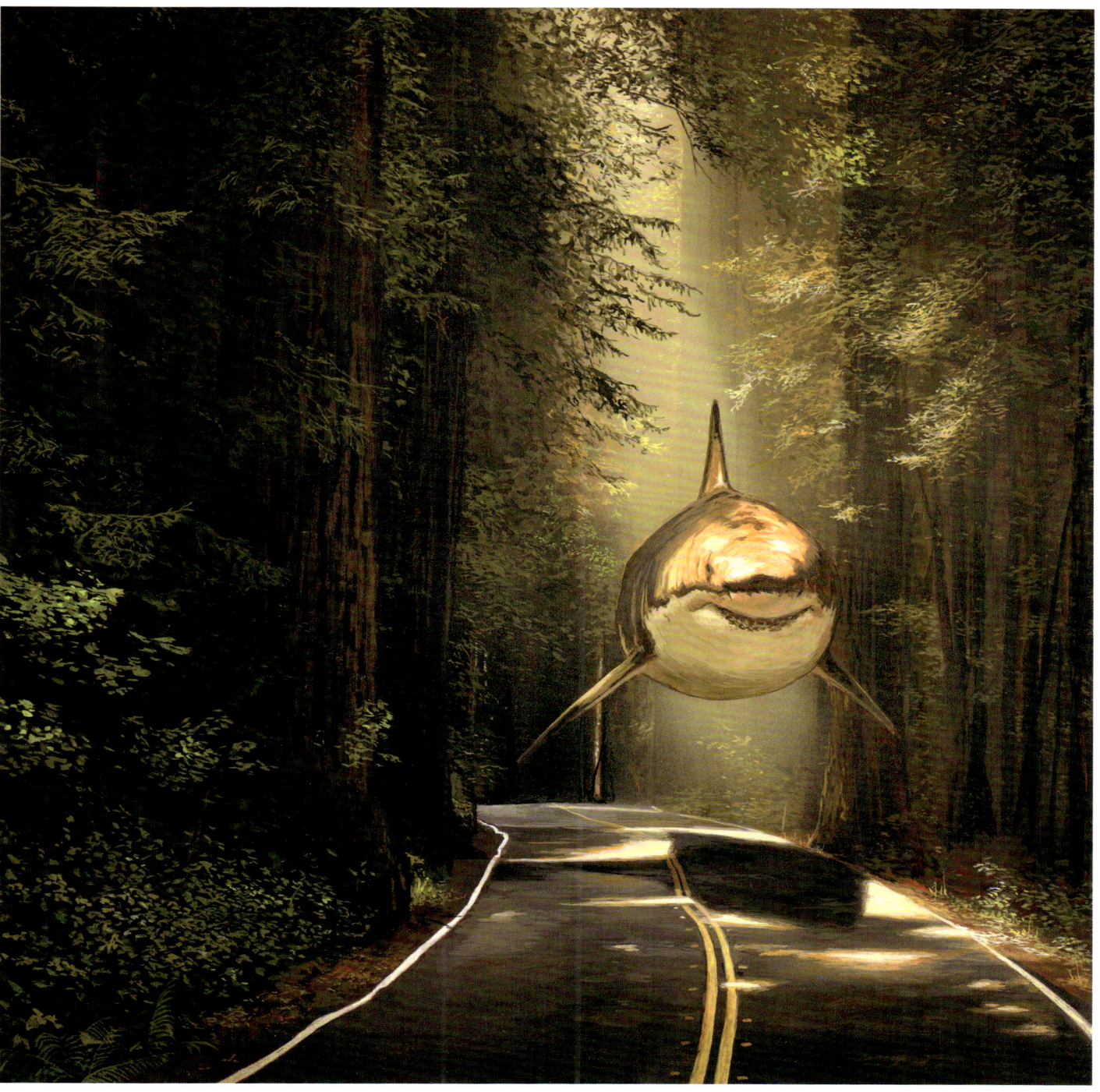

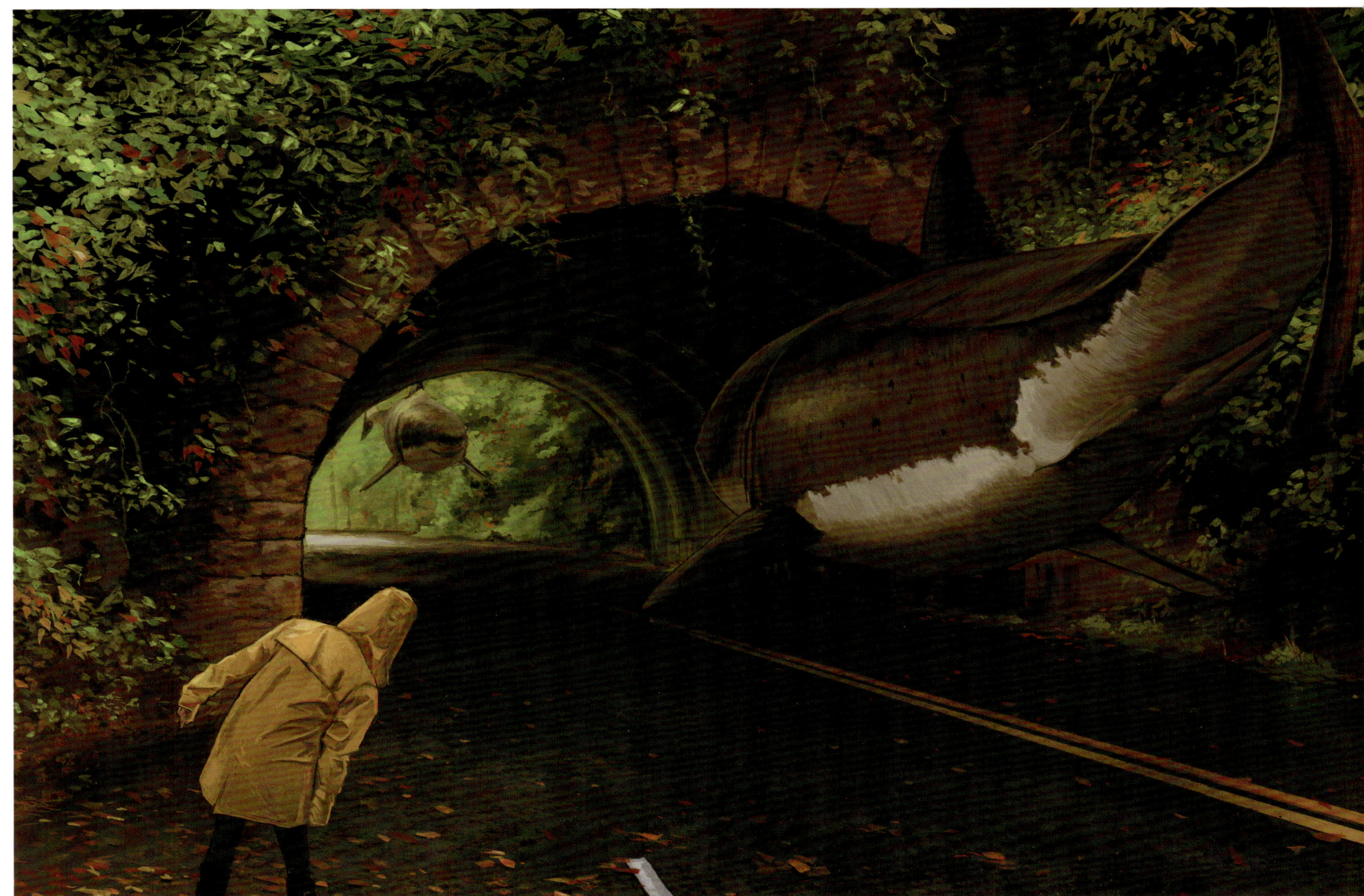

And You Cried Out To Me | 12" x 24" | gouache on wood | 2020

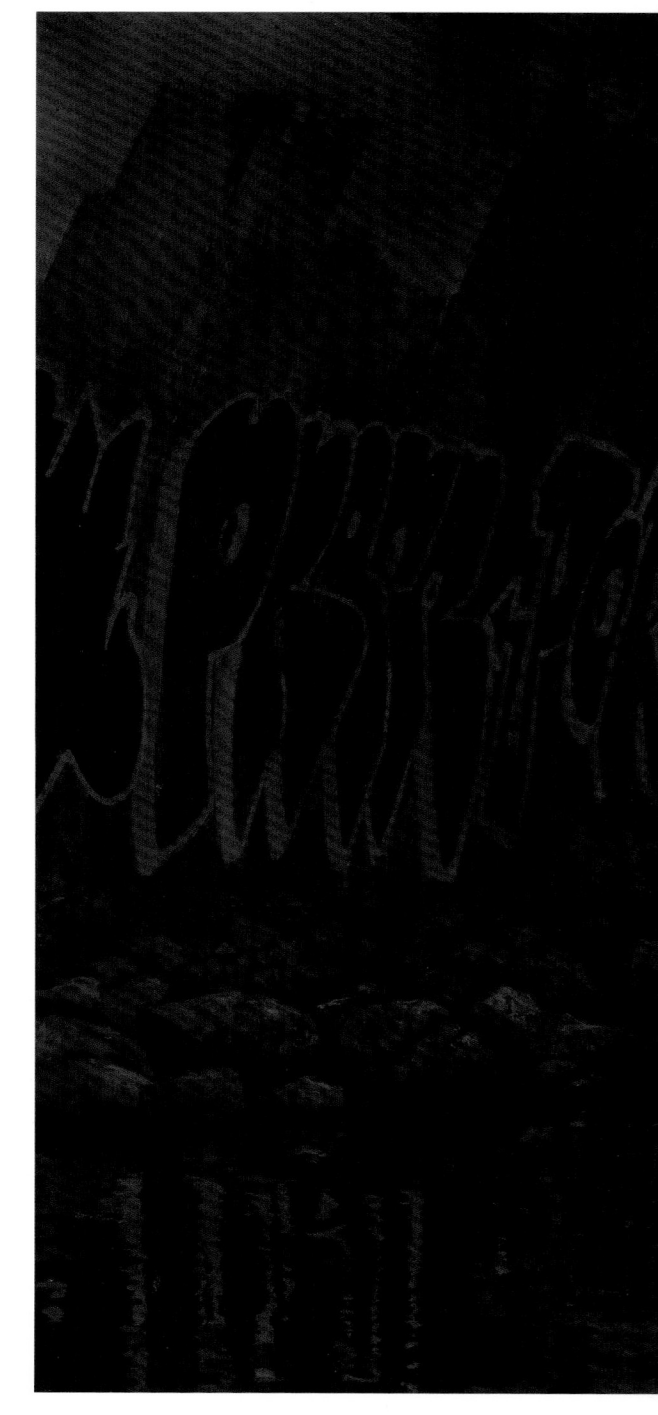

It Was You I Was Dreaming Of | 10" x 20" | gouache on wood | 2021

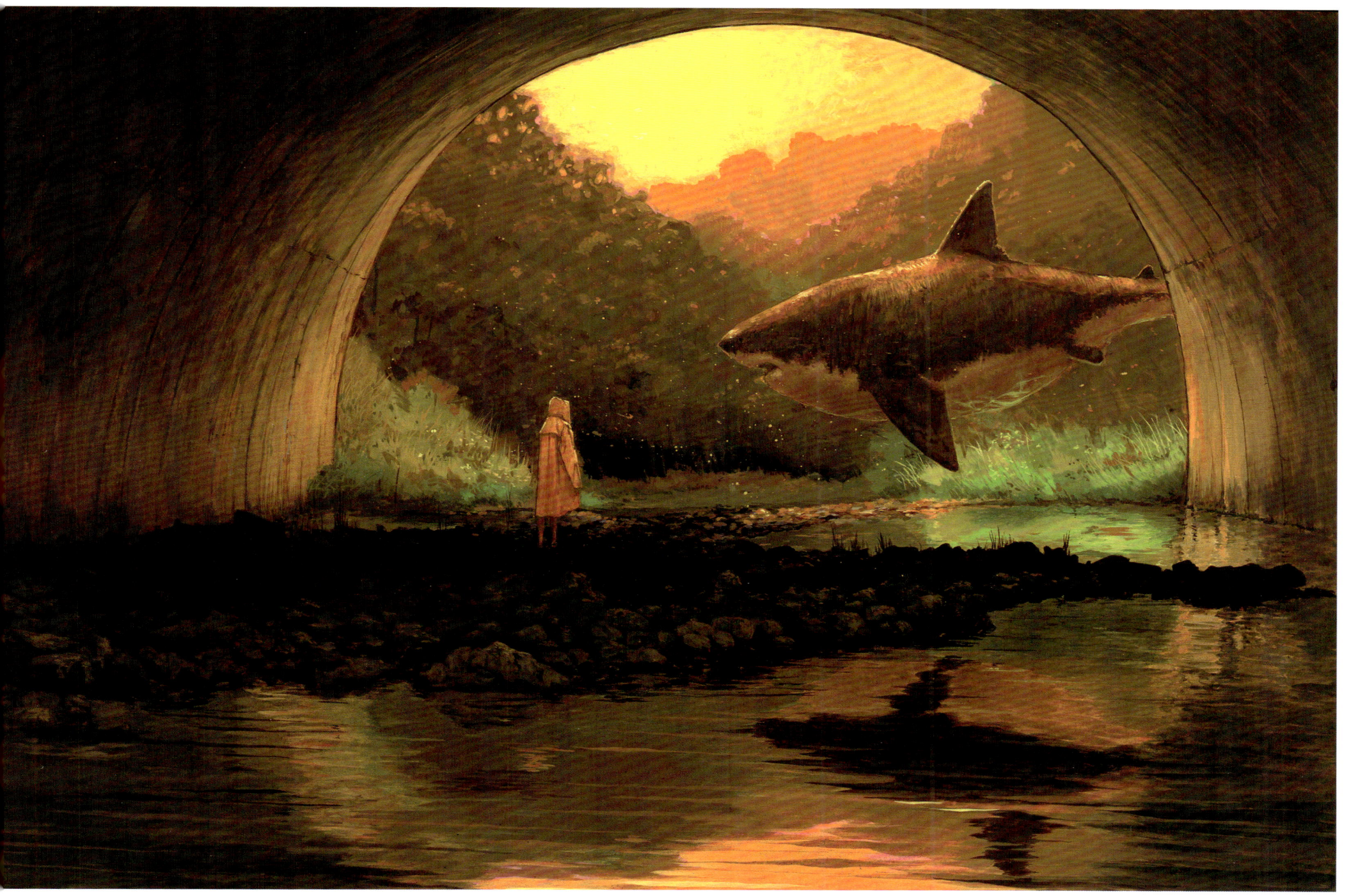

I see my work as a visual diary, using animals and contrasting environments to explore the complexities of my youth. The constant movement between the wrong crowd and moments of escape mirrors the interaction between different wildlife in bizarre, impractical settings. The unnatural pairings reflect how I was often in environments that didn't suit me, yet I found ways to navigate through them.

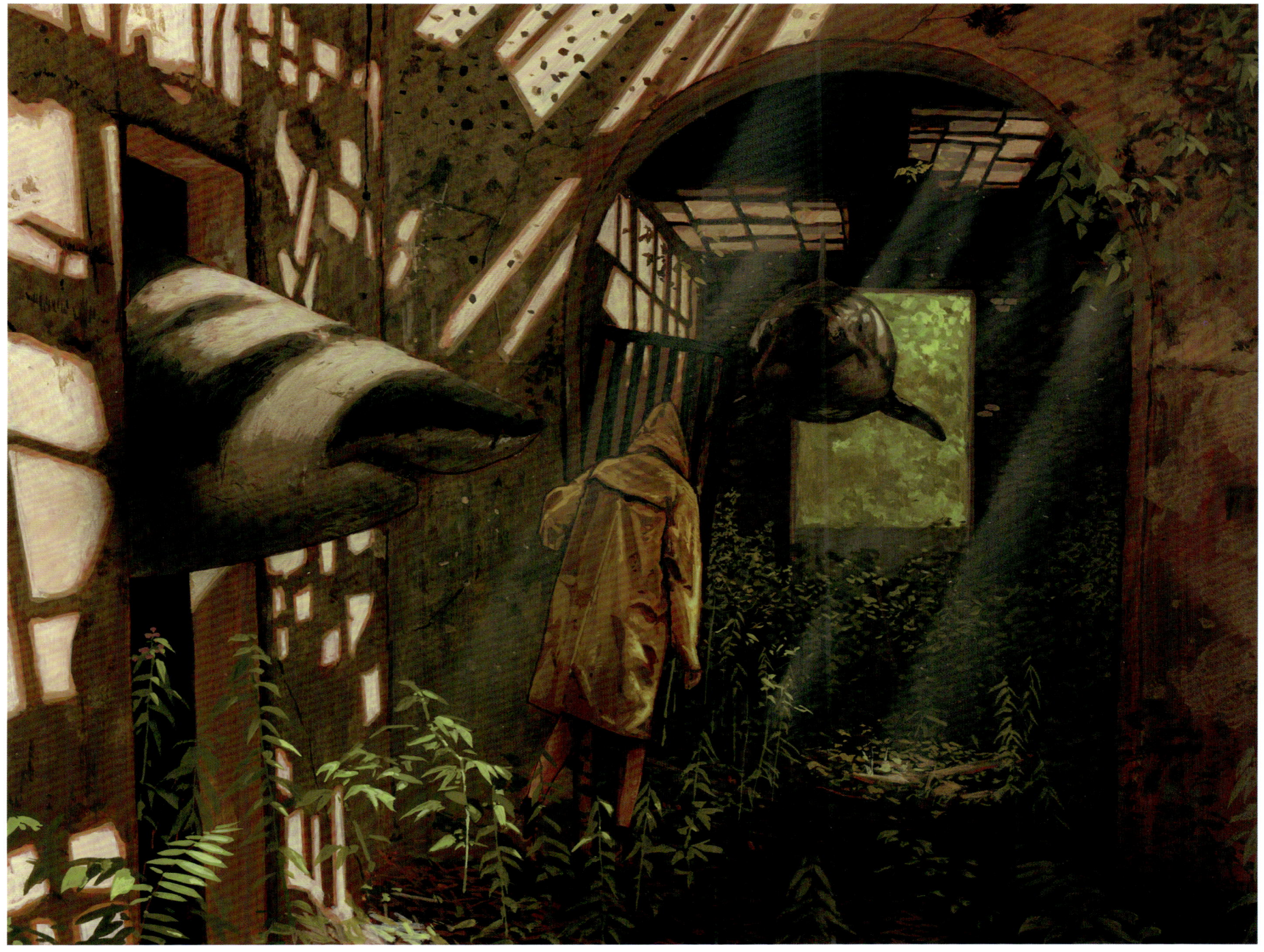

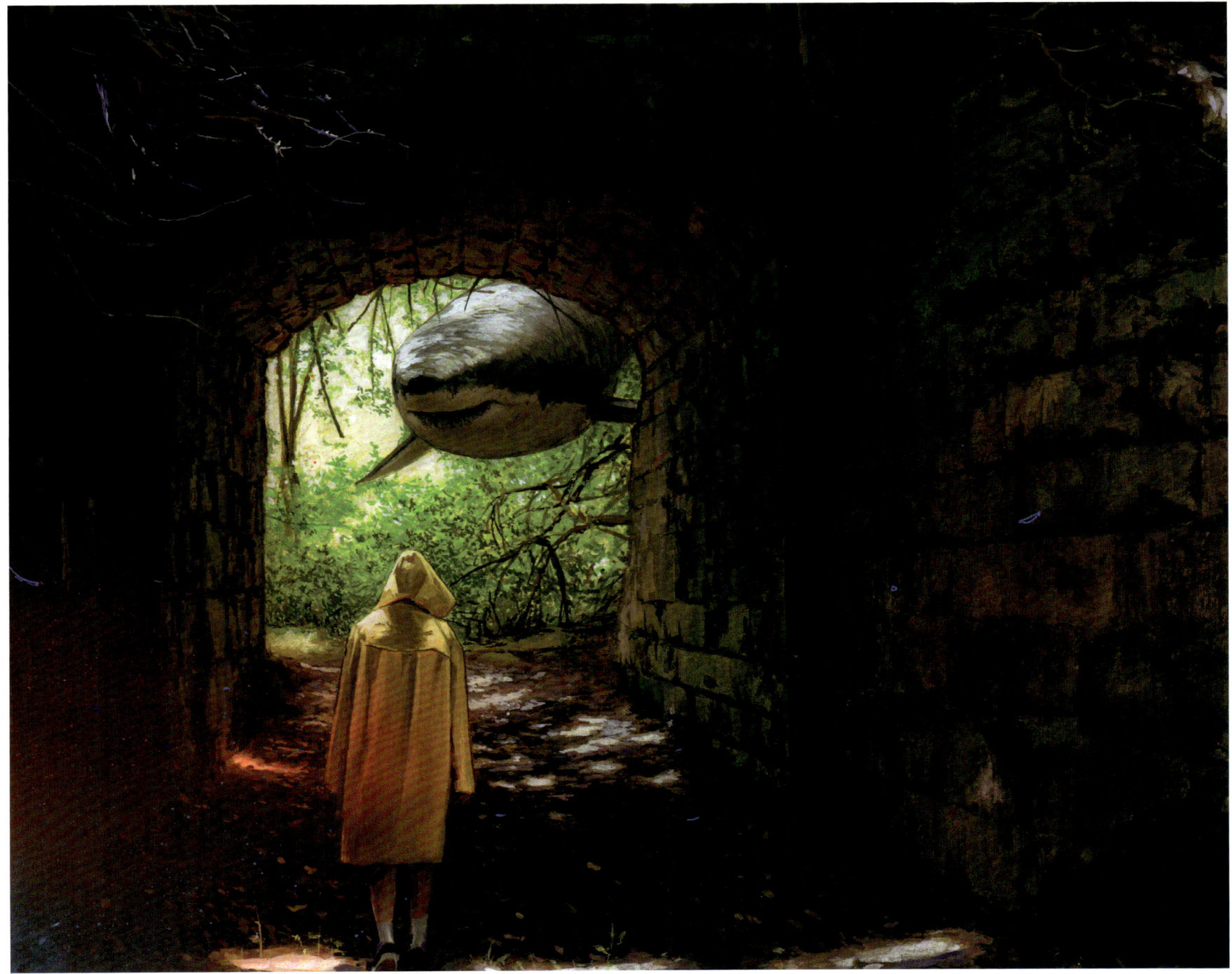

Little Dream One | 6.5" x 4" | gouache on paper | 2023

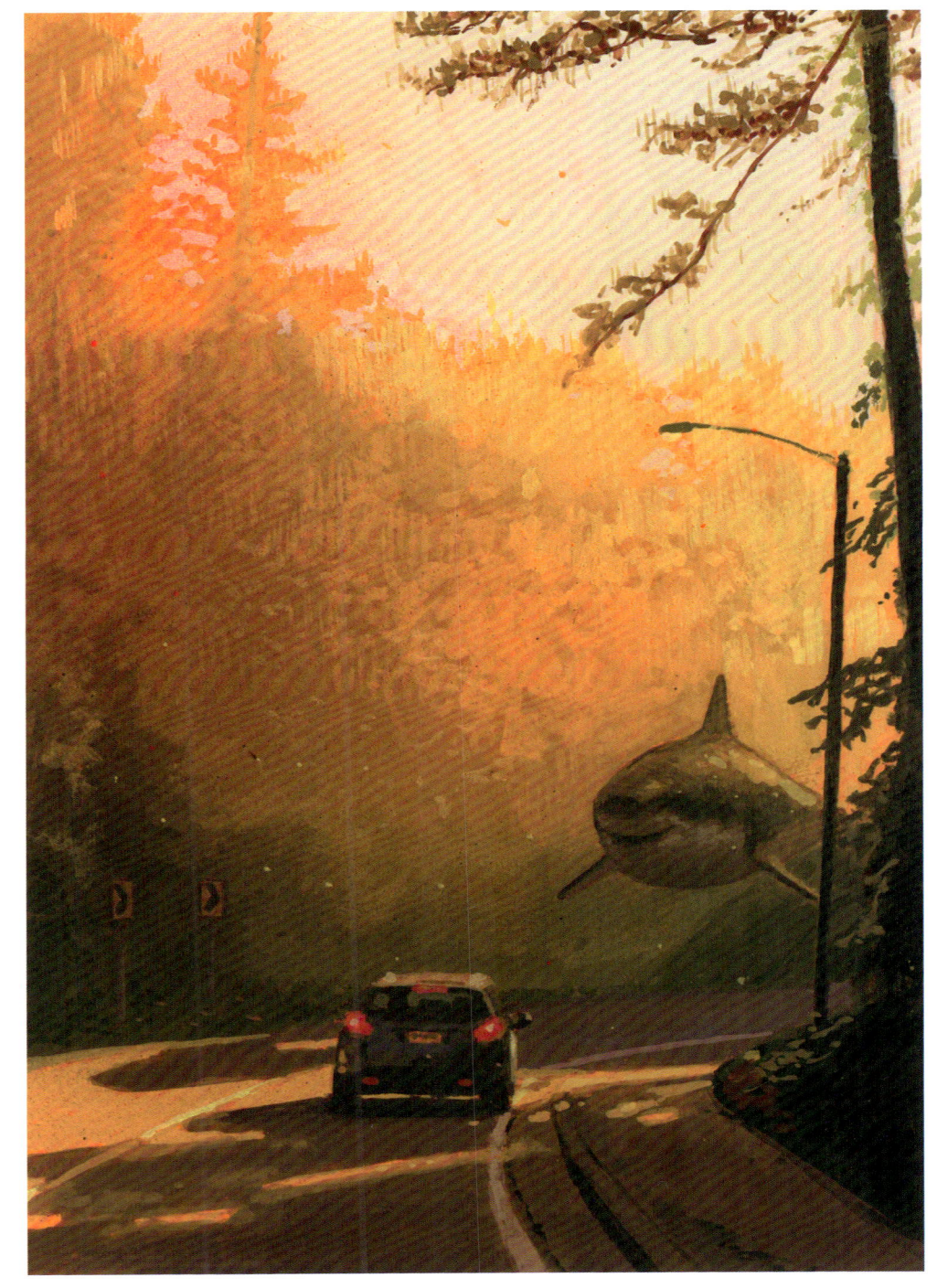

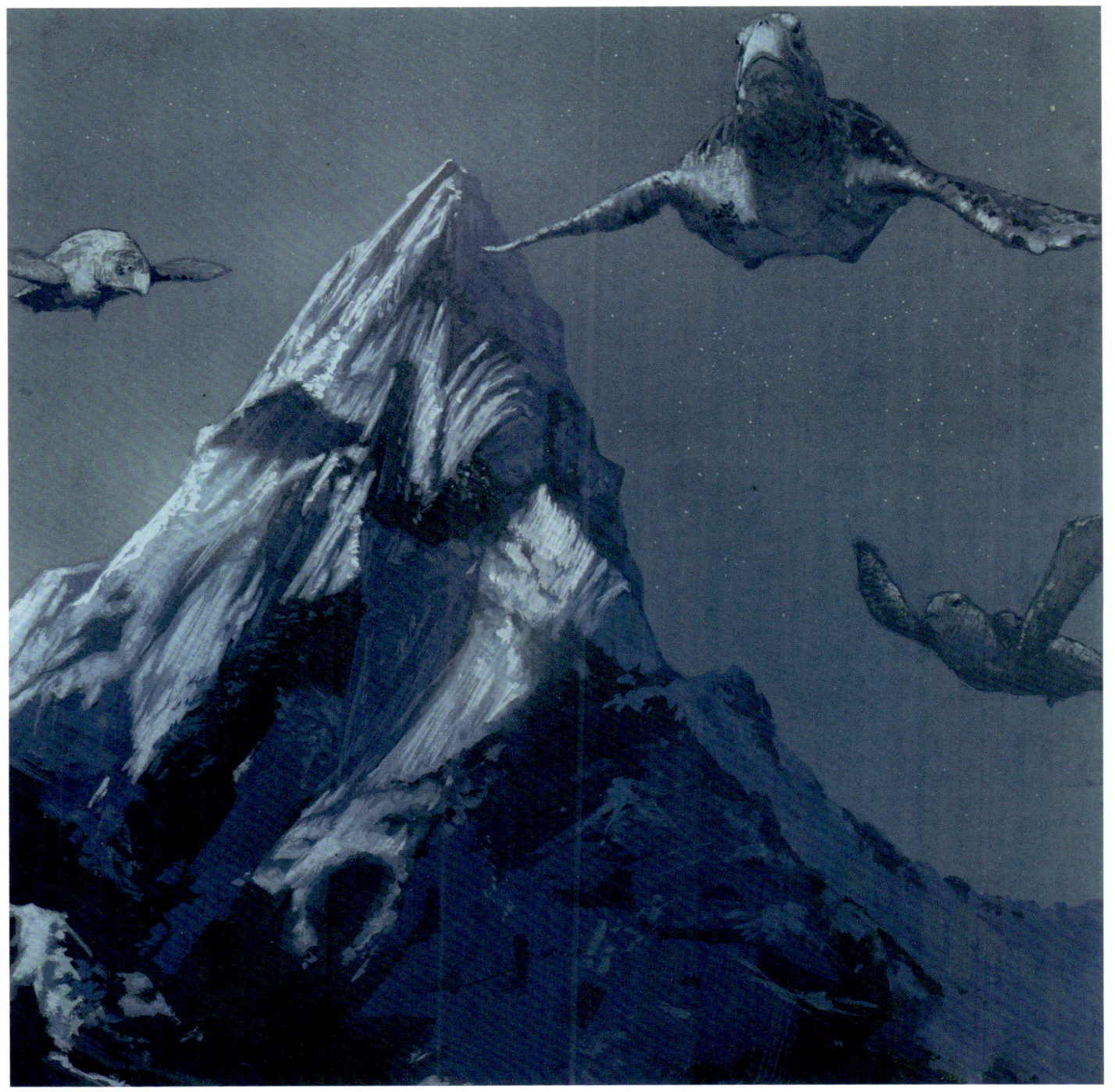

The marine life is particularly significant.
Water, often a symbol of depth, emotion,
and subconscious, and represent the higher
awareness I tapped into as a child. The
marine creatures stand for moments of
serenity and insight, offering me perspective
and understanding in a chaotic world.
They serve as guides, subtly leading me
away from darker influences, much like the
quiet moments of introspection that helped
me find clarity.

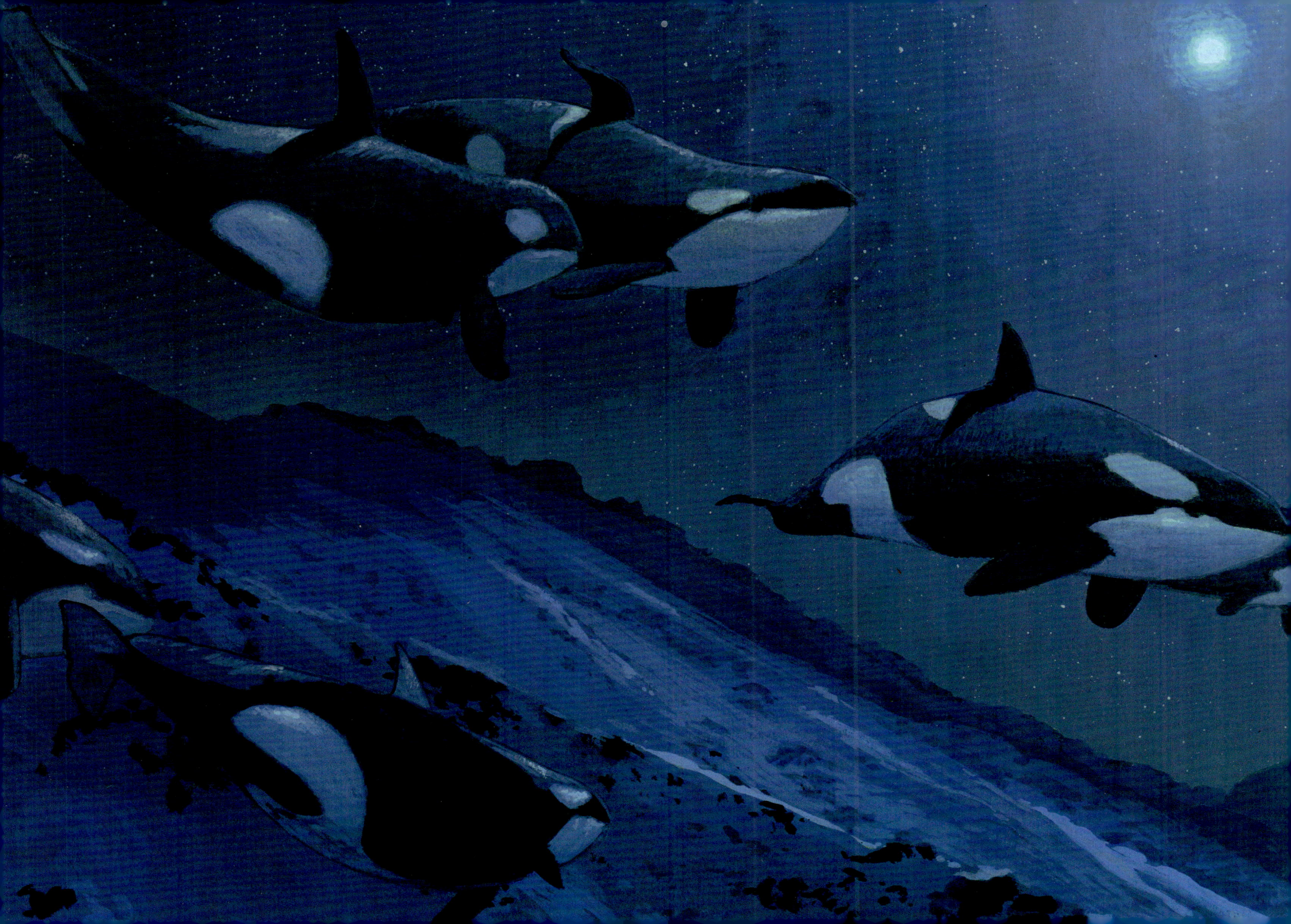

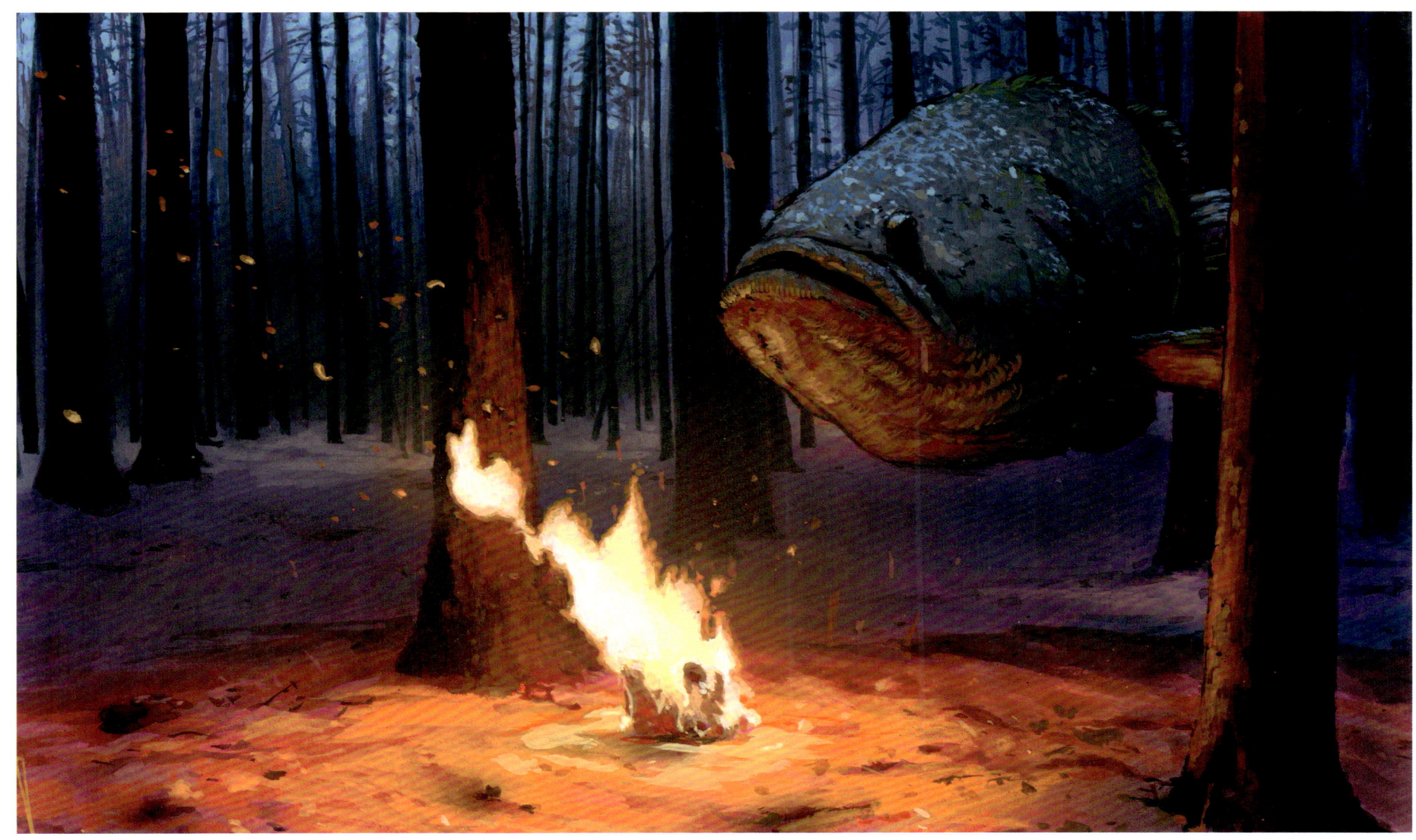

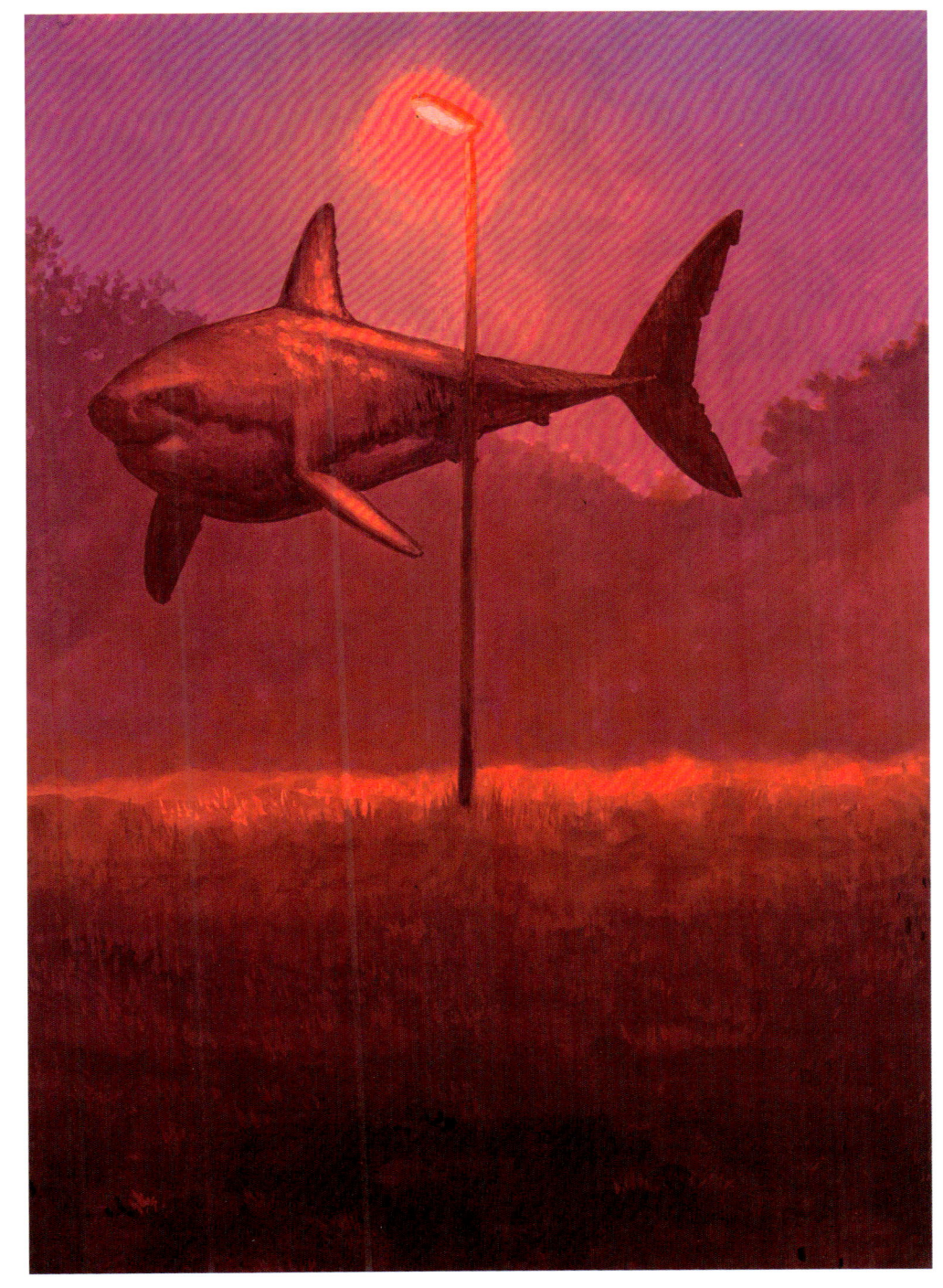

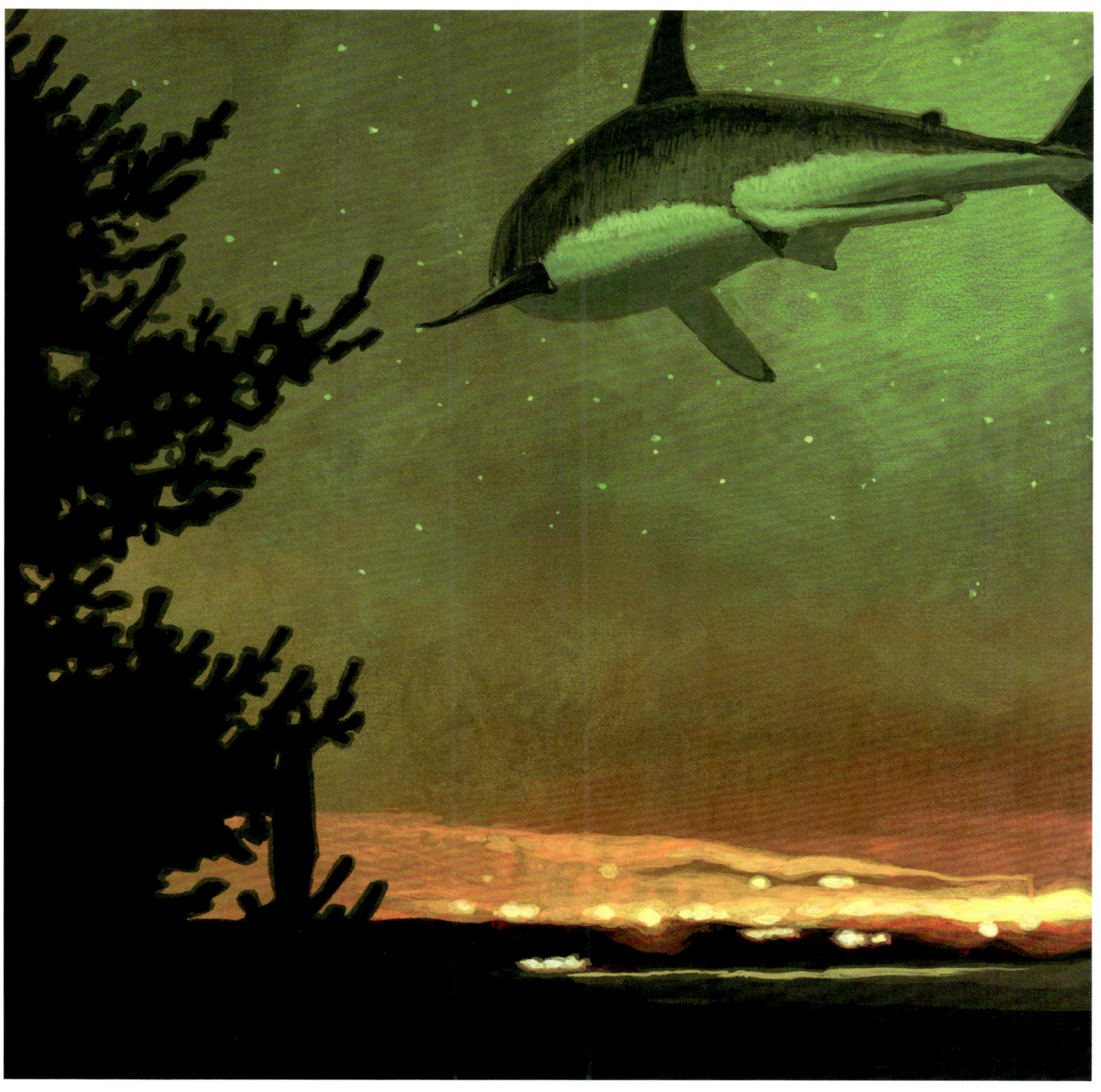

The unnatural scenes and bizarre juxtapositions capture the turbulence of my upbringing while also highlighting moments of awakening or rescue. The absurdity and contrast serve not only to question reality but also to explore my personal evolution and the internal forces that have shaped me.

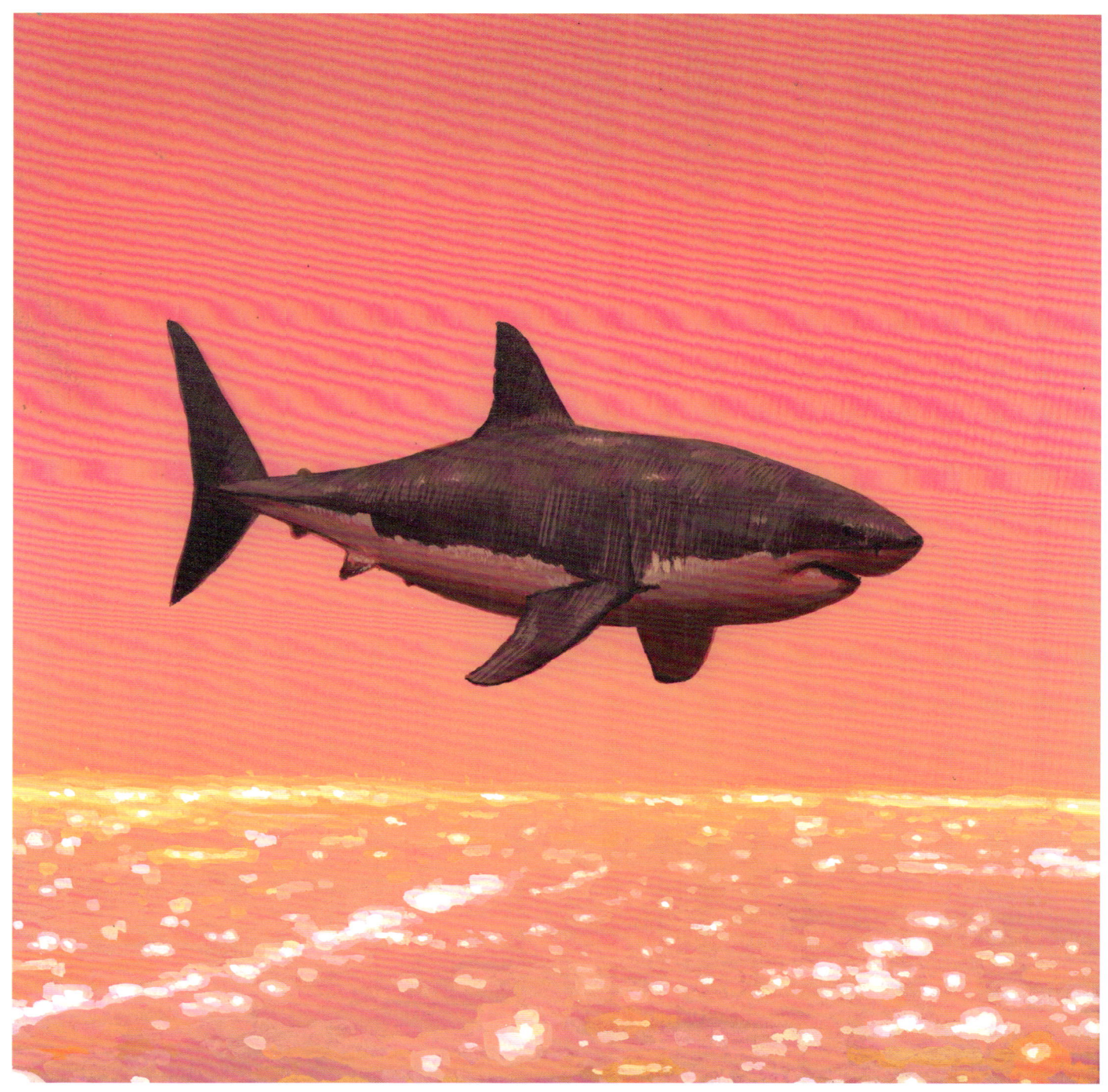

ESSAY
Reflections on The Work of Chris Austin
Luke W. Barrett (Collector, & Writer for Beautiful Bizzare magazine)

The first time I interviewed Chris Austin was in 2020 for Beautiful Bizarre magazine, during the early months of the COVID-19 pandemic. It felt appropriate that Chris was being interviewed right then. In terms of his career arc, the timing coincided with Chris having become one of the most well-known and respected names in the new contemporary art world. By then, his distinctive aesthetic was already instantaneously recognisable amongst a surging fanbase, both in the real world and the virtual world of social media and online previews. That was also a moment in time when there was considerable uncertainty and unease in the world over the future and our place in it. Whether intentional or not, Chris' body of work invites dystopian interpretations through his depictions of a familiar world that is unfamiliarly bereft of humans and being reclaimed by nature. Those themes resonated with the unsettling mood that was lingering in the world then and, some may say, now still.

While those moons were aligning, fate was not without a sense of humour. That issue of the magazine was itself destined to fall victim to the pandemic. To this day, it is the one issue that was never released in print format. With global supply chains disrupted, that issue, along with the feature story on Chris, could only be released in digital format. This wrong was somewhat put right years later, when that issue was included in a time capsule installed on Earth's moon, etched in platinum that will endure for centuries to come. This was part of the Lunar Codex initiative.

Against that backdrop, this book is a symbolic and tangible artefact that, for the first time, documents and celebrates what Chris has been able to achieve so far. This book has gathered some of the finest examples of Chris' work and offers glimpses into the ideas and emotions being expressed through these paintings.

While Chris has said that he came out of the womb carrying a pack of crayons, this book's release comes about a decade after the birth of the body of work for which Chris is best known. It has been a prolific decade. While he has long since lost count, Chris estimates there must currently be over one hundred of his paintings scattered across the globe. While Chris paints from the home he built with his own hands in Canada, he regularly exhibits with some of the world's most prominent galleries, from the United States to Australia.

Chris' oeuvre exists within the context of several concurrent movements within the contemporary art world. There is no perfect name for these movements. 'New-contemporary' seems too utilitarian and its second-aunt 'pop-surrealism' does not seem quite right either. Despite lacking a well-settled name, there is defi-nitely an identifiable genre (for want of a better word) and Chris exists at its epicentre and is one of its leading proponents.

In terms of Chris' success, this is absolutely an outworking of his unique aesthetic and outstanding execution. There is a cinematic quality to every painting which could easily be a frame taken from a motion picture. From foreground to background, protagonist to antagonist, every detail is rendered with photographic-like realism. One of the hooks within Chris' work is the uncanny surrealism that Chris is able to create with his photorealism. There is nothing abstract or impressionistic or cartoony about these works. Chris weaves his surrealism from strands of photorealism. The effect is a double-take or a fleeting belief within the viewer that the scenes depicted are in fact happening or have occurred, at least until our mind catches up and talks sense into us. There is a beautiful moment every time you look at one of Chris' paintings, before our left-brain or frontal lobe chimes in to spoil the party, where our inner-child is open to the possibility that orcas and sharks might be casually drifting through previously-human-inhabited cities and the neighbouring forests. Whether the world has been flooded or these creatures have evolved an ability to float through air, the rationalisation and the myth is of our own making and personal to each viewer.

At the same time, it is fair to say that the last decade has also coincided with a fascination within the genre with nature and the planet. During the last decade, the world finally accepted, for the most part,the science of climate change and the negative impacts that post-industrial humans have had on the environment and the other lifeforms we share our planet with. While nature has always featured prominently in art, the last decade has been one where themes involving nature and animals have been particularly embraced and have enjoyed a resurgence. Indeed, there are galleries, artists and collectors exclusively focused on art that is nature-focused. It seems fair to say that this has been a serendipitous tailwind for Chris that has also shaped some interpretations of his paintings.

Chris' paintings are certainly open to cautionary or even dystopian interpretations that see a premonition of what might transpire if we do not change our relationship with the environment and other lifeforms. These interpretations arguably stem from a human-centric mindset that infers something unworldly from the absence of humans. His work can be analysed and appreciated on that level. Equally, his paintings can be enjoyed more straightforwardly as an aesthetical celebration of nature and some of the majestic creatures that inhabit the planet. Speaking to Chris, however, it becomes apparent that his paintings are explorations of fundamentally human themes and meditations on his own childhood.

Chris has found peace and smiles when he reflects on his childhood and his parents. There were difficult times in his childhood though. As happens with too many families, his parents separated when he was very young. Chris' father was initially granted custody of Chris and his brother. Unfortunately, there was an extra member of the household that lived in a bottle and that was better at attracting his father's attention. Fear was a feeling that Chris and his brother learned to live with.

As a child, Chris would often escape the house and spend many hours out on his own. He would spend whole days exploring the nearby forest, discovering abandoned houses and wandering through dark tunnels. These were defining experiences for Chris. If the situation had been different at home, he might never have been allowed to have these experiences, but nor would he have needed them.

Returning to his paintings, it becomes apparent that these are scenes from Chris' childhood. These are the forests, the abandoned buildings and the dark tunnels to which Chris would escape to get away from the situation at home. But these are not sad memories. These places were his sanctuary. Chris remembers those times as golden years that shaped him as a person. These were the life experiences through which he found his sense of self-sufficiency, resilience, compassion and love of nature.

The abandoned scenery evokes the loneliness of a child left to their own devices to raise themselves. The orca whales and the sharks that drift through the scenery enhance that theme. They are the imaginary friends that would keep young Chris company during his childhood adventures. The fact that they are apex predators hints at the sense of constant fear and vulnerability that Chris and his brother lived with. The young character wearing the yellow slicker is overtly young Chris, exploring his surroundings either alone or with his imaginary friends and a sense of fear.

Fast-forward and there was eventually a happy-ending of sorts. Chris' father found his sobriety, but the piper must be paid and diabetes took his sight. It is a cruel irony that, having reestablished their relationship, Chris' father has never actually seen any of the art that was inspired by those childhood years and that has driven Chris' artistic success.

A book like this can assist with identifying subtle thematic variations across the broader body of work. First, there are the paintings that feature a world or an environment that is devoid of humans. Second, there are the paintings that feature the lonely child in the yellow slicker, exploring their surrounds in conjunction with those apex predators. These first two groupings have been discussed already, but there are two other groupings that can be discerned.

Third, there are the paintings in which congested human cities and streets are shared with nature.Circumstance has required Chris to find his own way through life. At almost every turn, he has taken the road less travelled. This third group of paintings, where humanity and nature cross paths, makes the point that, after all is said and done, no matter how we all go about life, we are all still here. There is more than one path through life and to success.

Fourth, there are paintings that convey a political or social message, through images of climate-related fires and riot squads and the like. These days Chris is aware that he has an artistic voice—one that will be heard—that he can use to express his opinions on causes that are important to him.

Many will be relieved to hear that Chris intends to keep pursuing this body of work for years to come. That said, there will be subtle evolutions along the way, as we have seen in recent years. Until a few years ago, the yellow slicker character had never revealed their face, but now they have. The giant grouper fish is a relatively recent introduction to Chris' world. If you thought this character was a more pleasant or happier symbol, you are mistaken. The grouper is a throw back to a past relationship in which his former partner kept pet grouper fish, which brings back all manner of unpleasant memories for Chris.

In the future, Chris envisages introducing a new, recurring character into his paintings. The new character will be an explorer-father-figure who will feature in the ongoing narrative with the yellow slicker character. Again, there will be parallels to Chris' own childhood. In terms of the symbolism, the character in the yellow slicker and the new explorer character will both be Chris. There is something courageous, moving and simultaneously sad about someone becoming the father-figure they never had, but always needed and wanted, to themselves.

Chris has succeeded in creating a distinctive aesthetic which is immediately identifiable as the work of Chris Austin. While visually captivating, these paintings subtly tell a deeply moving and very human story through symbolism that is not necessarily immediately obvious. This book hopefully goes some way to unlocking the secrets within these paintings. As for whatever consciousness unearths the images of Chris' work on the moon in centuries to come, they will need to figure it out for themselves.

Until then, what a wondrous and beautifully mysterious place the Earth would seem. And it is. We should take care of it. If Chris' work tells us anything, it is that sometimes it is up to us to take care of ourselves.

Luke W. Barrett, January 2025

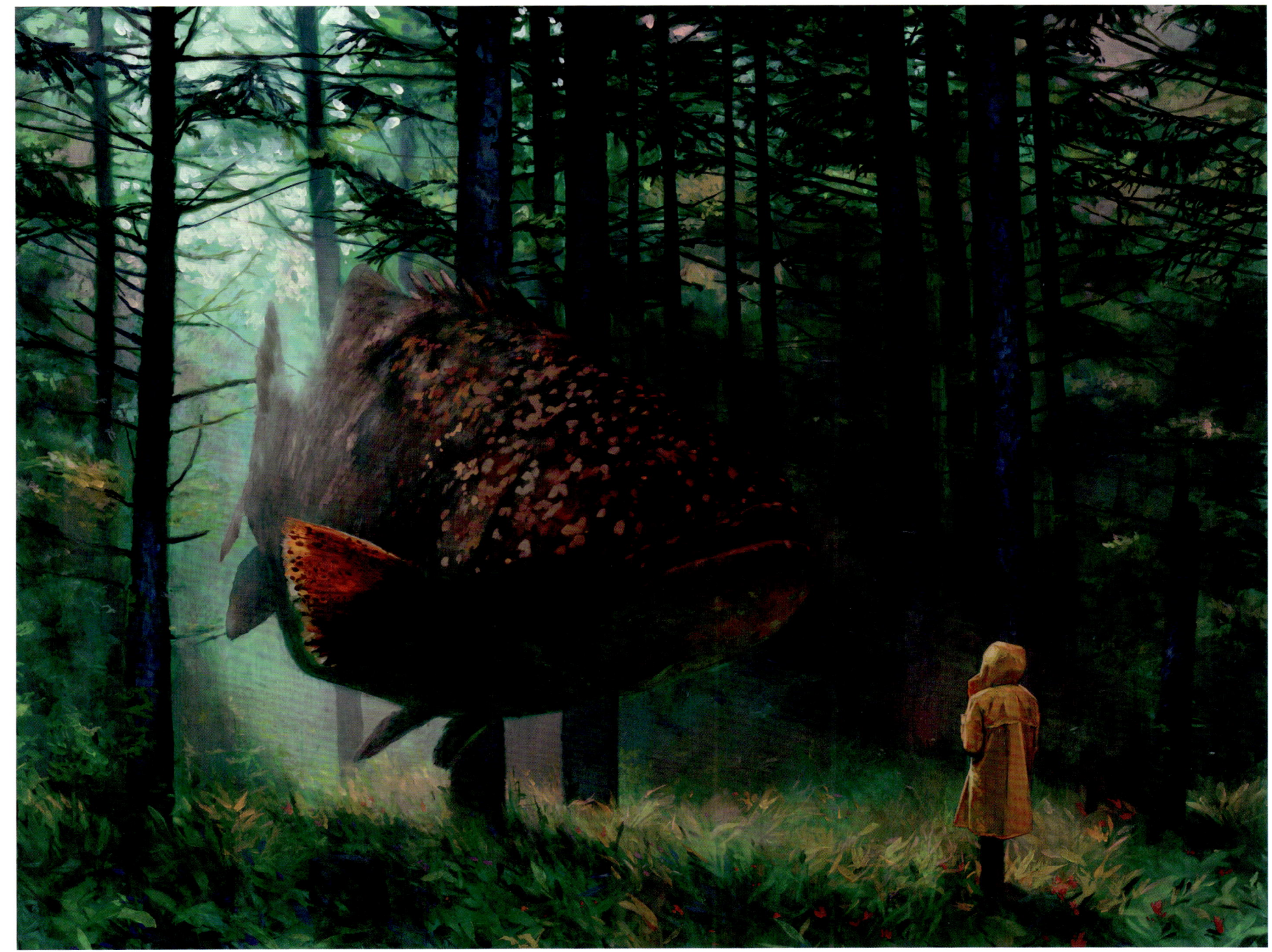

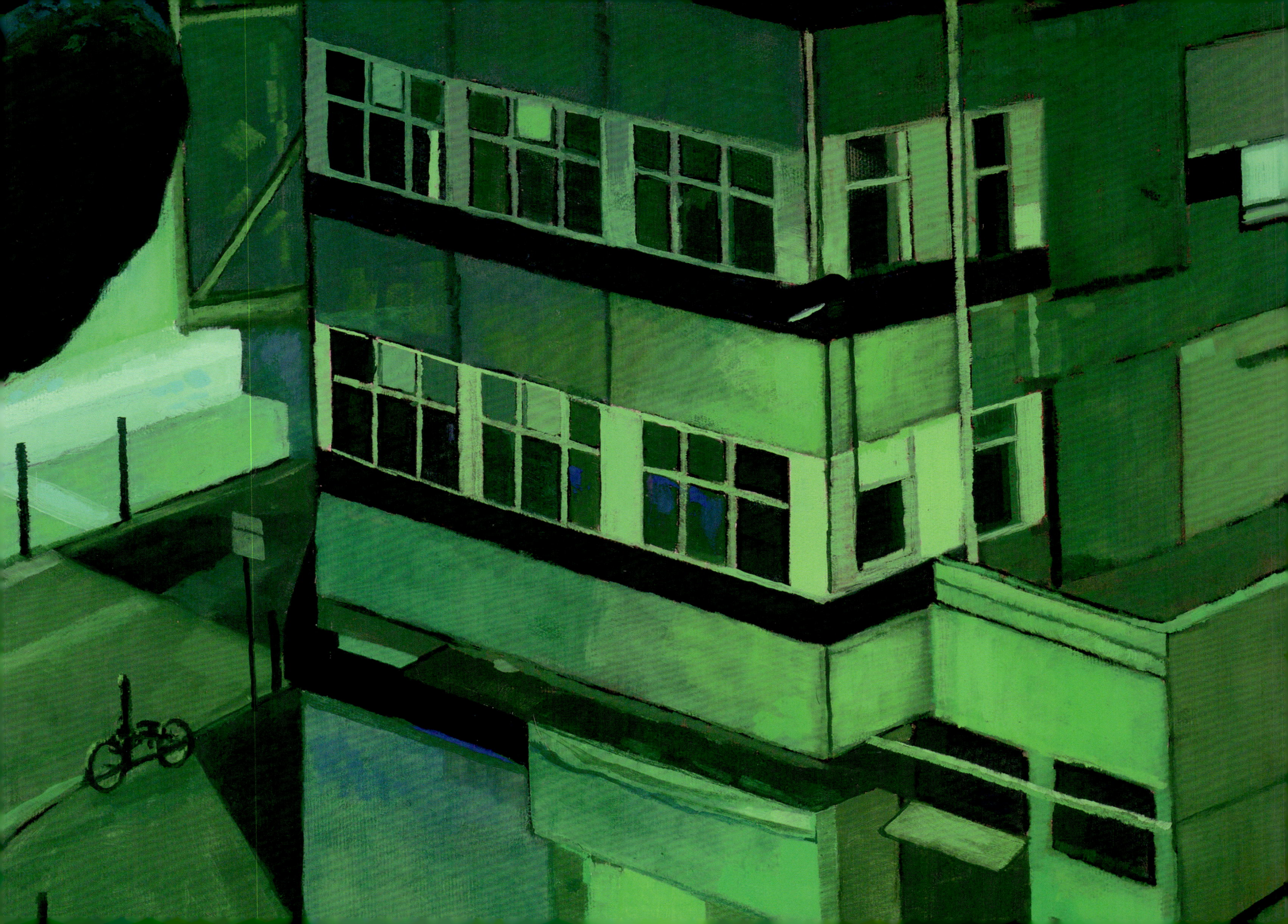

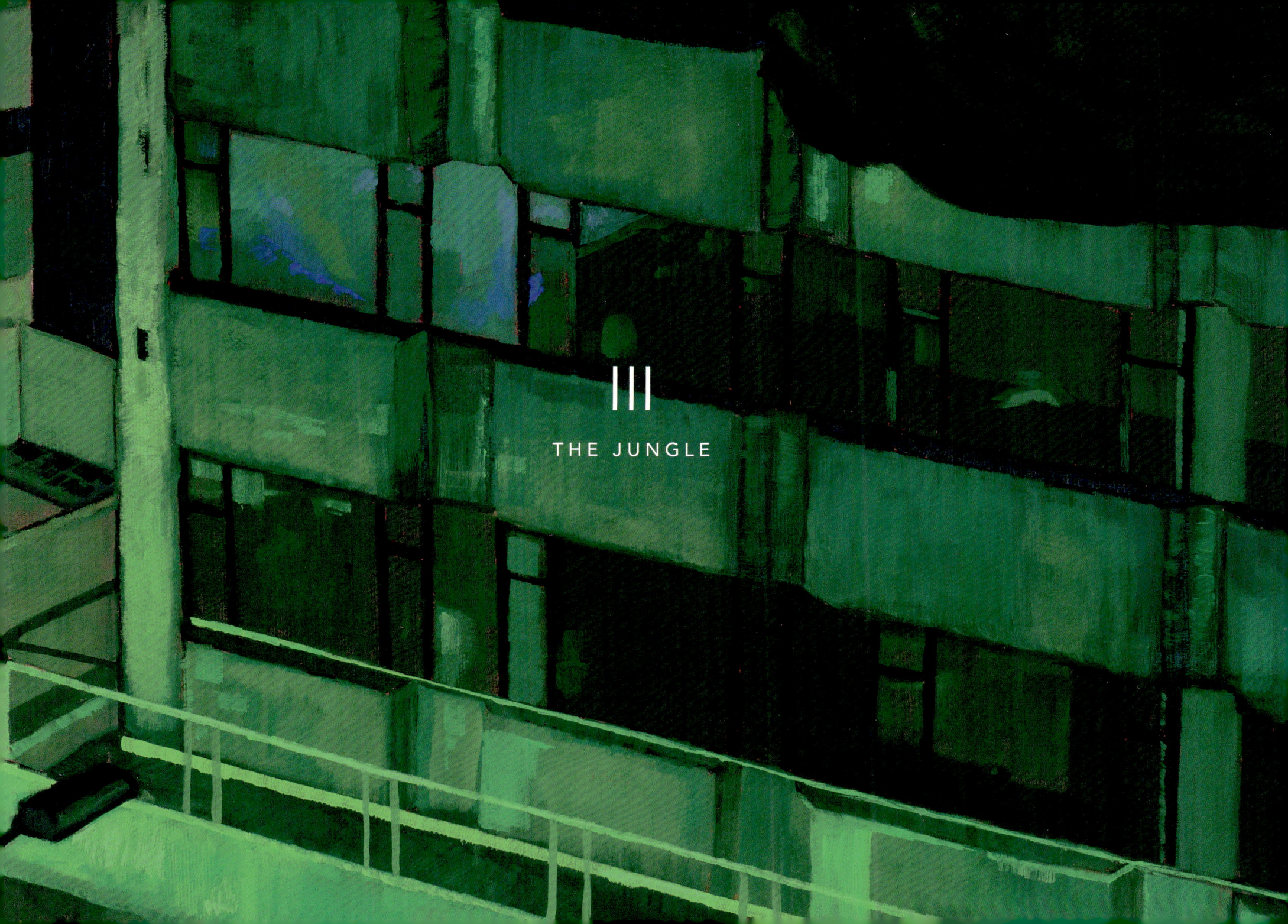

III

THE JUNGLE

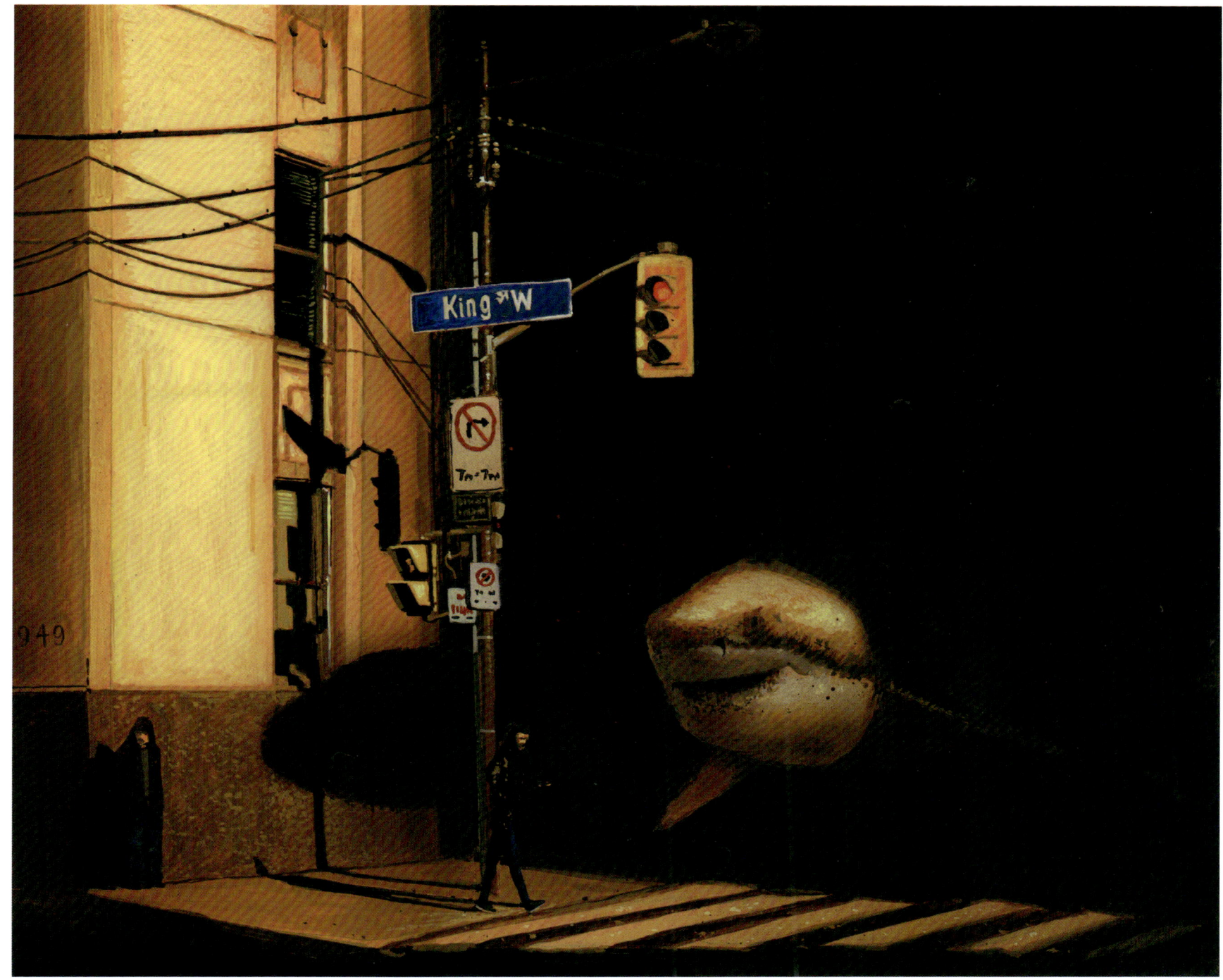

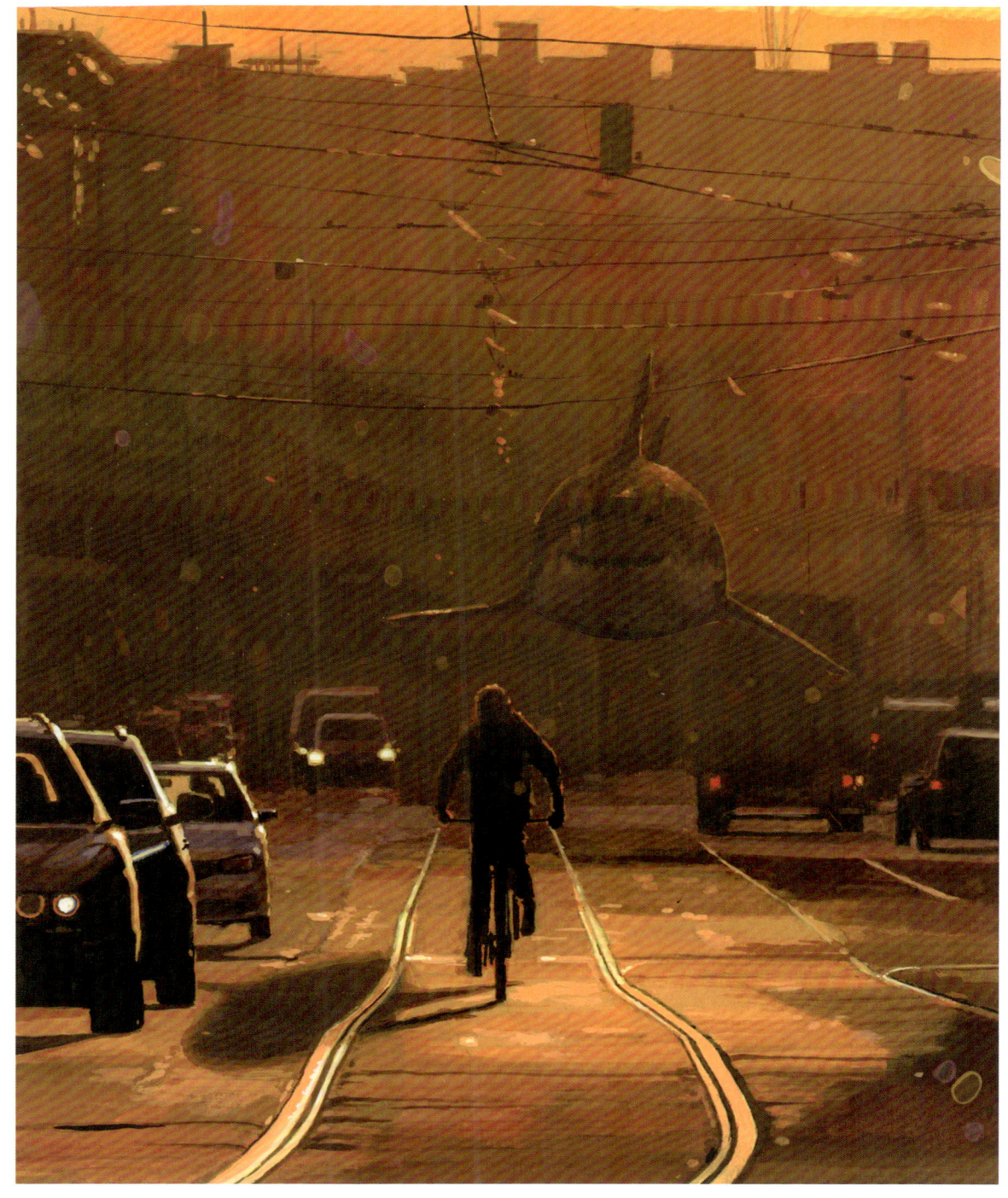

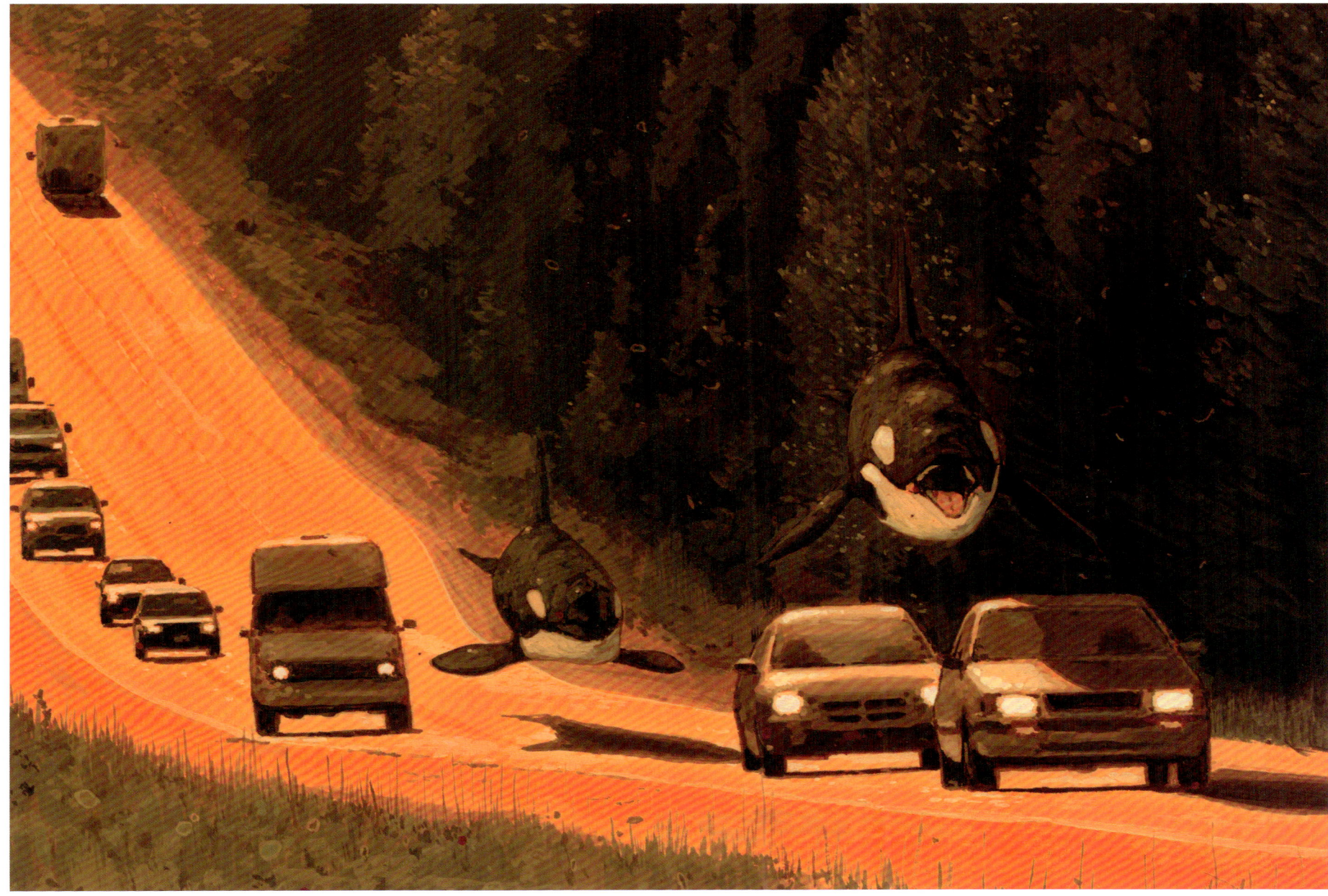

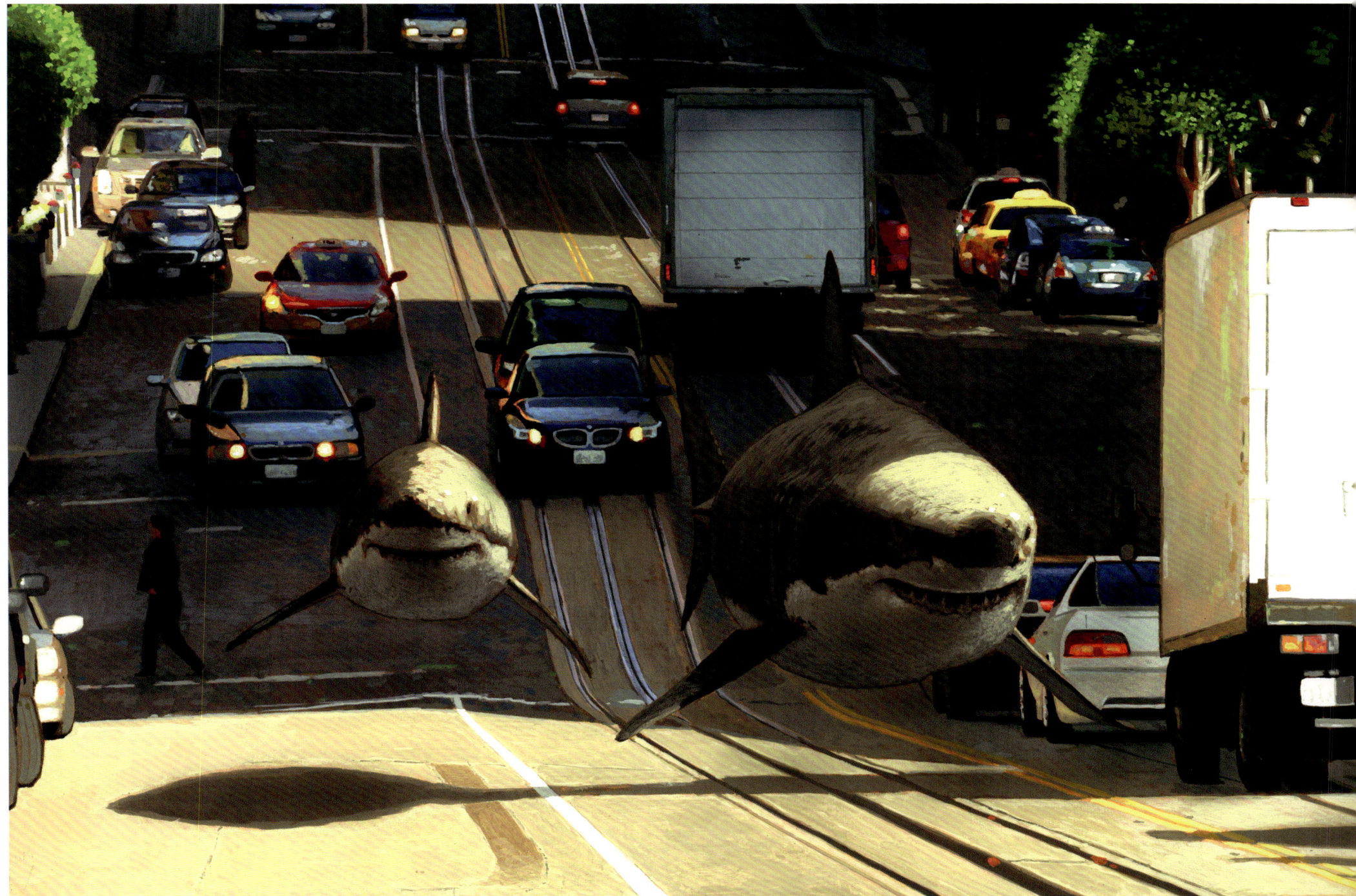

Thriving Cities | 12" x 24" | gouache on wood | 2023

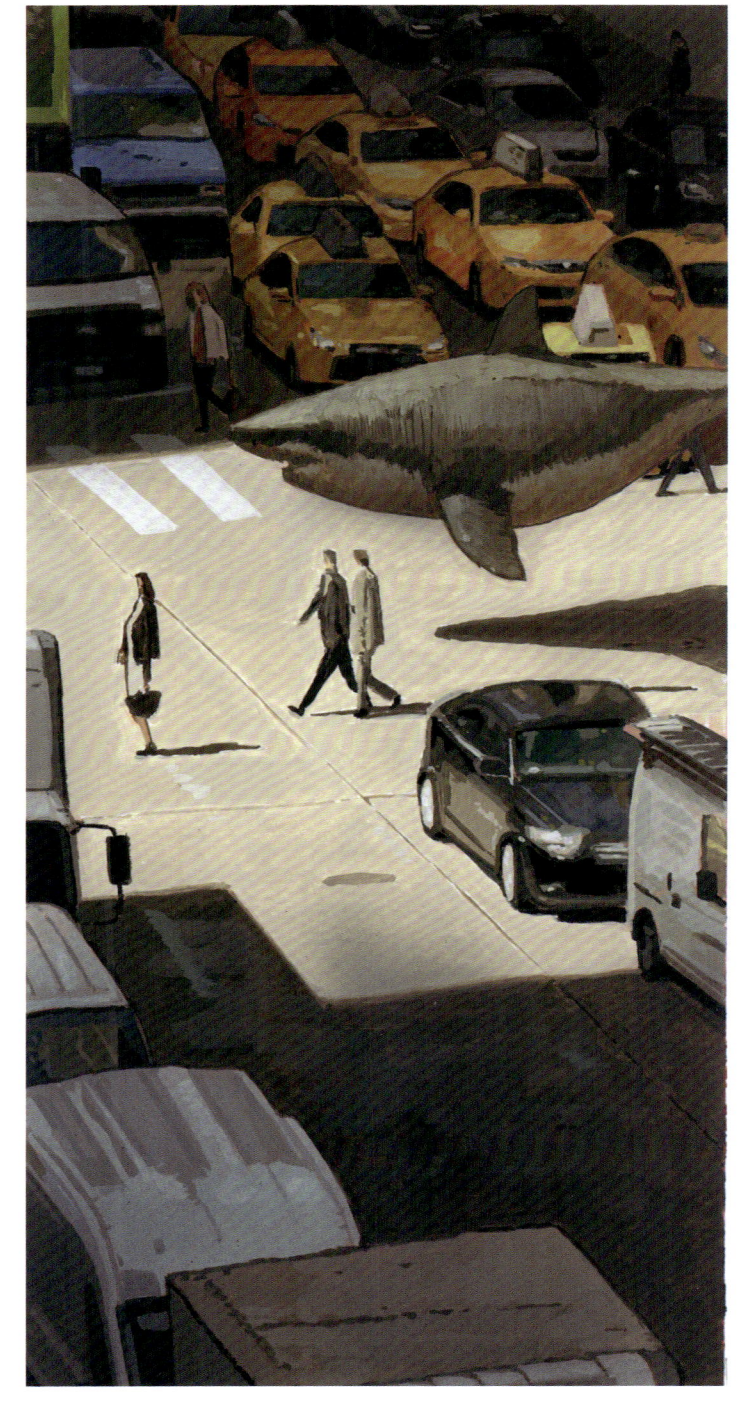

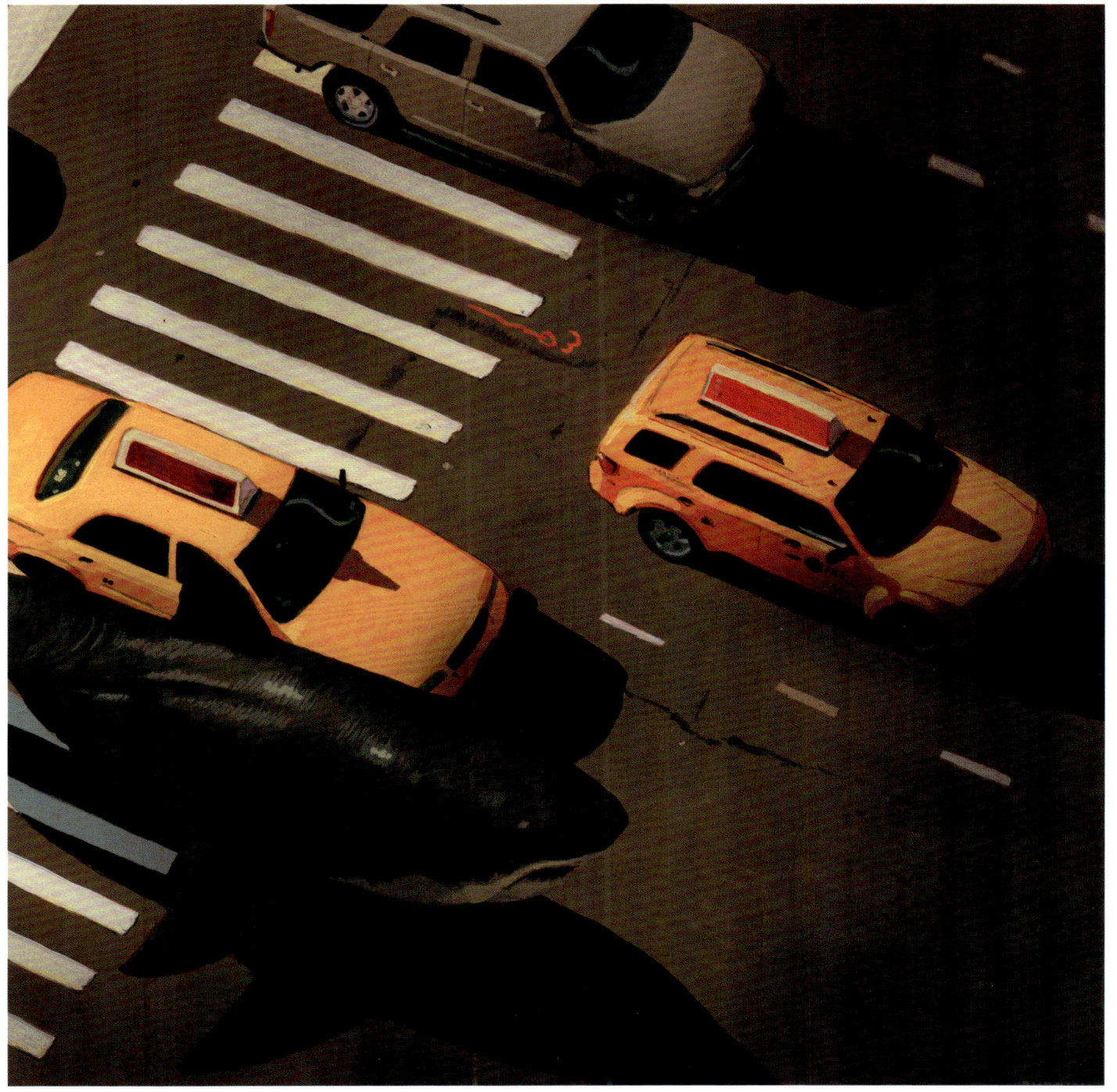

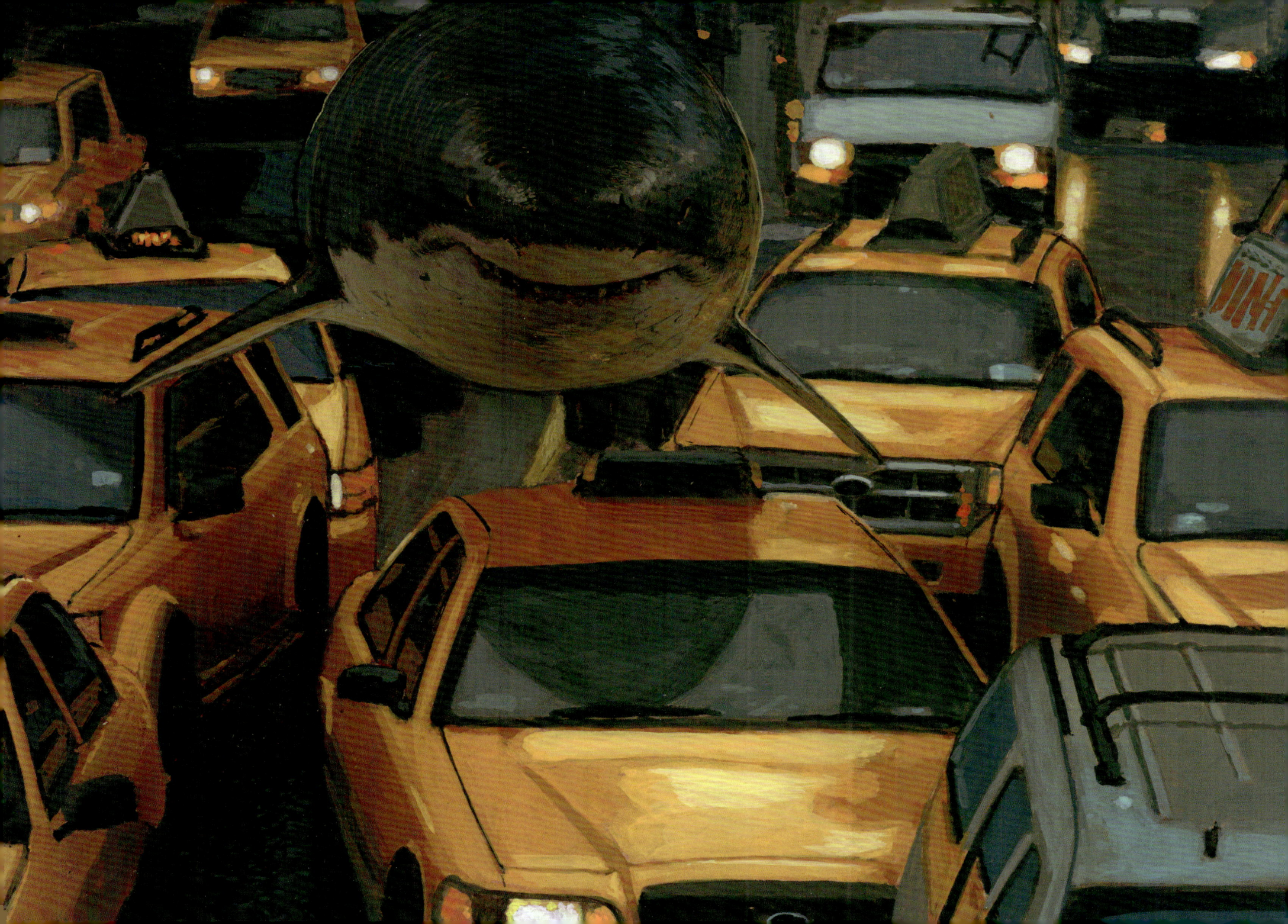

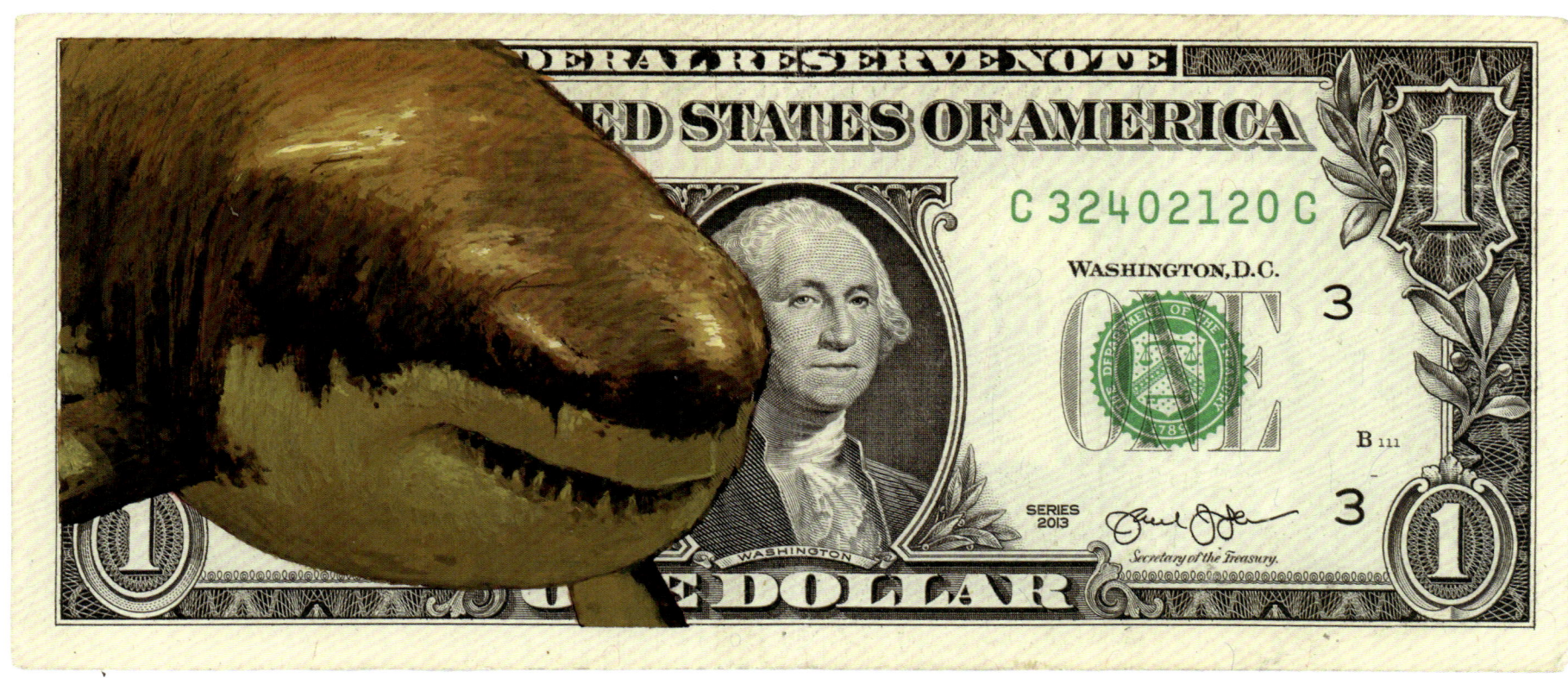

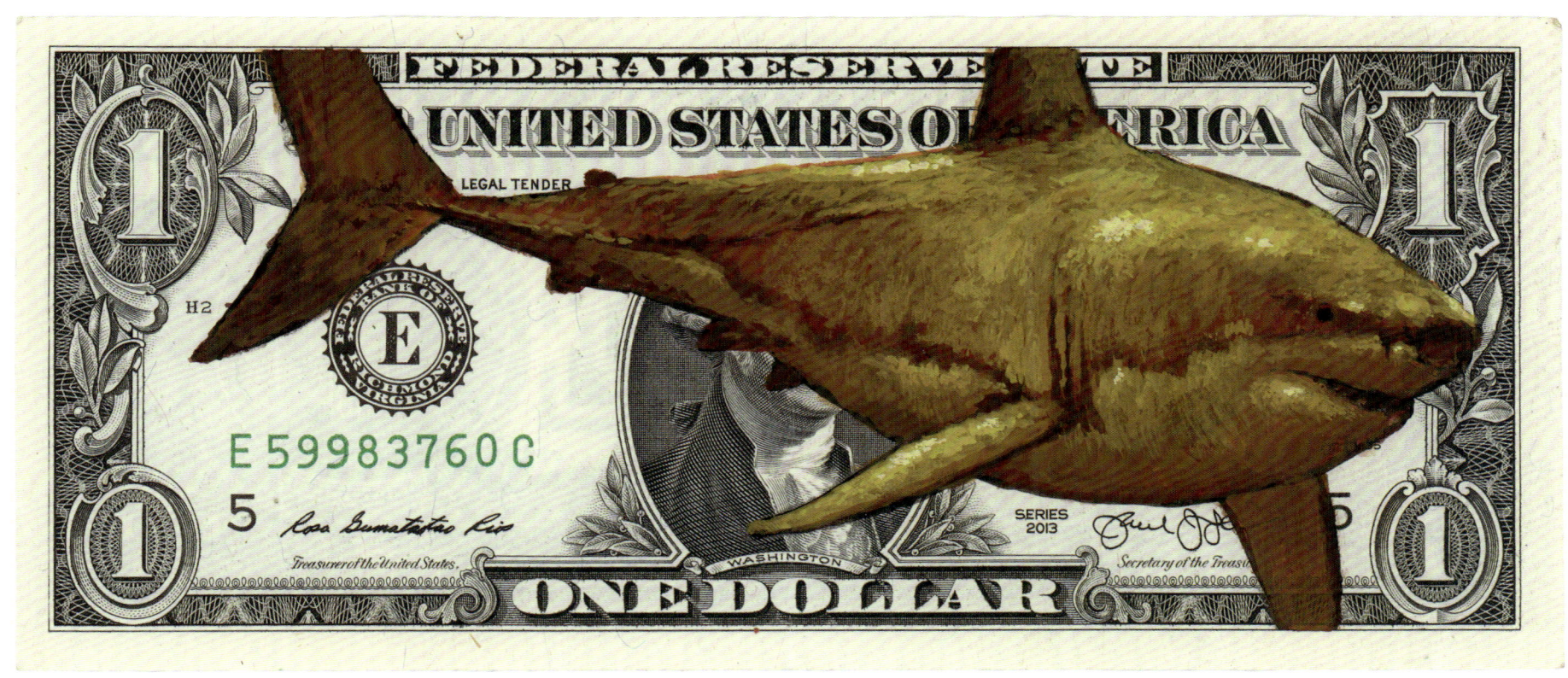

141

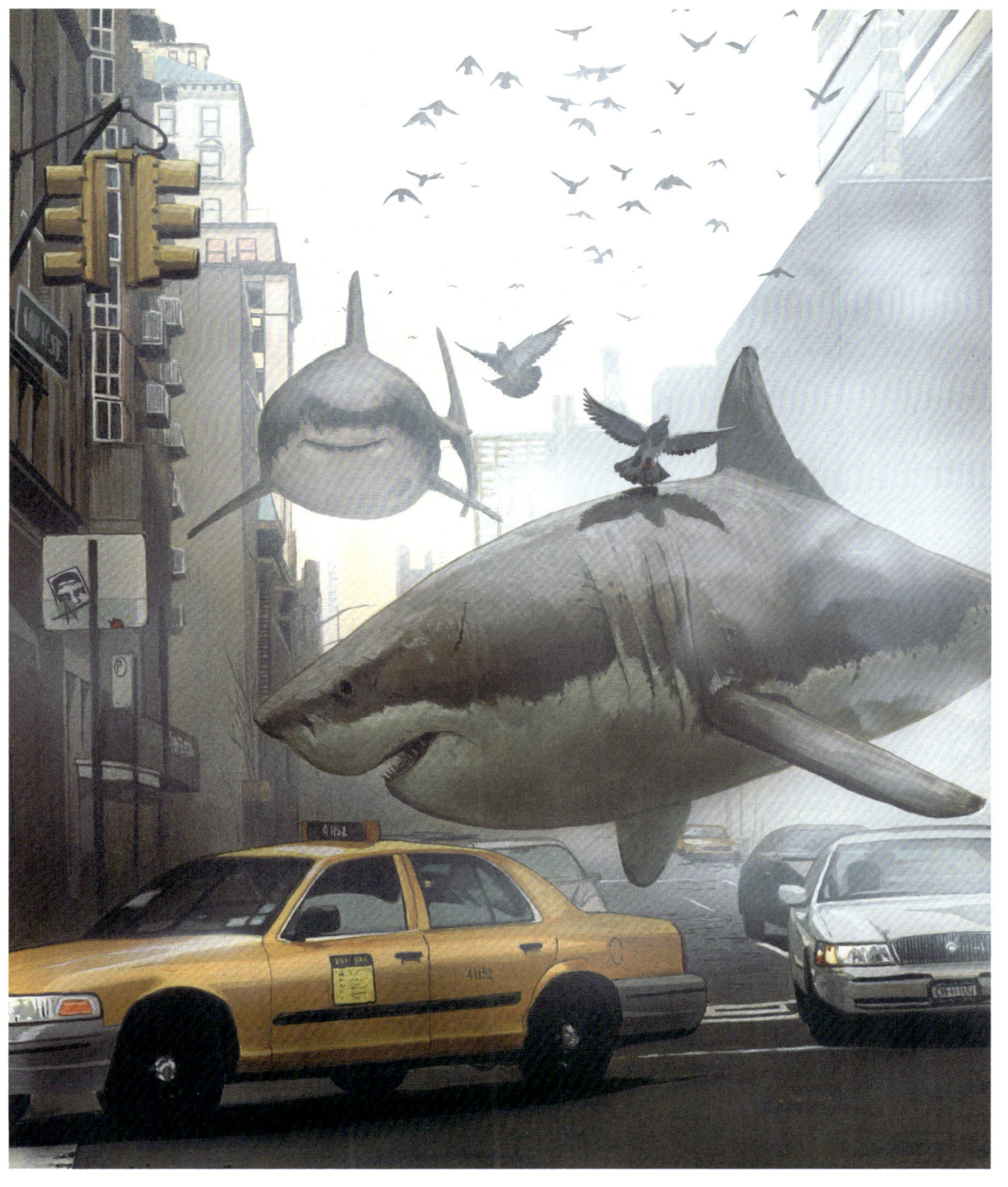

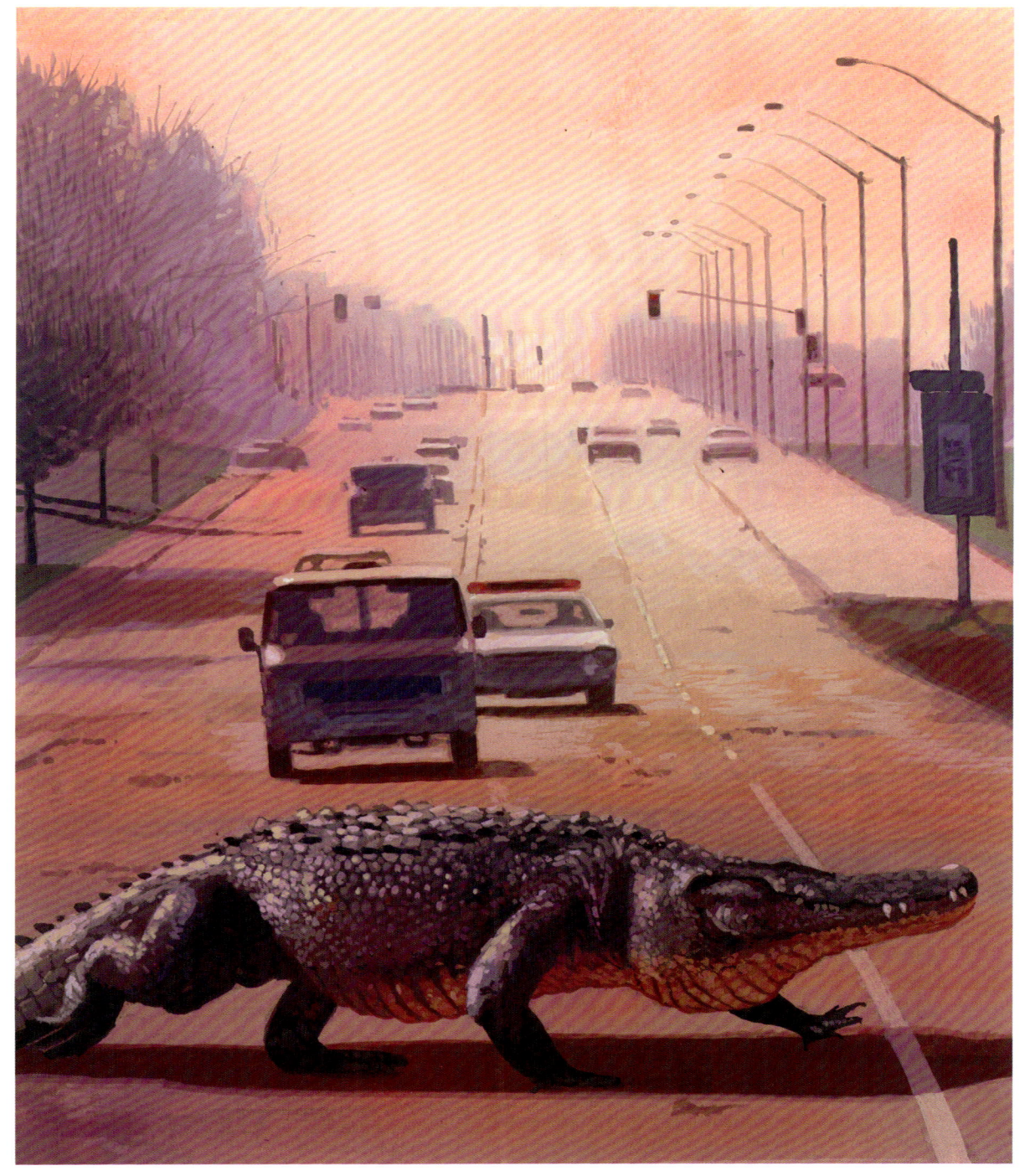

Queen Street Golden Hour (study) | 7.5" x 4" | gouache on paper | 2022

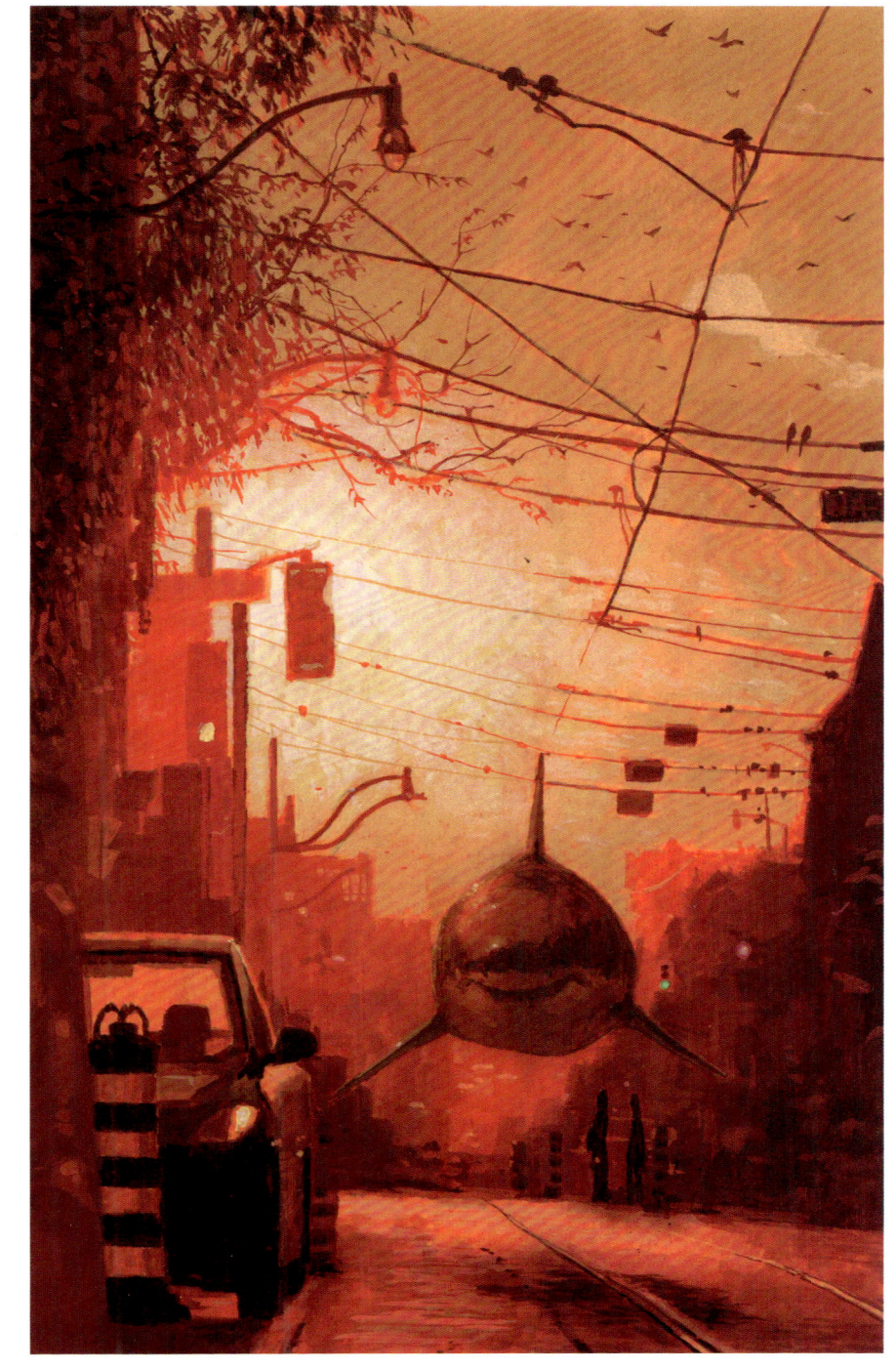

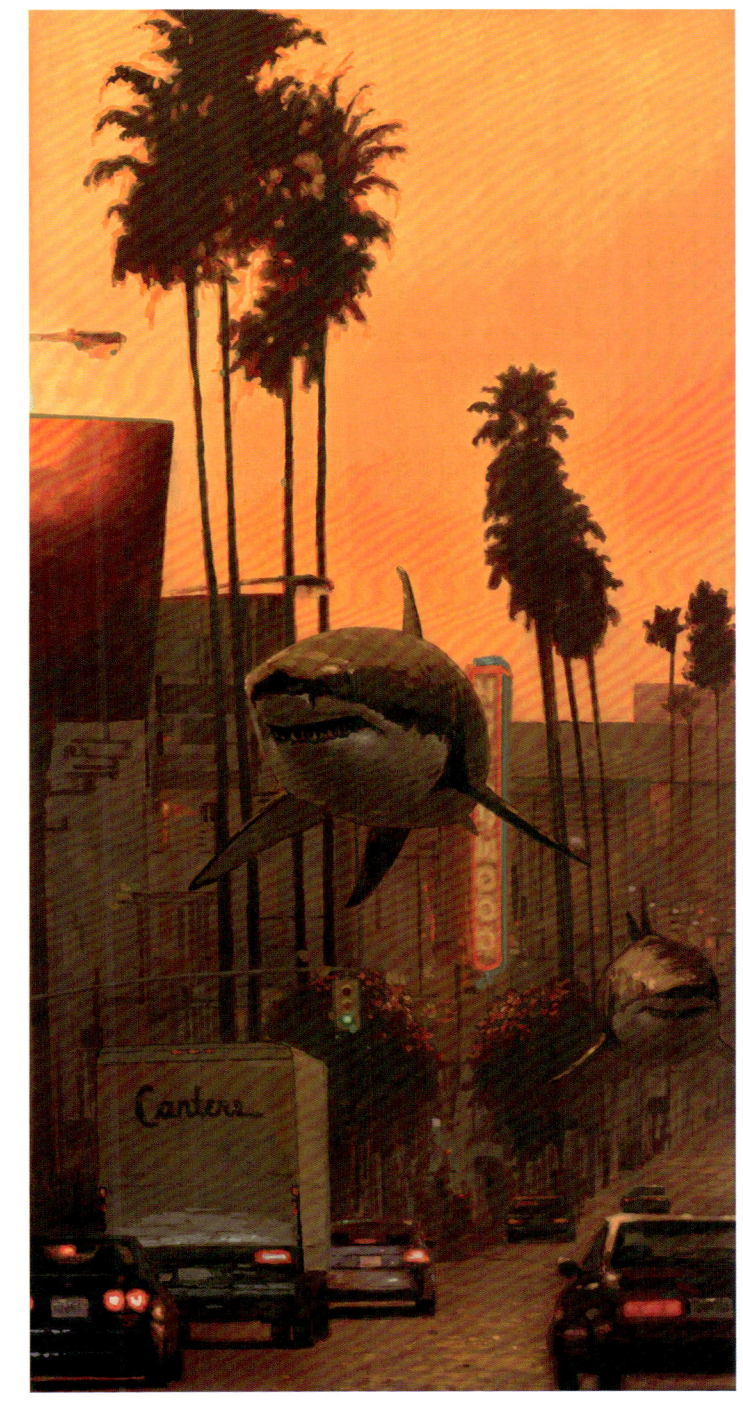

Subway (study) | 10" x 10" | gouche on paper | 2021

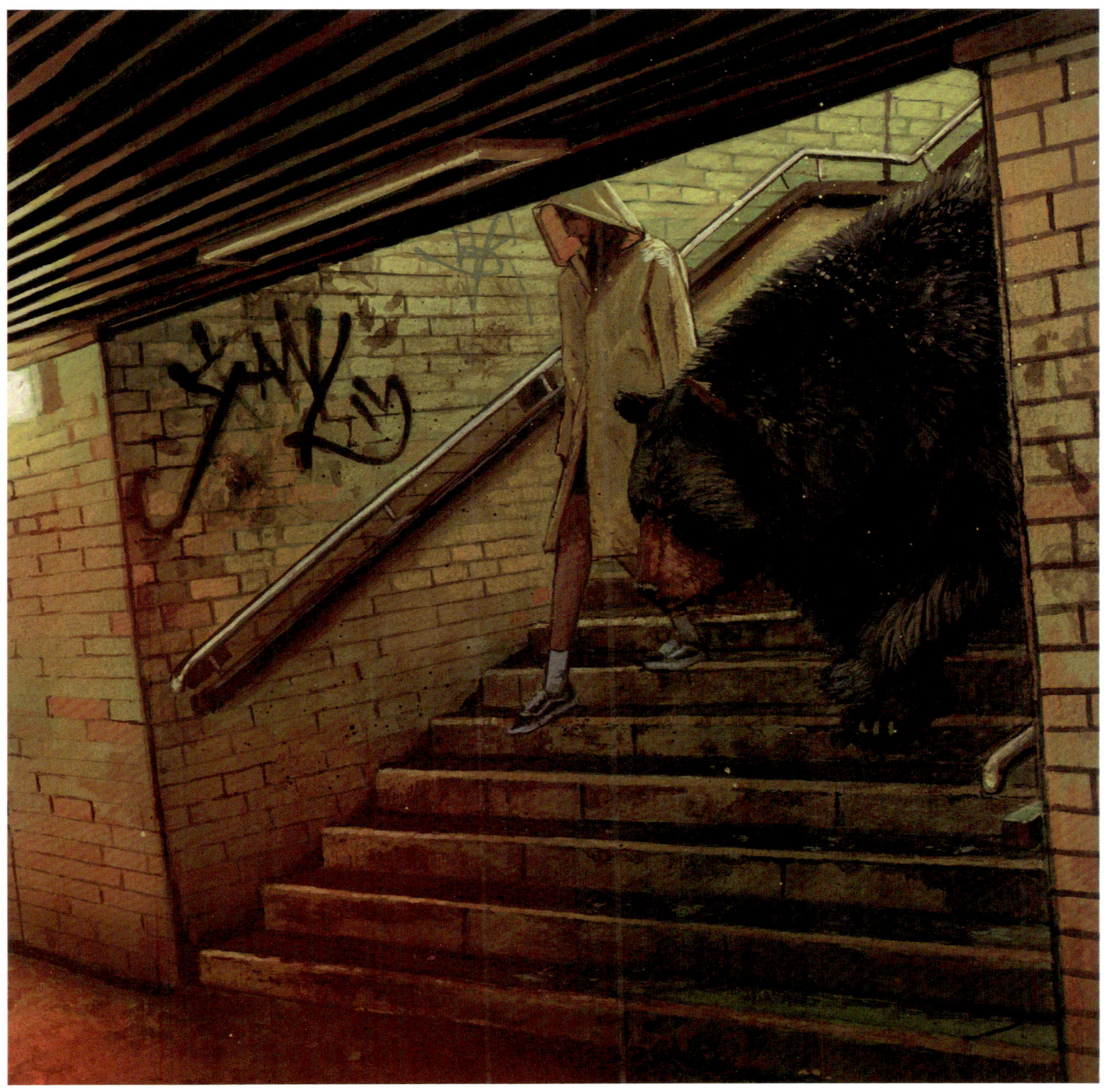

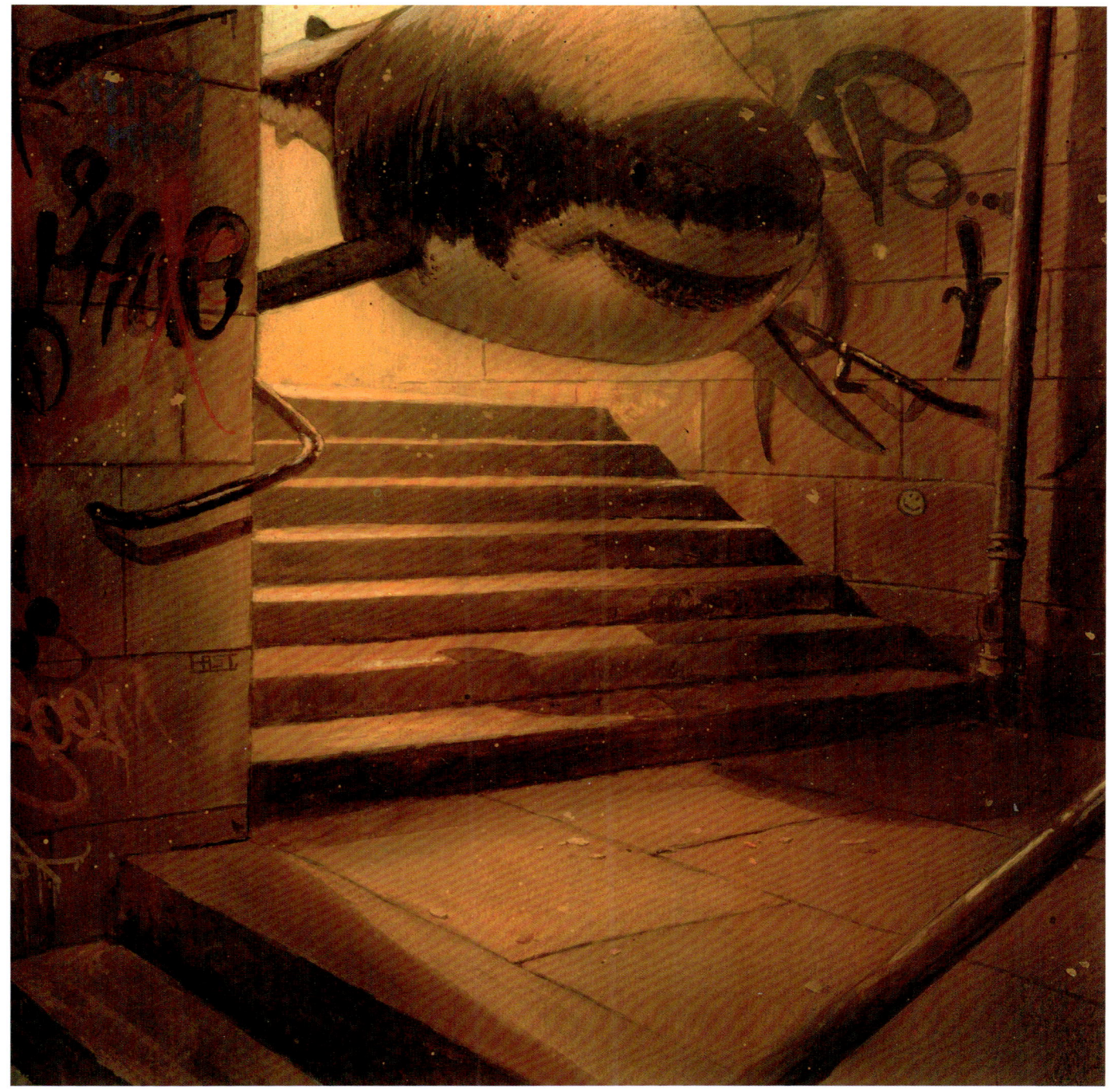

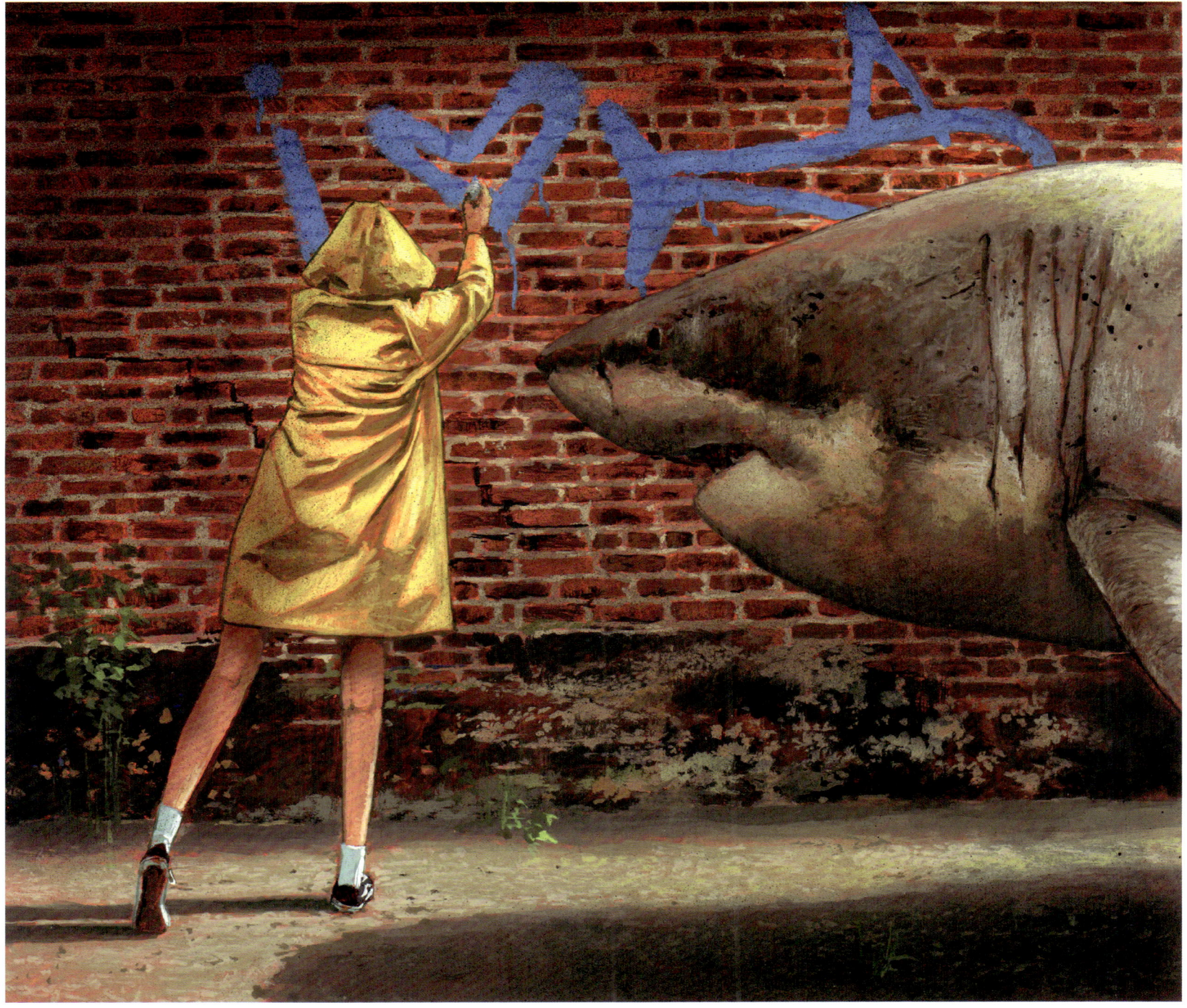

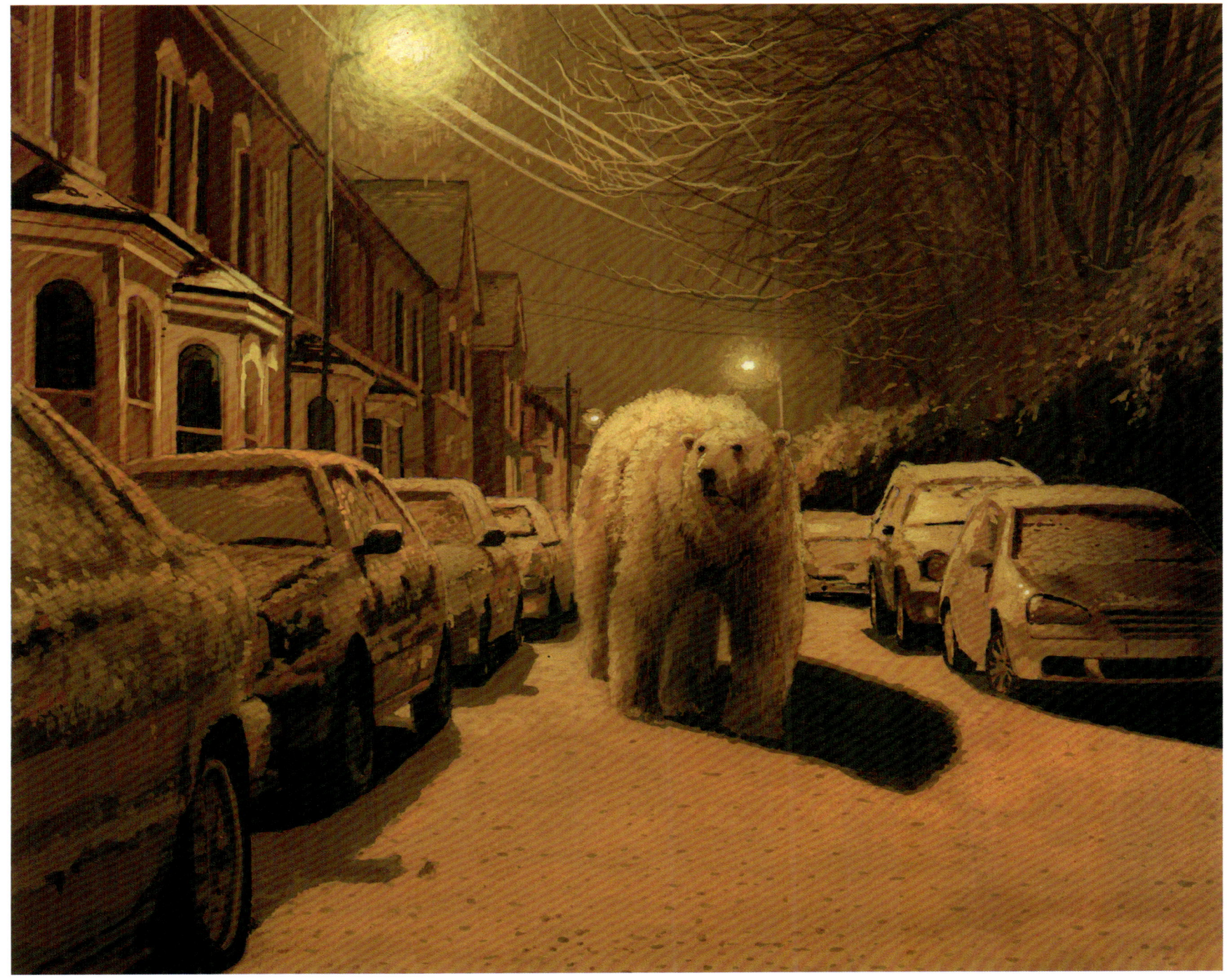

Weird Fishes (study) | 6" x 10" | gouache on paper | 2020

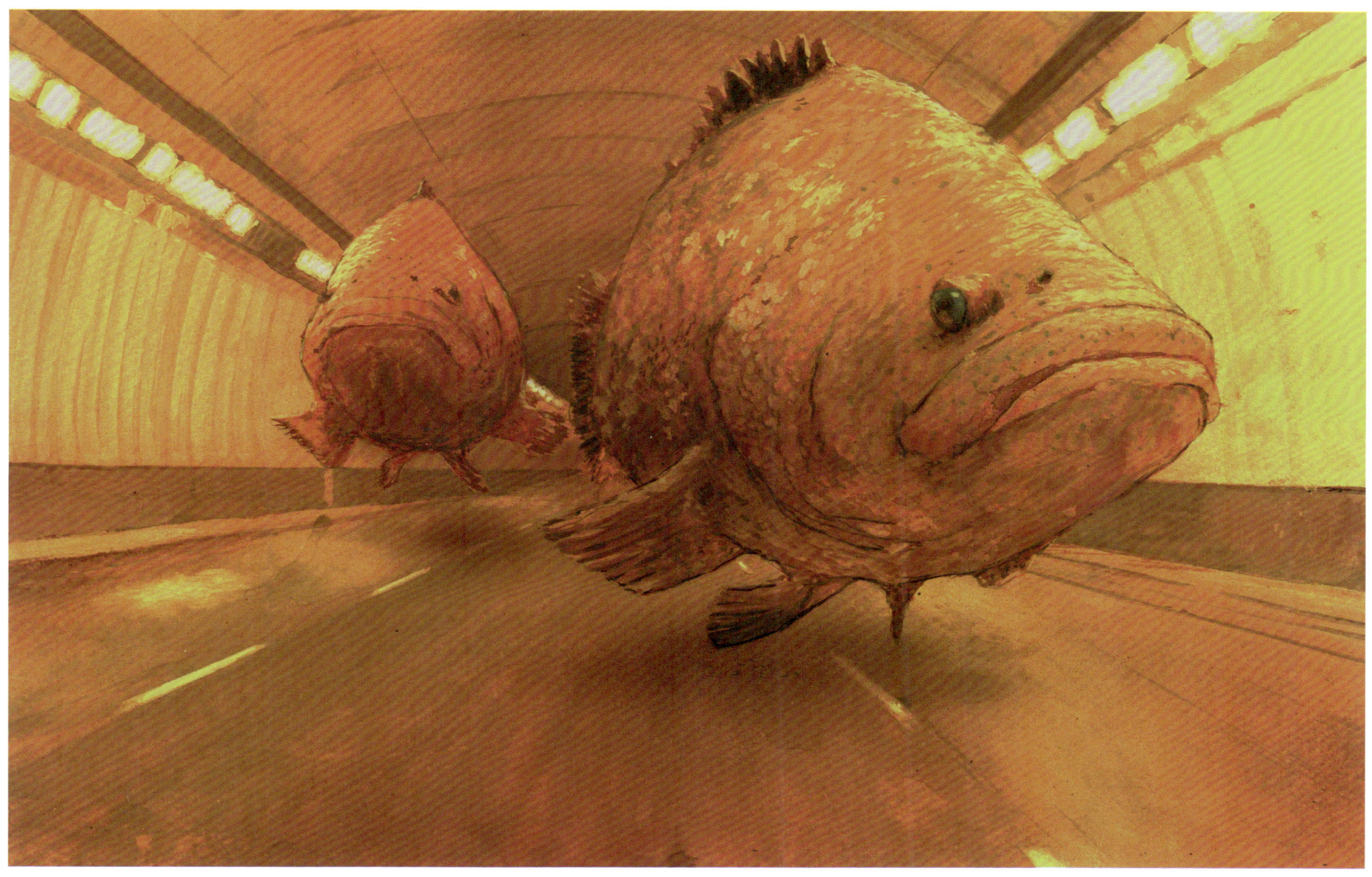

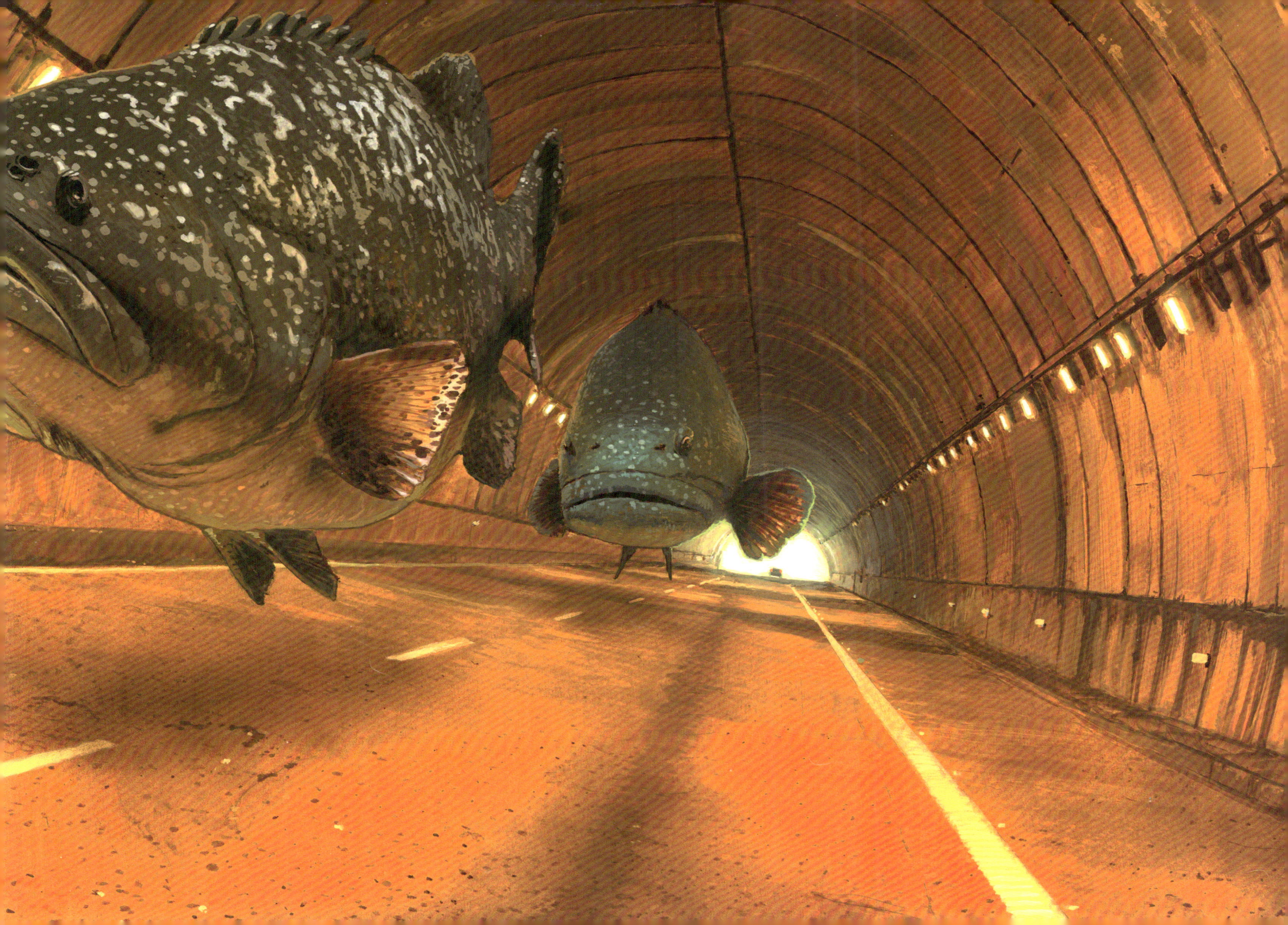

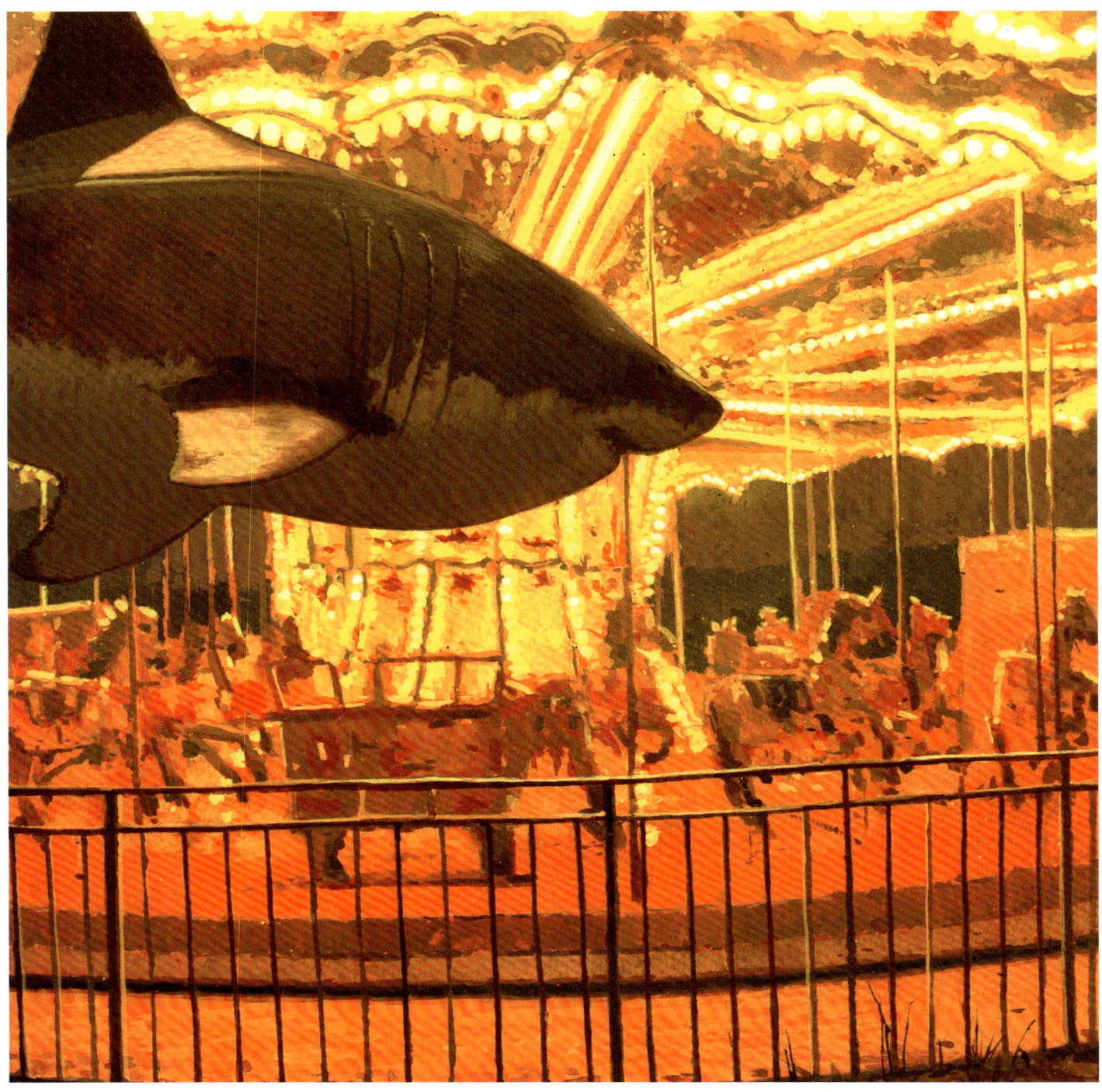

Summer Nights and Carousel Lights (study)
9″ x 9″
gouche on paper
2020

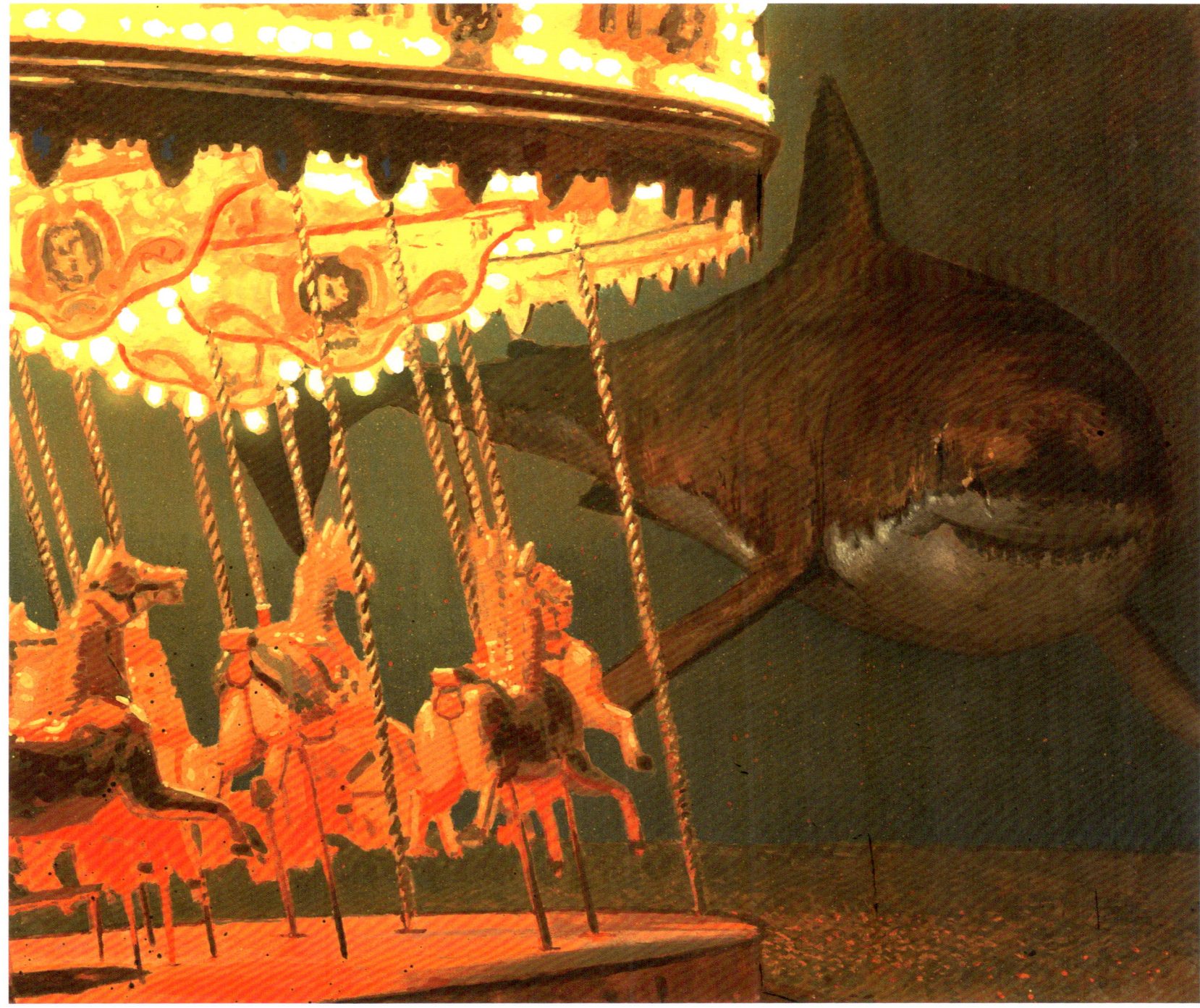

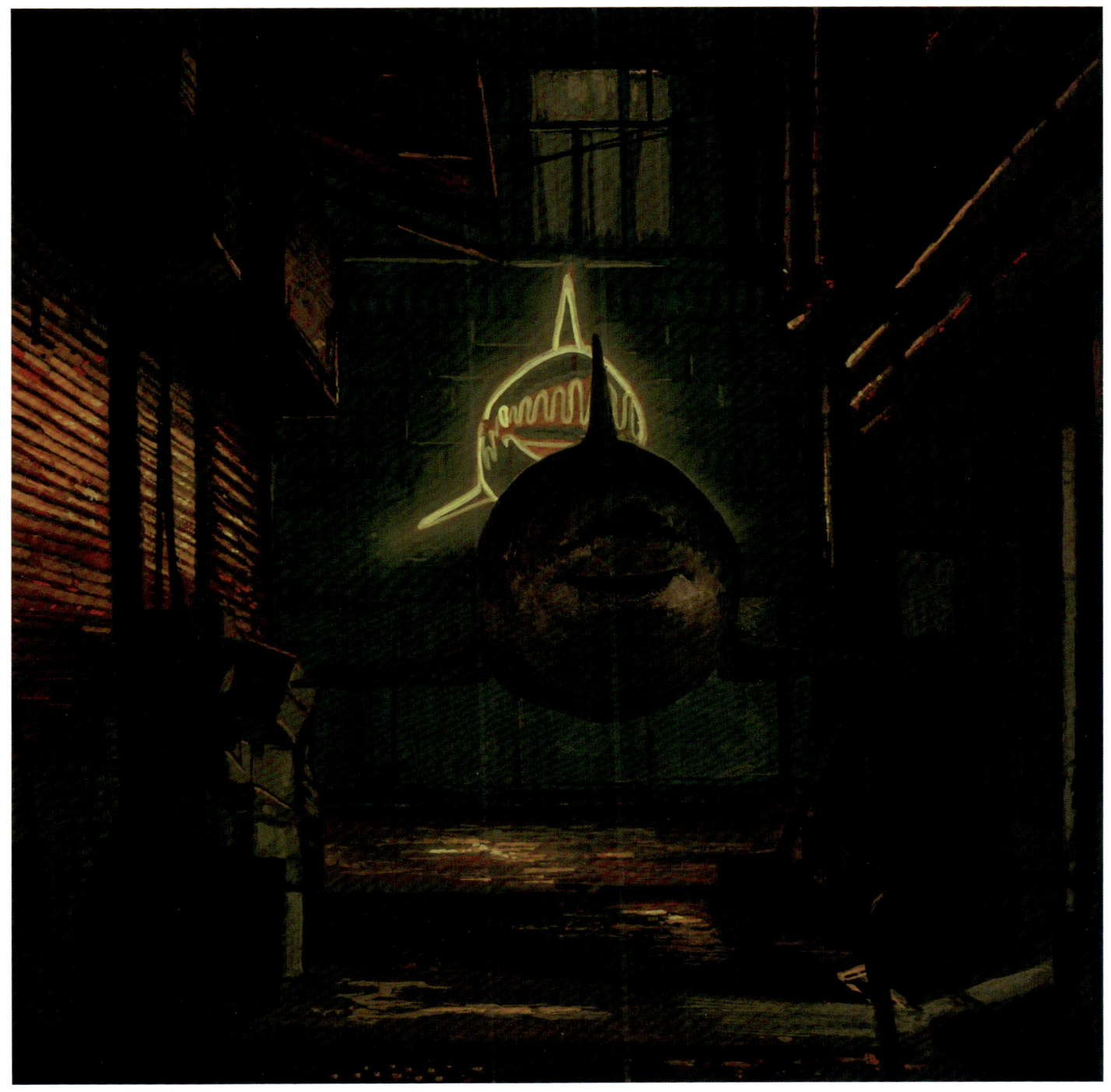

Long Winter's Night | 17" x 13" | gouache on wood | 2022

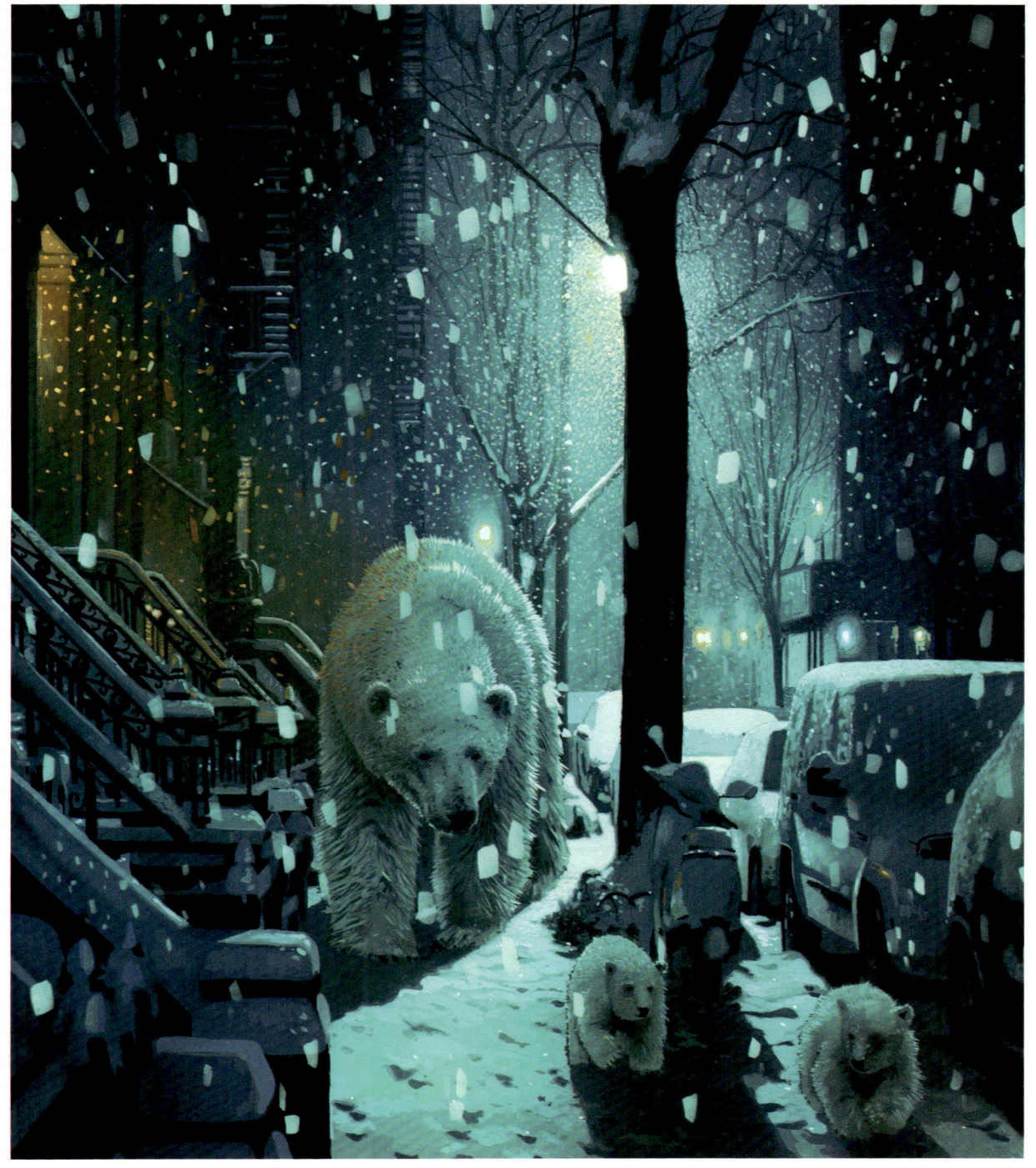

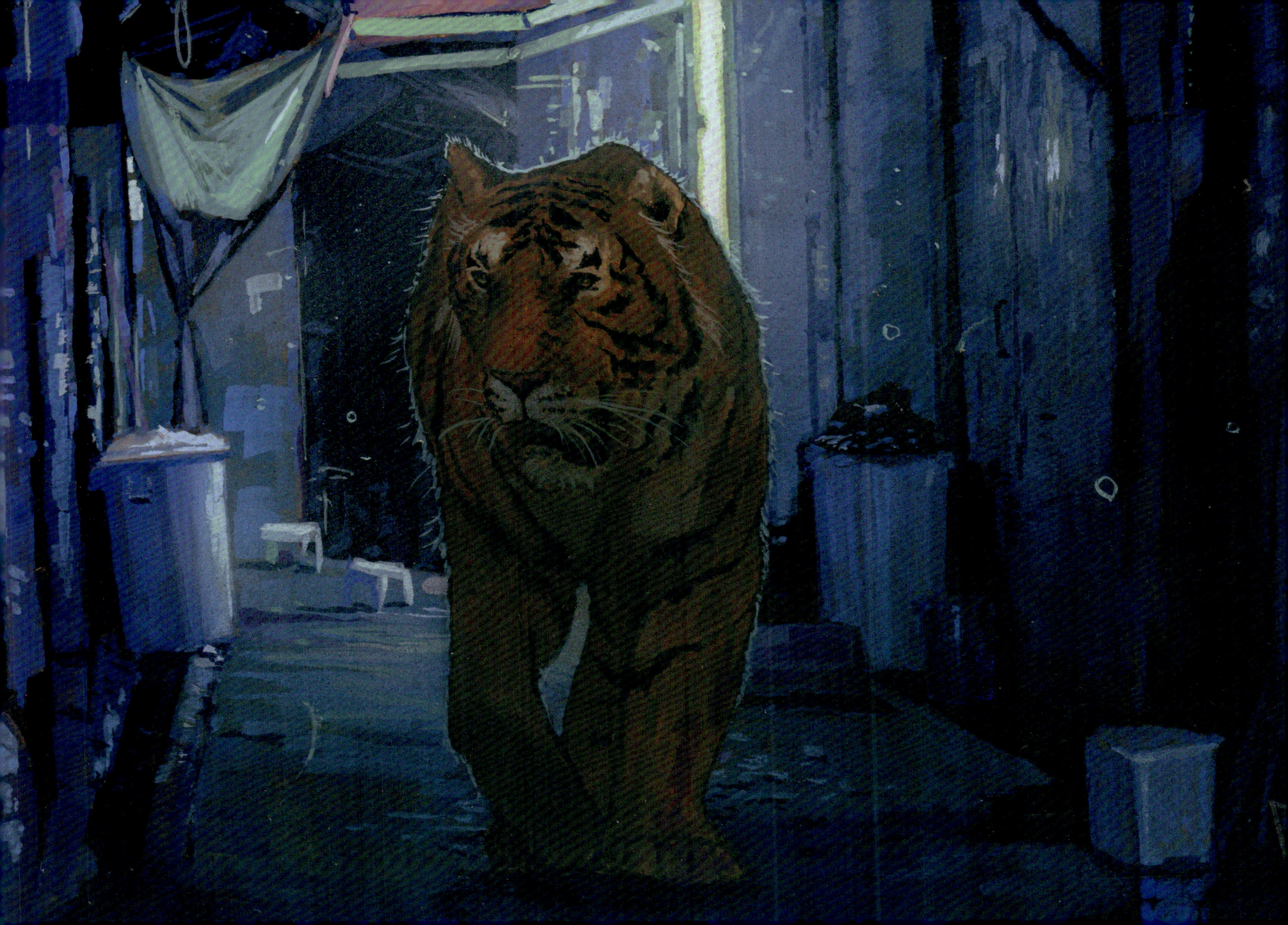

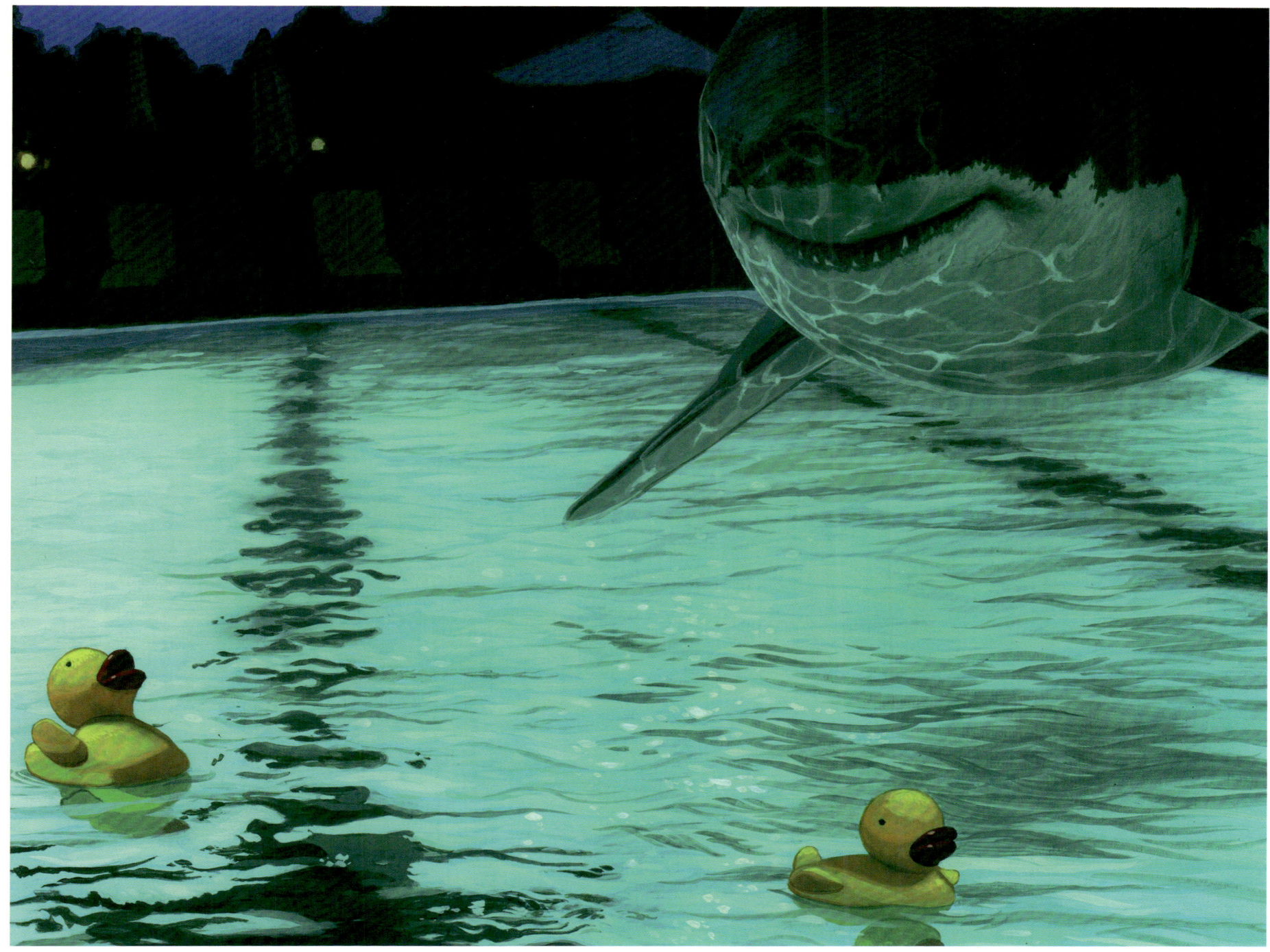

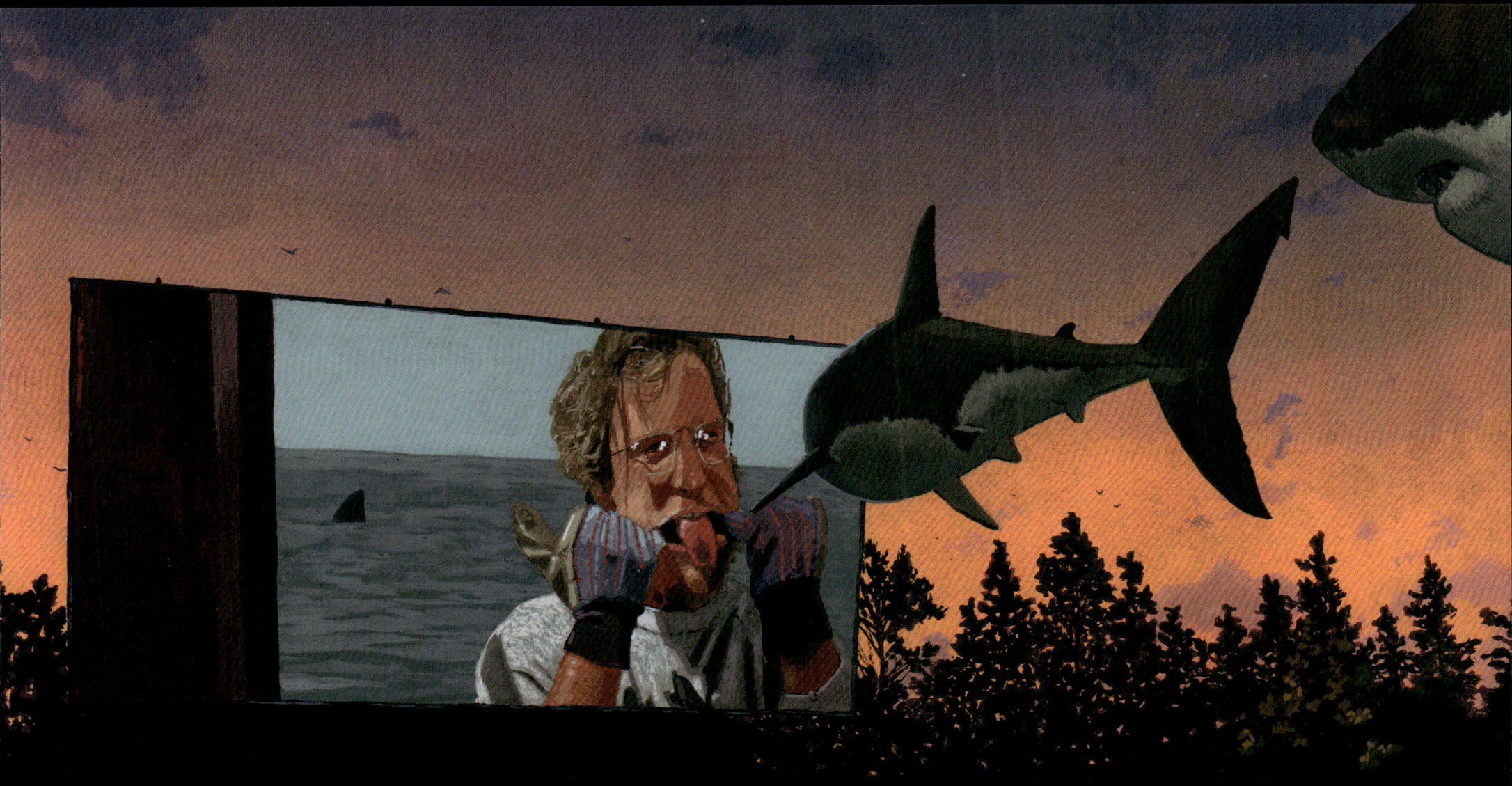

Here Now In A Place In Time | 10" x 8" | gouache on paper | 2023

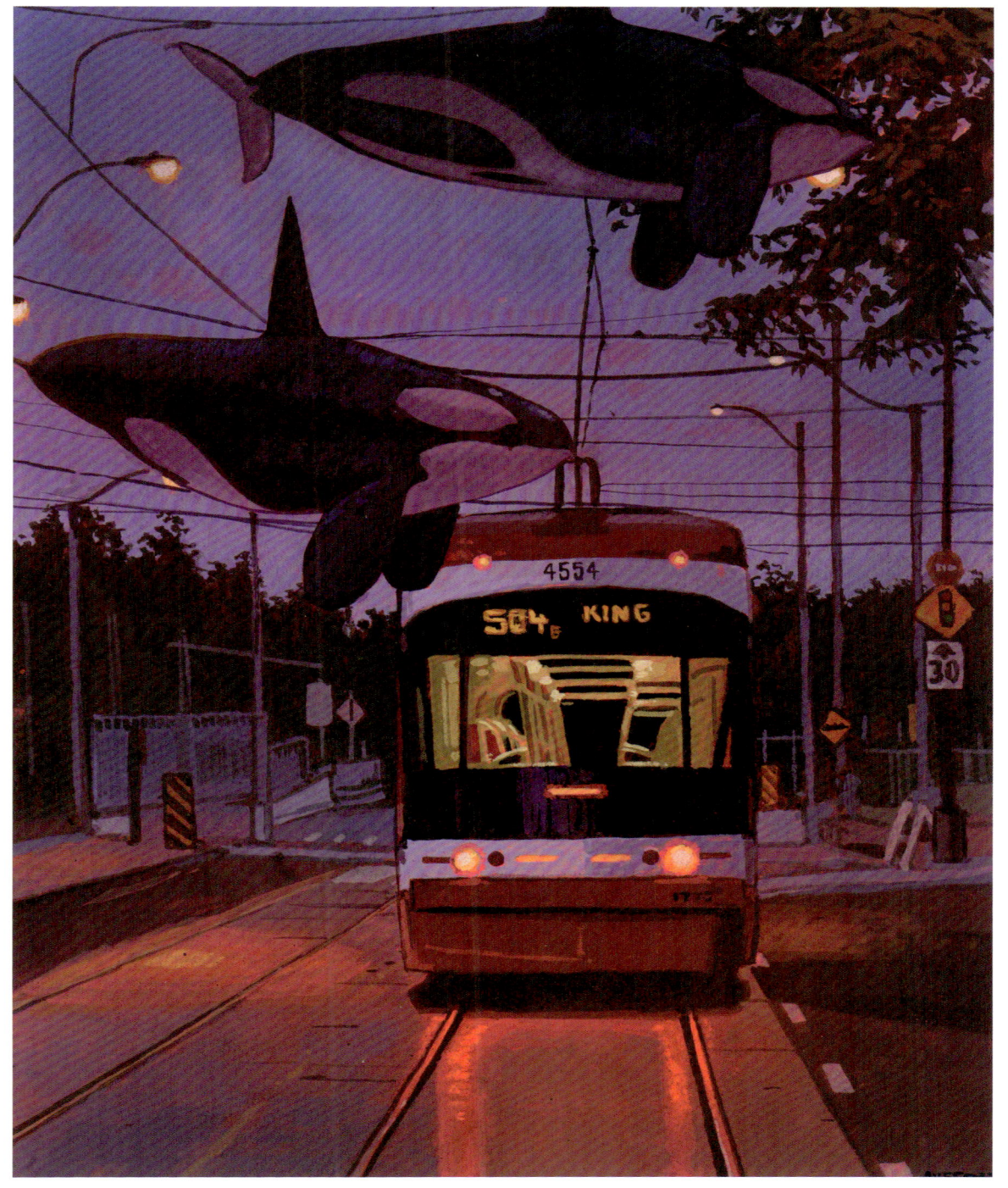

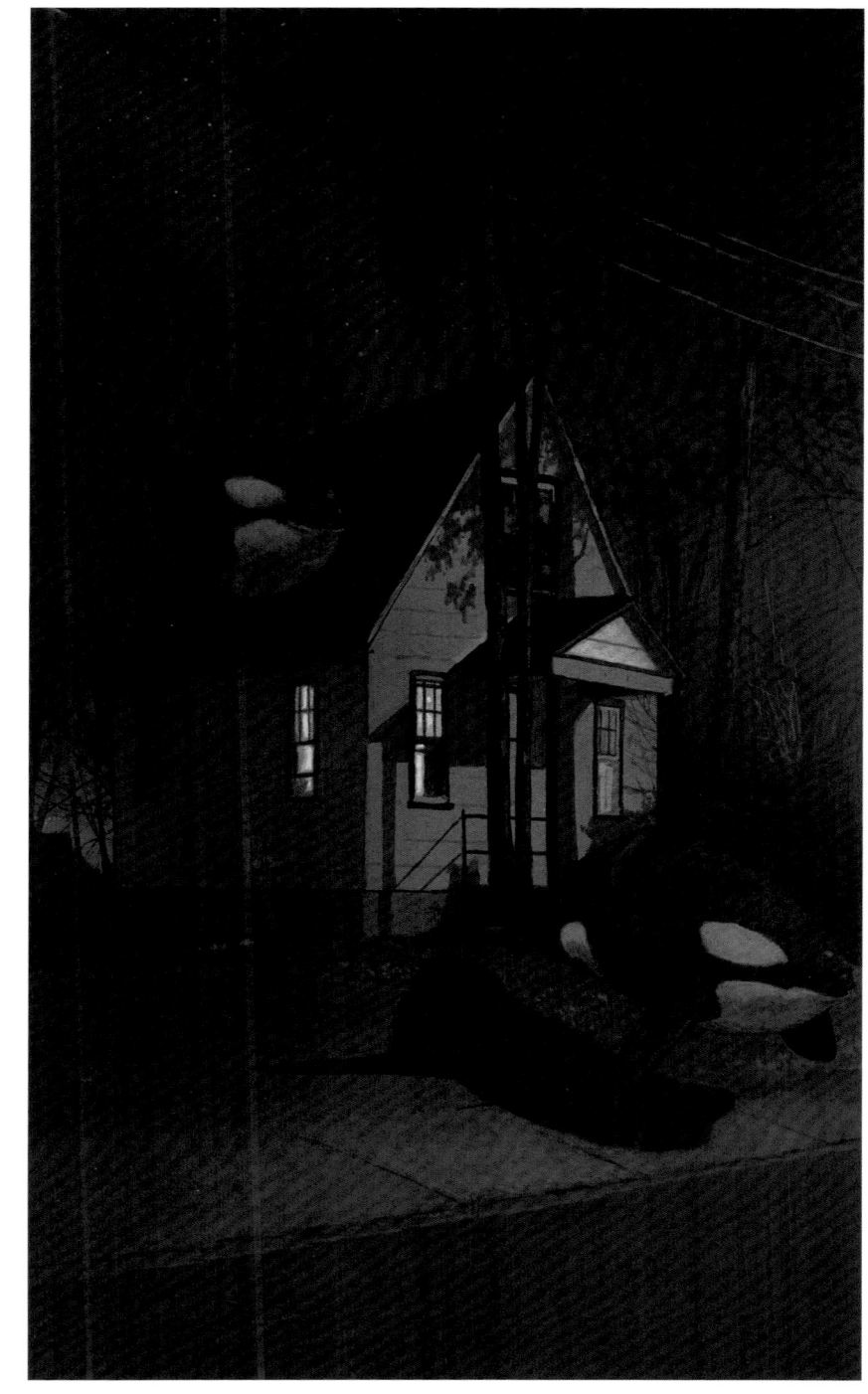

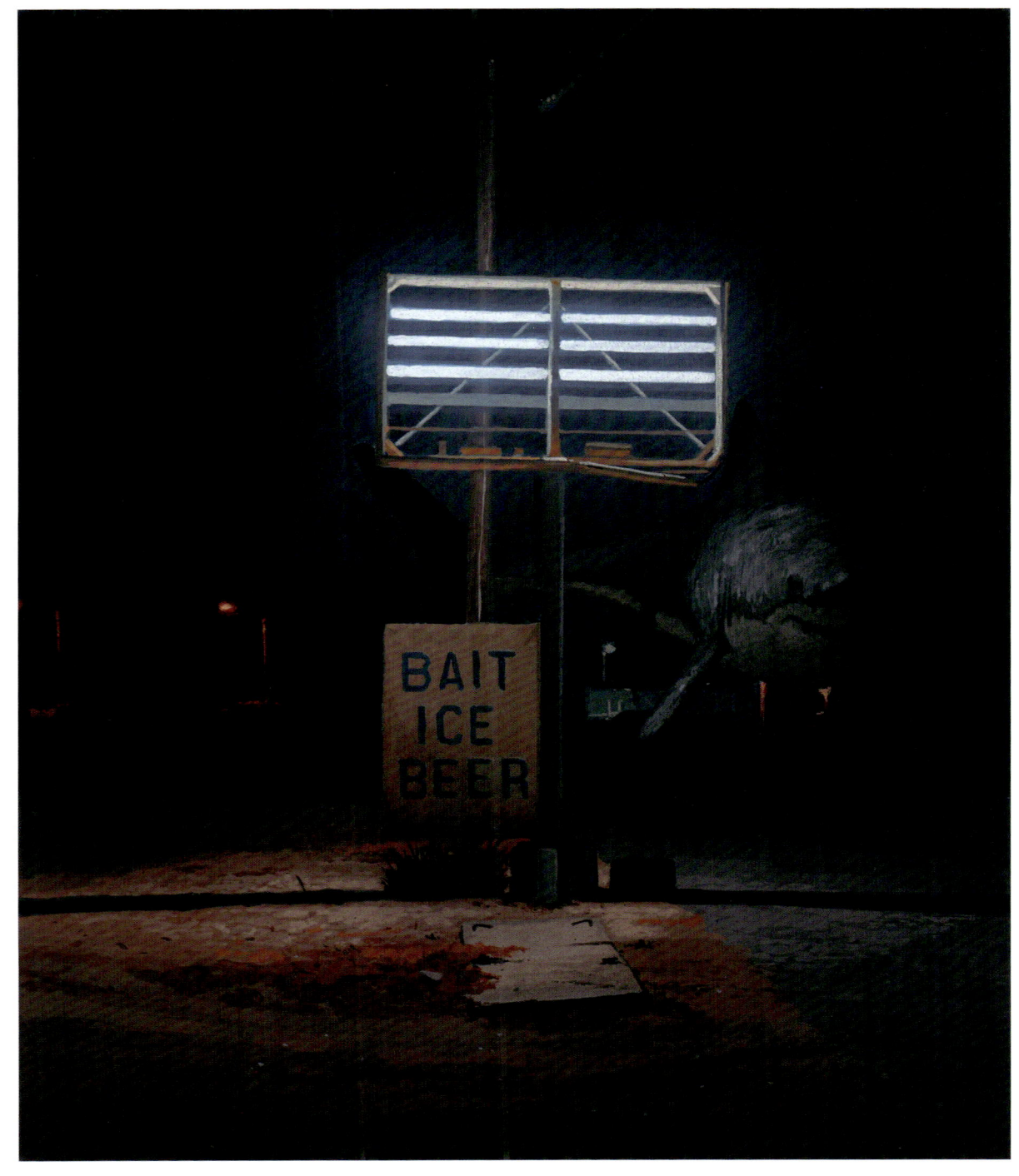

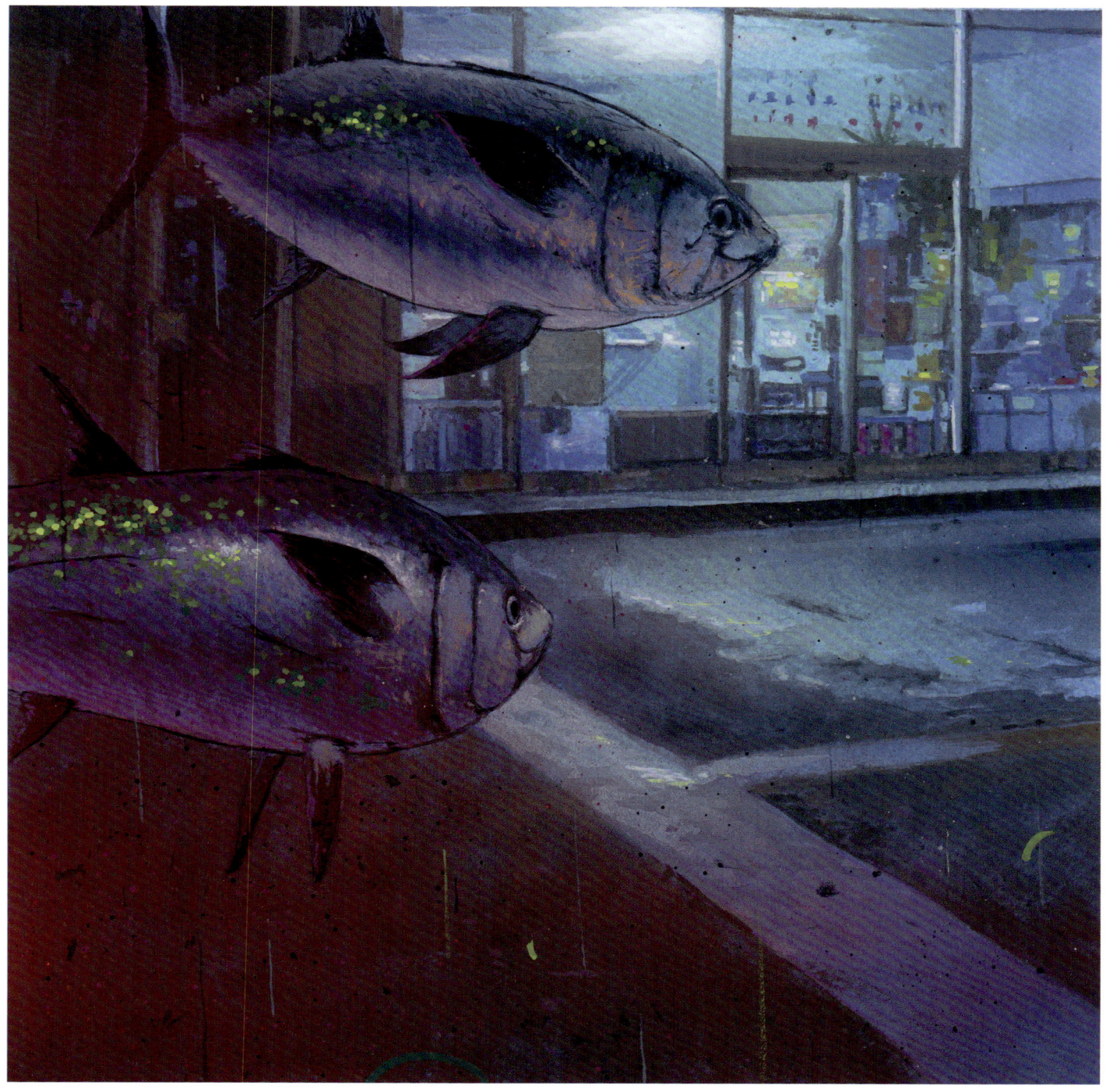

The Last Of Winter (study)
7" x 7"
gouache on paper
2022

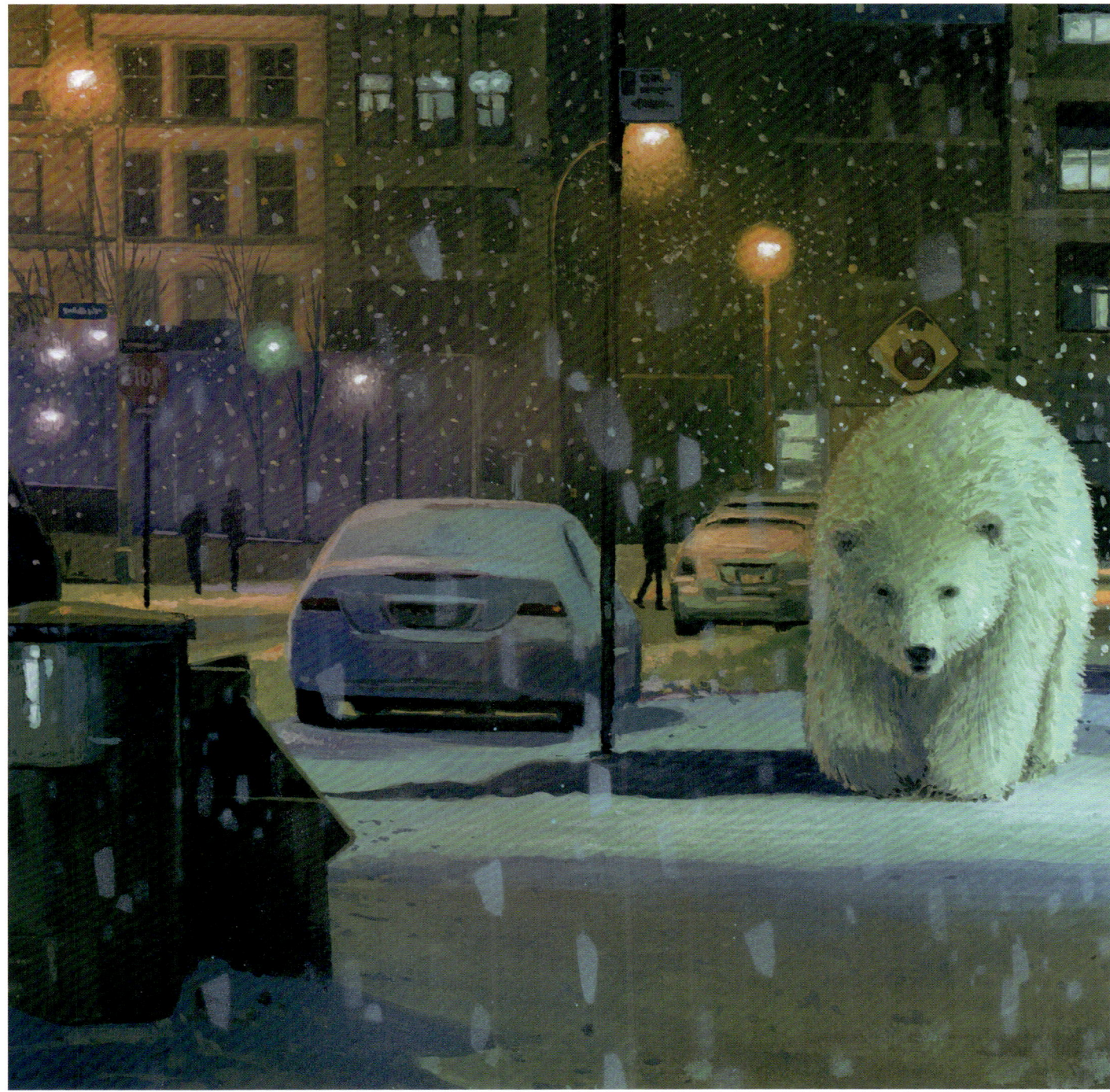

The Day That I Know (study) | 12" x 9" | gouche on paper | 2022 | detail

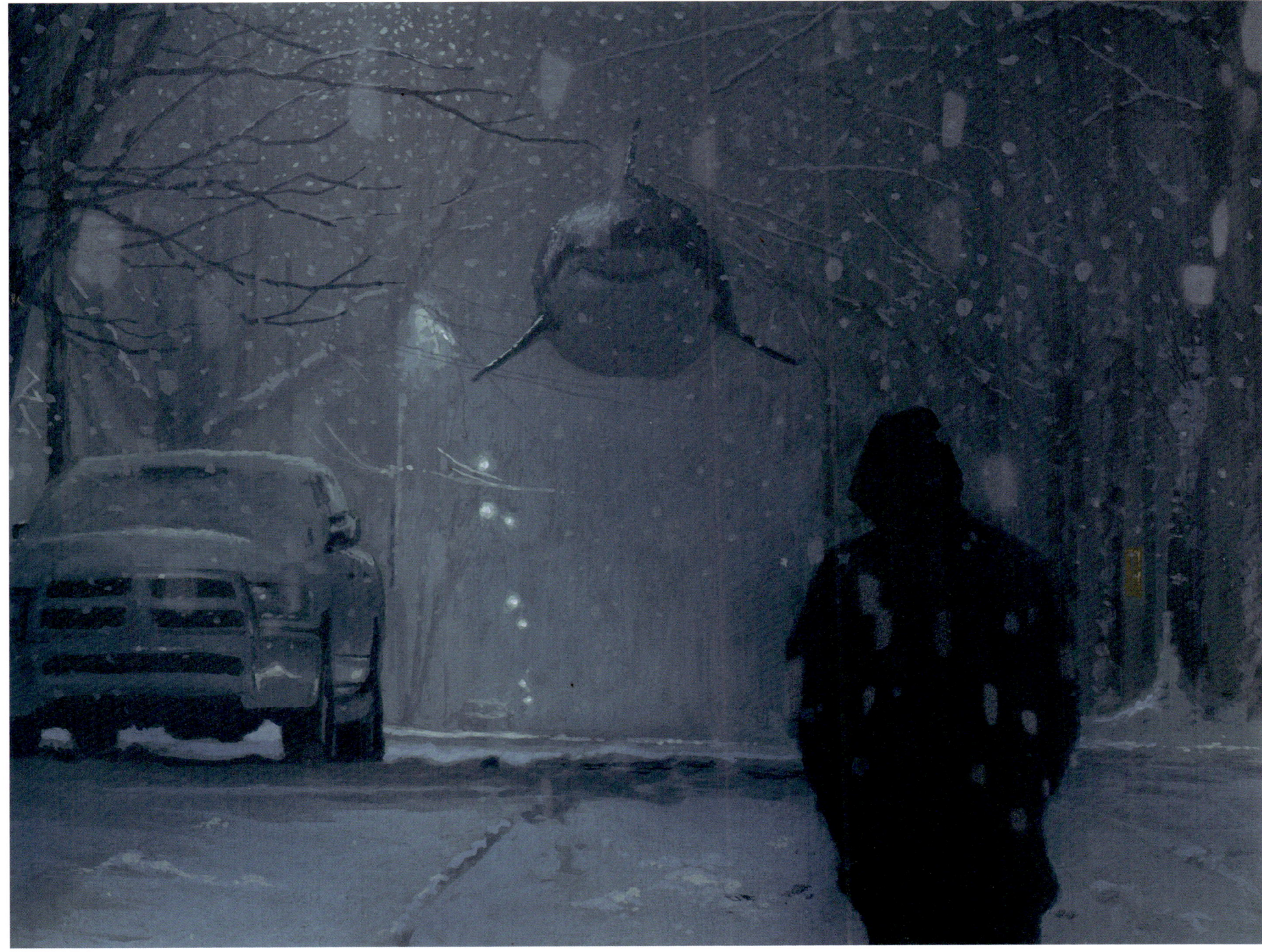

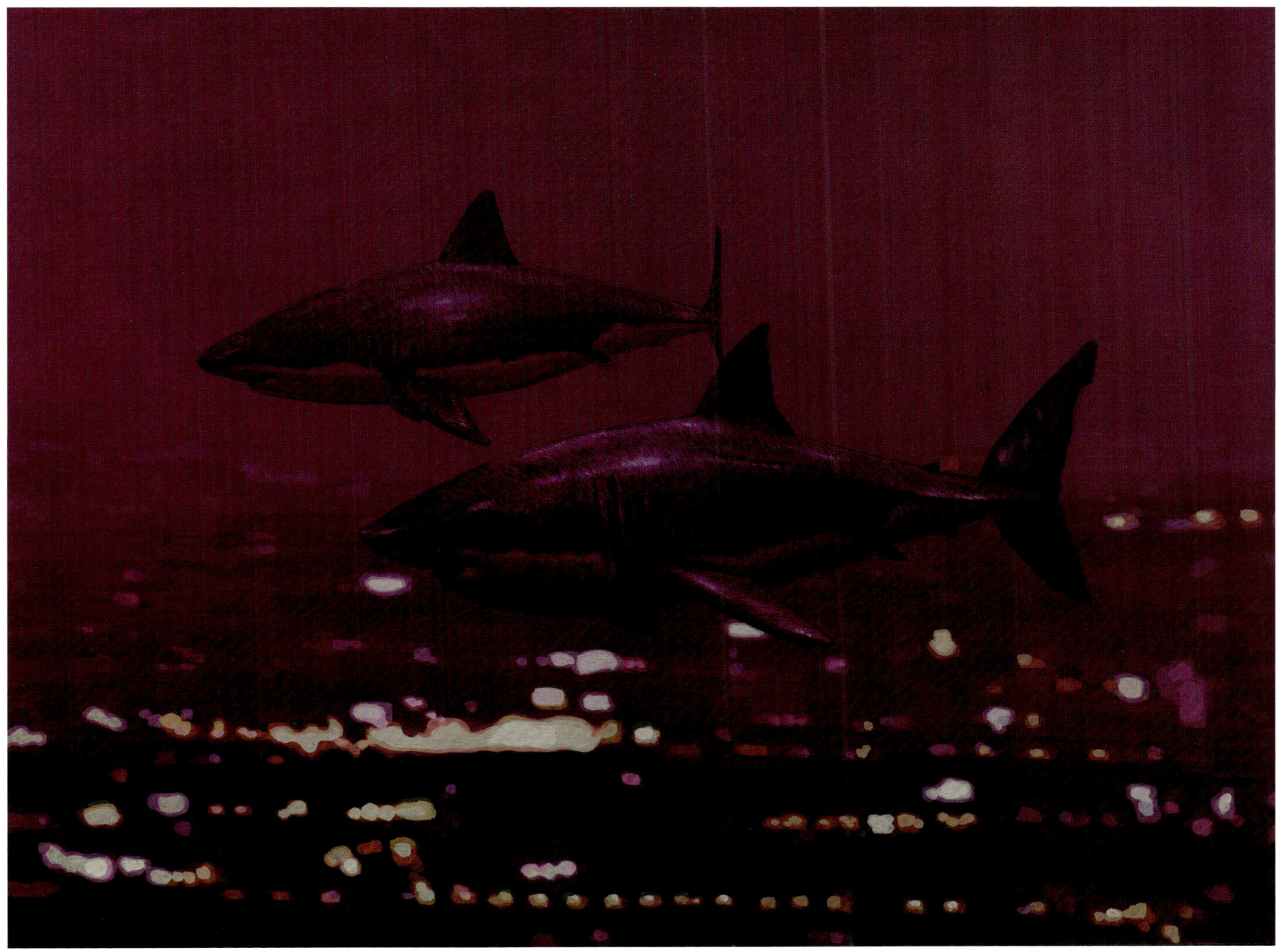

My work not only entertains with its absurdity but also sparks a deeper conversation about interconnectedness and adaptability, as animals are depicted thriving in environments where they don't naturally belong. These unlikely friendships between different species invite viewers to reconsider relationships and survival beyond logic or instinct, exploring themes of harmony and tension within nature.

Busy Lives | 40" x 40" | oil on canvas | 2022

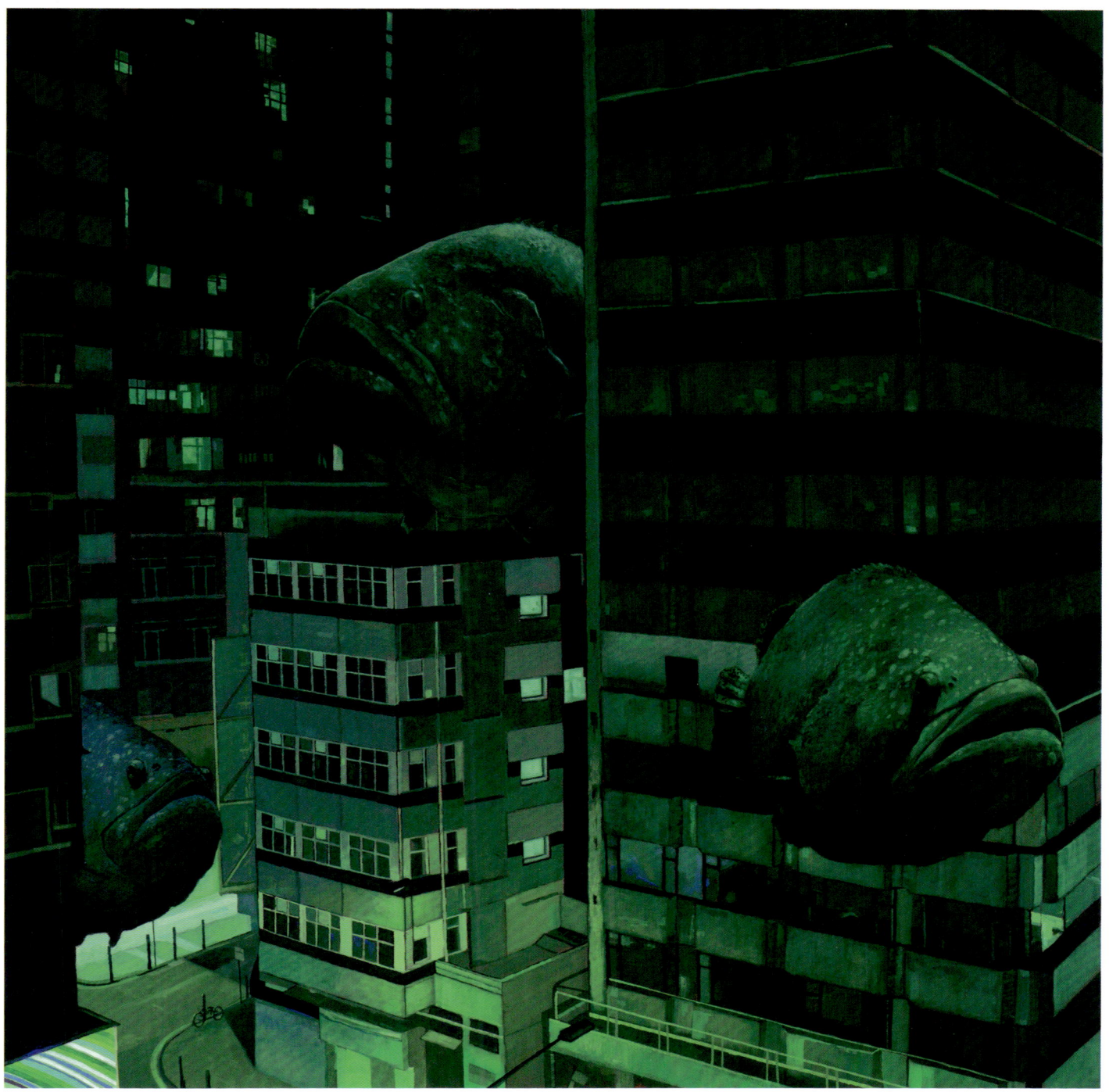

Only The Lonely (study) | 9" x 8" | gouche on paper | 2023

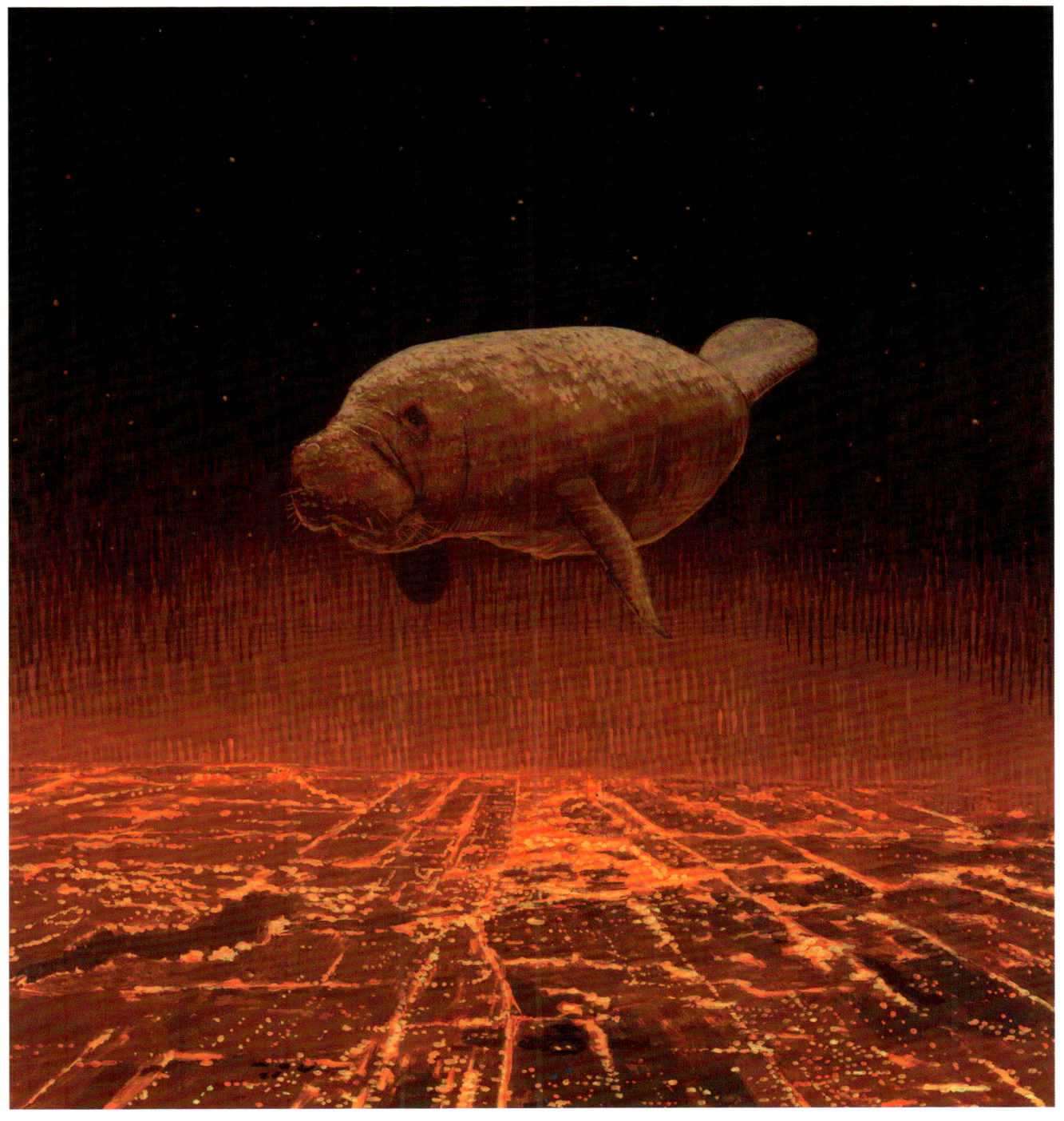

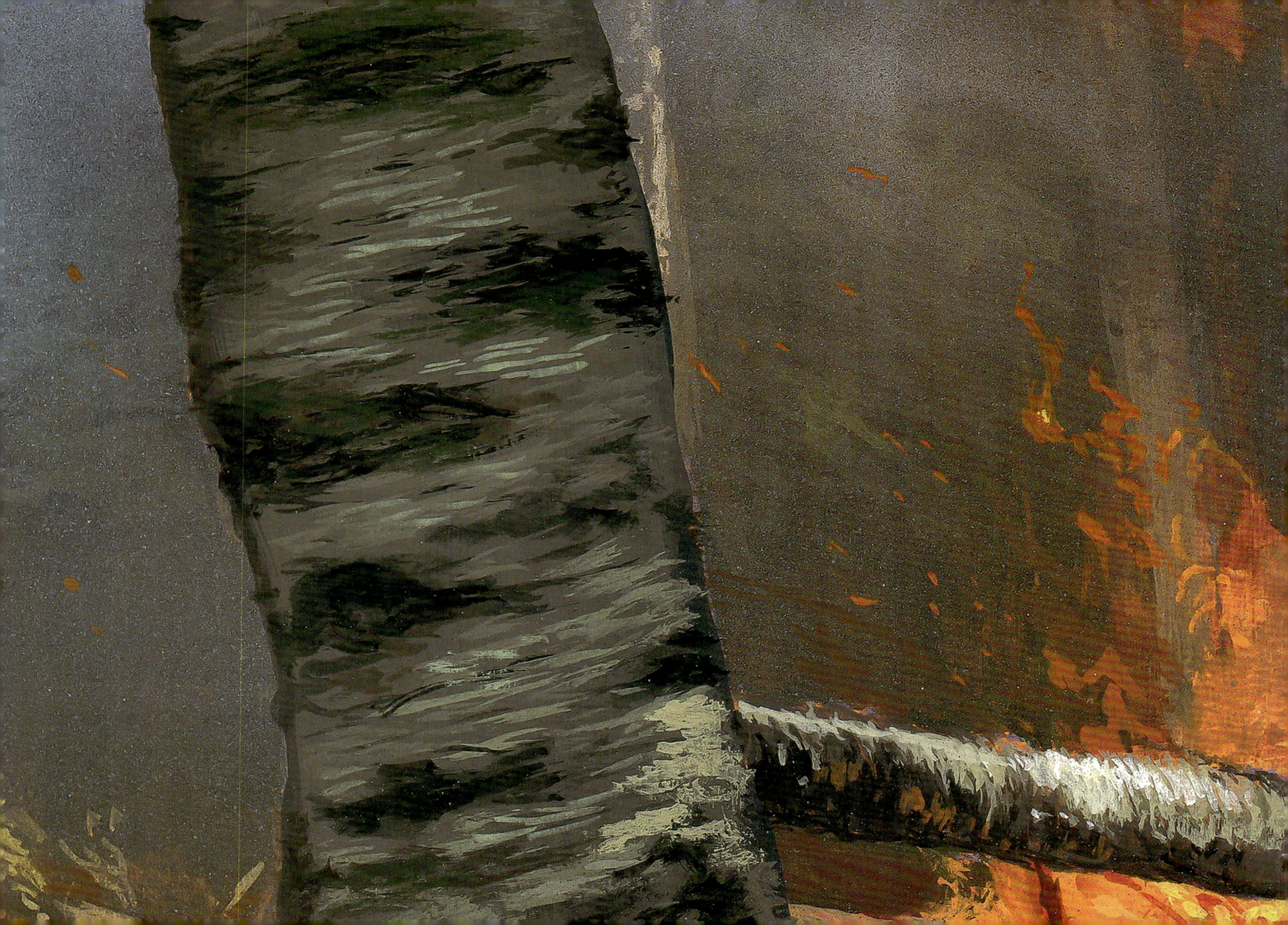

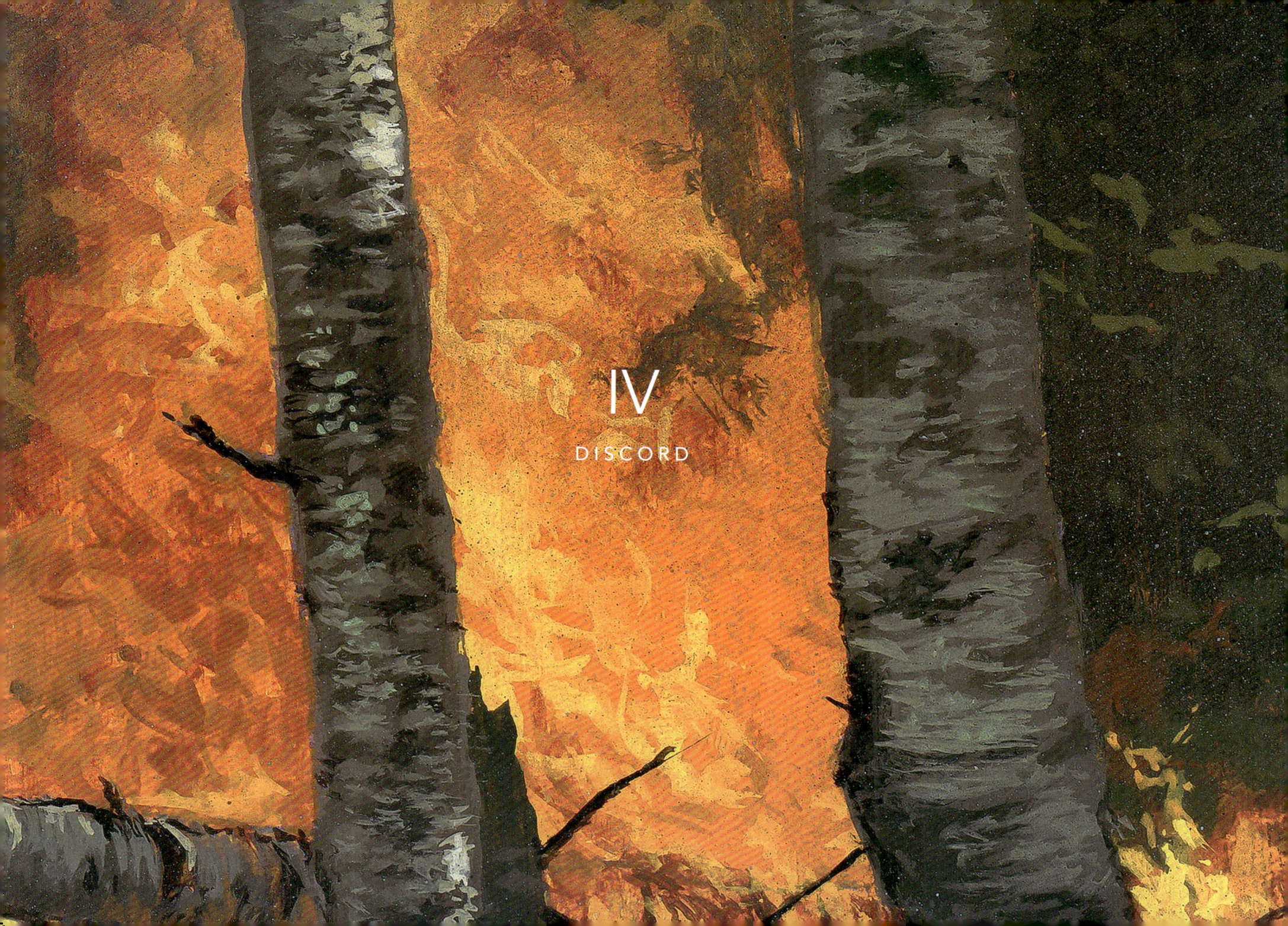

IV

DISCORD

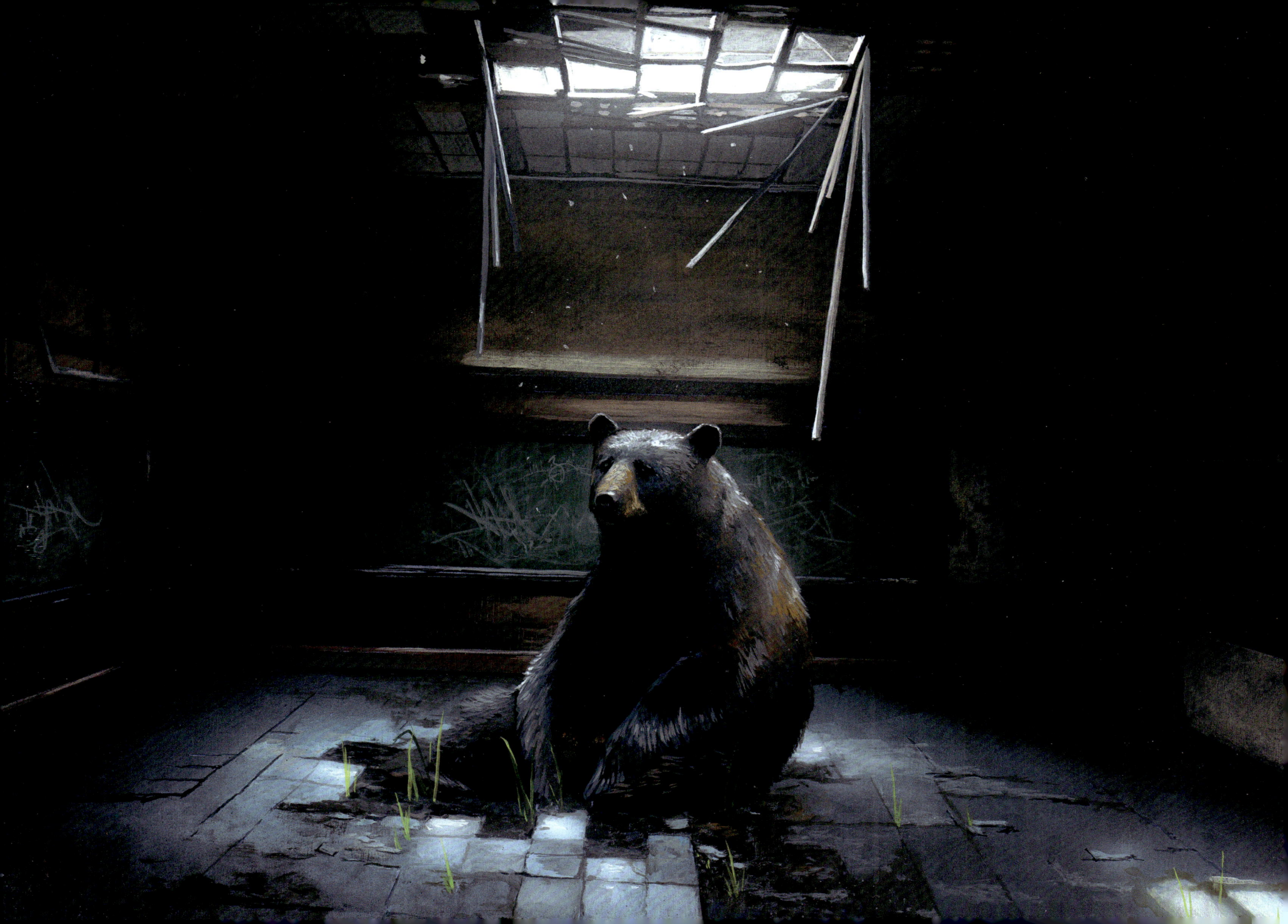

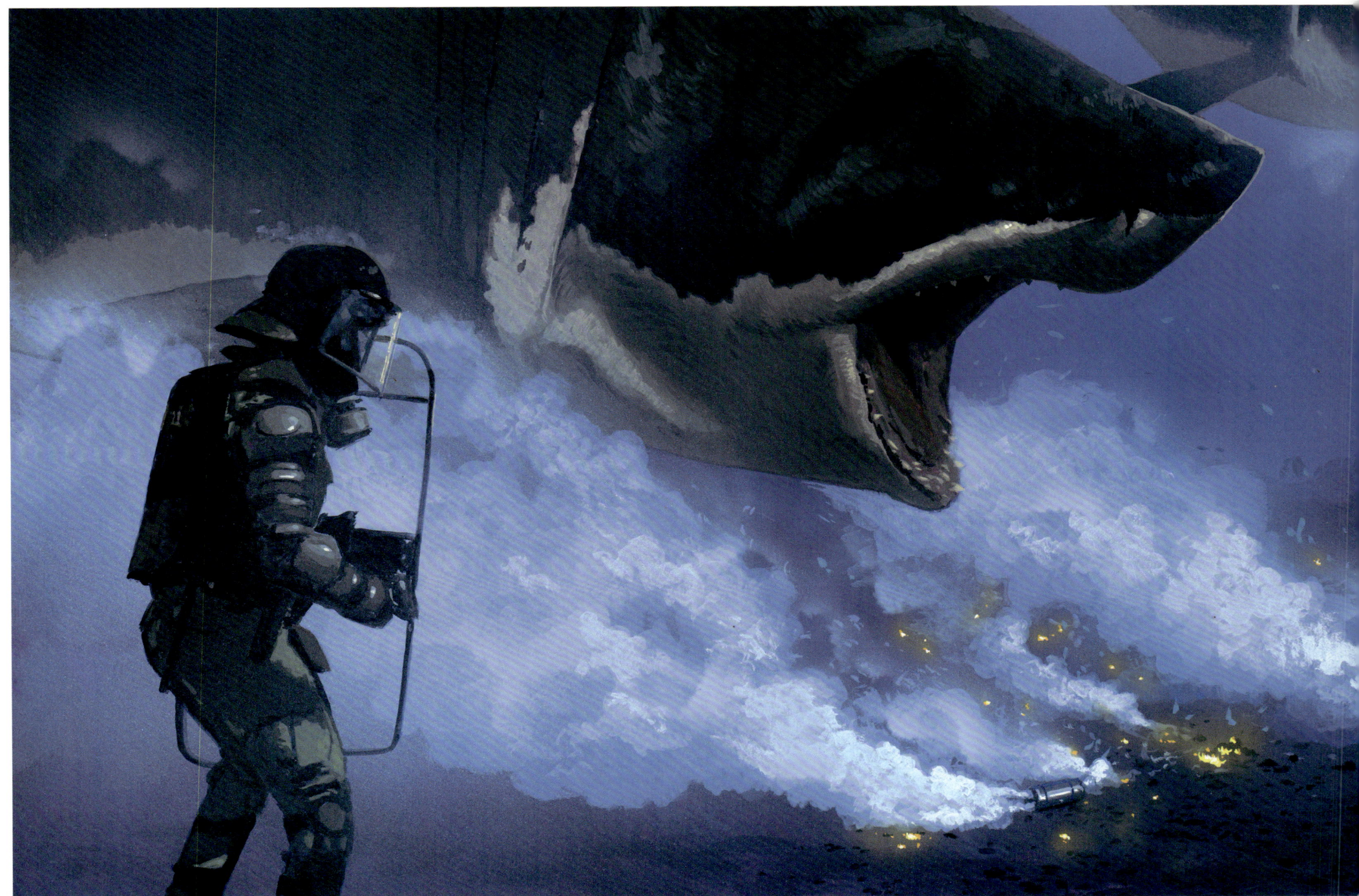

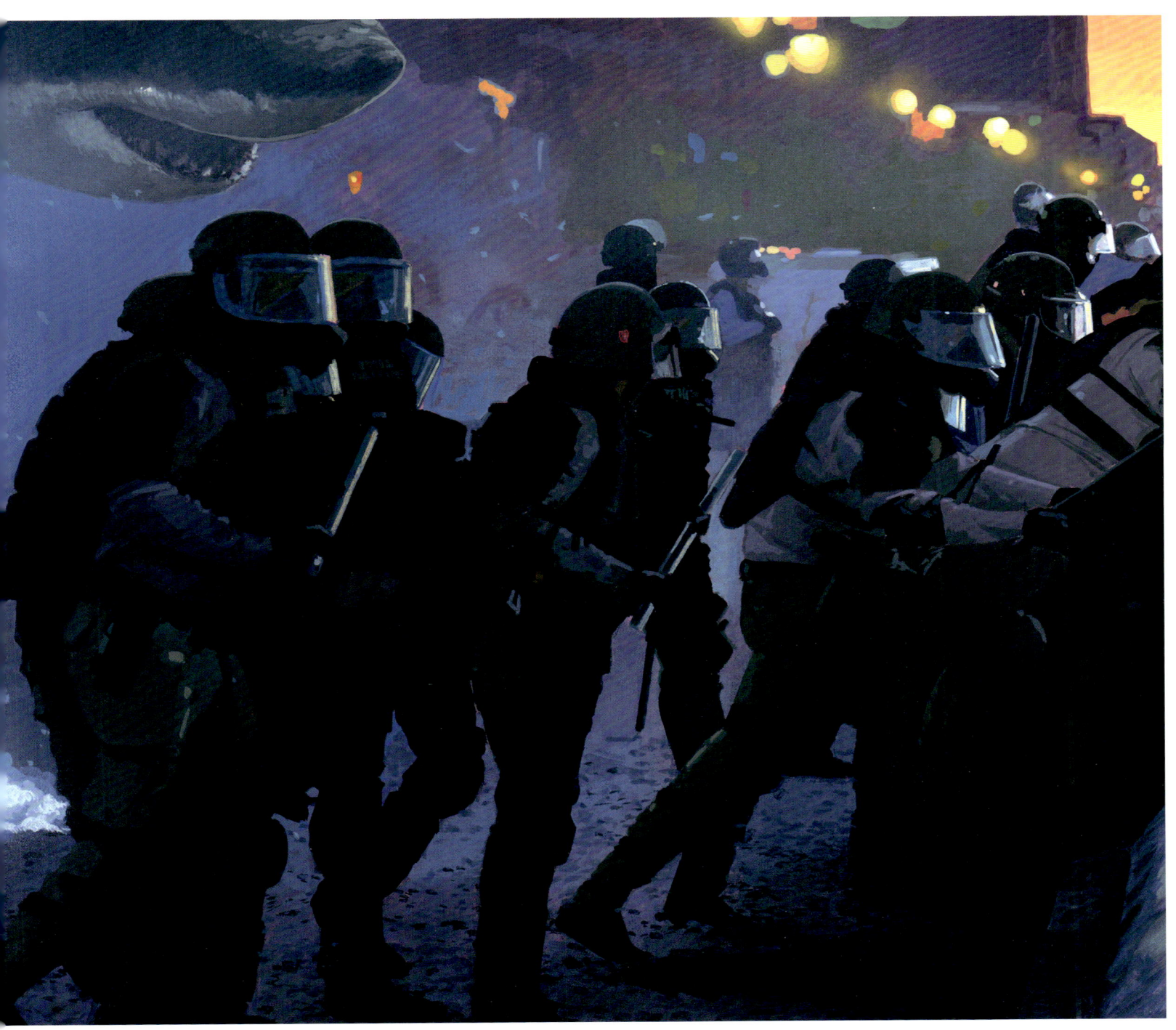

Language Of The Unheard
11" x 30"
gouache on wood
2023

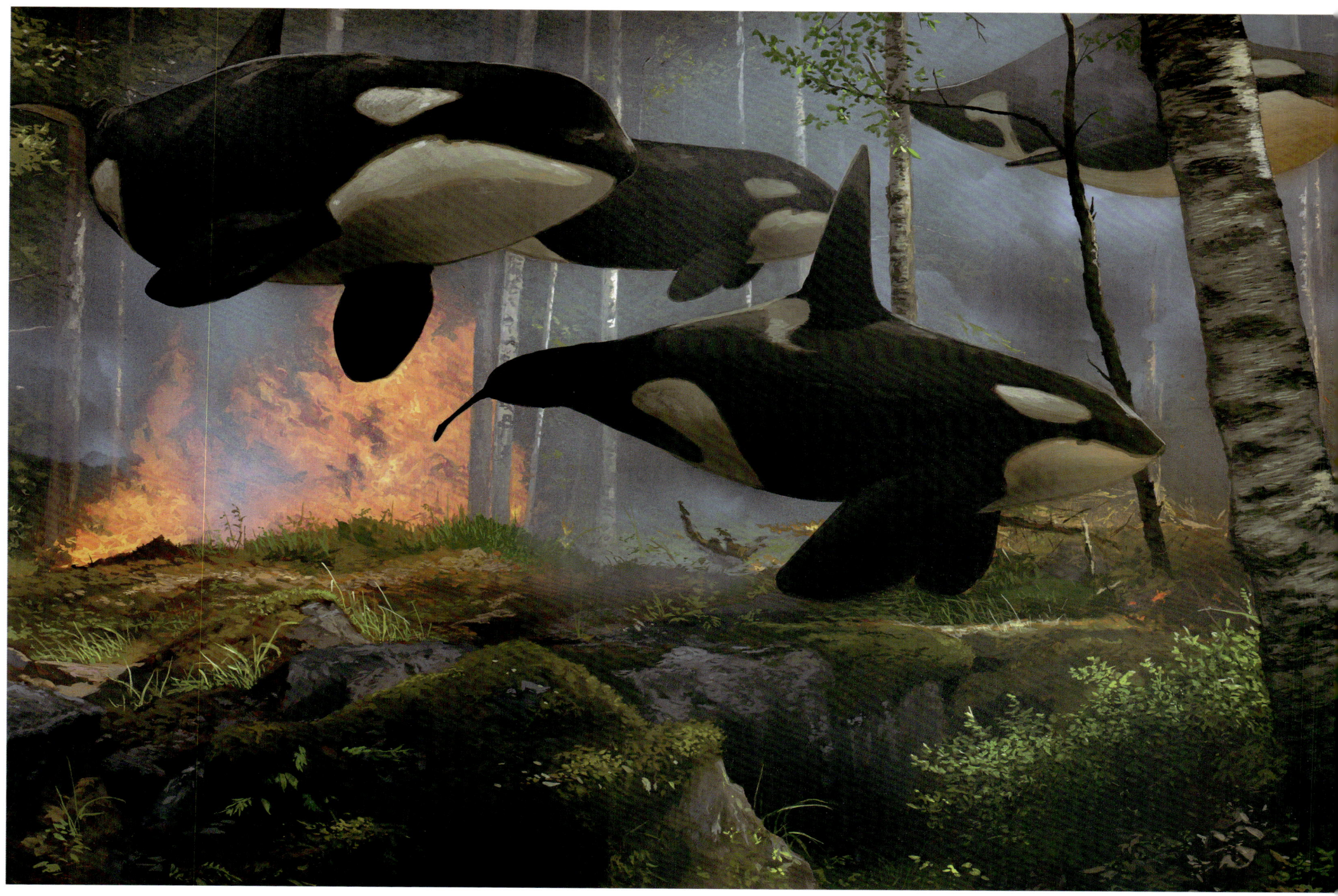

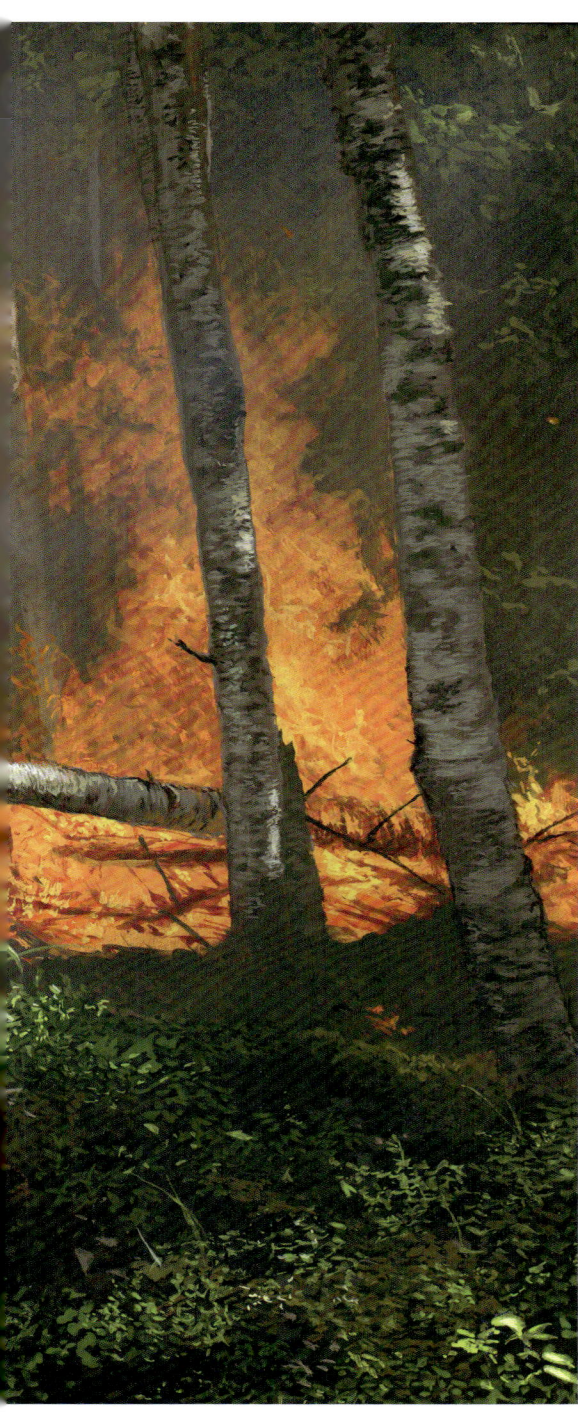

About Today | 10" x 20" | gouache on wood | 2020

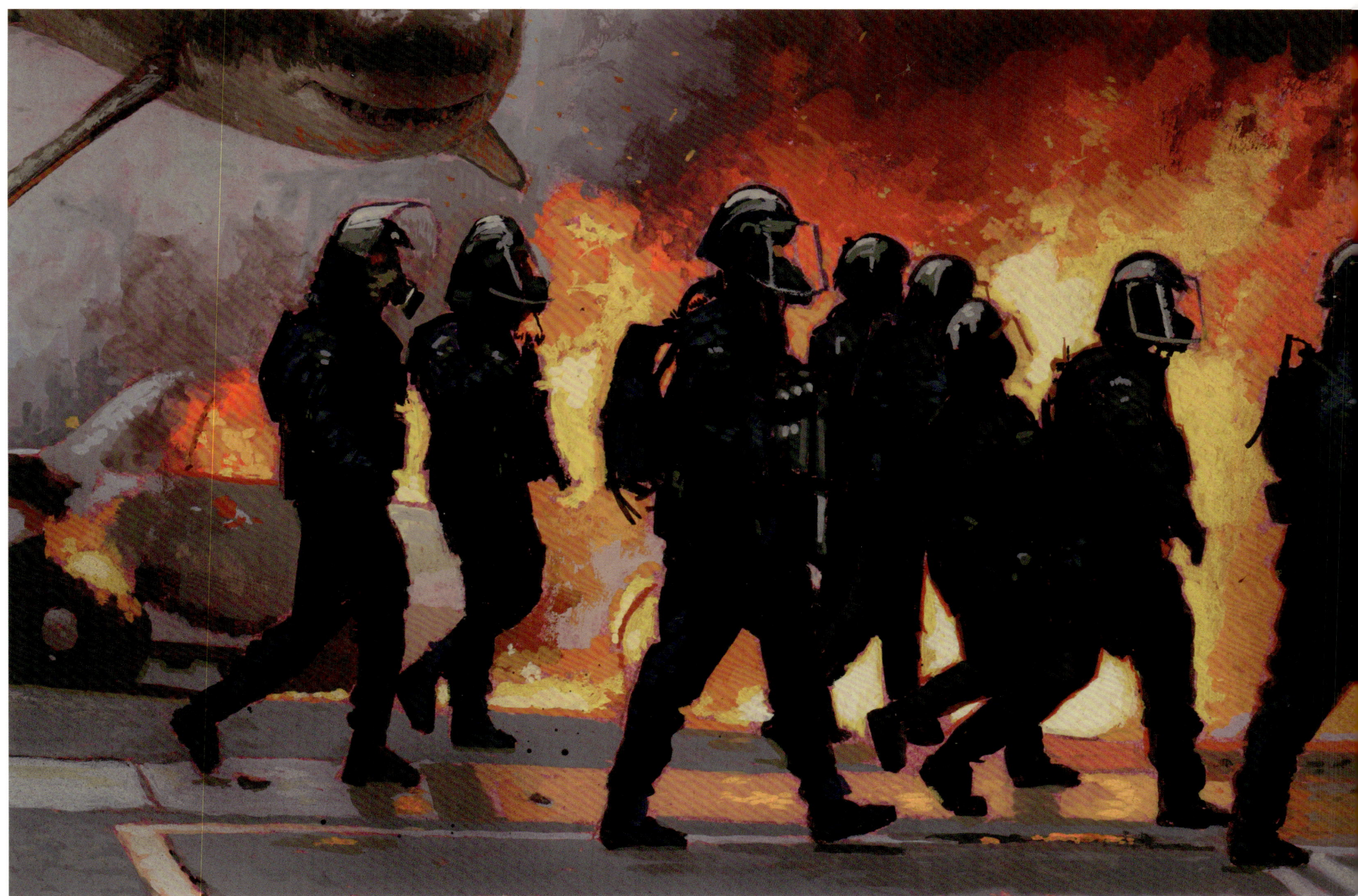

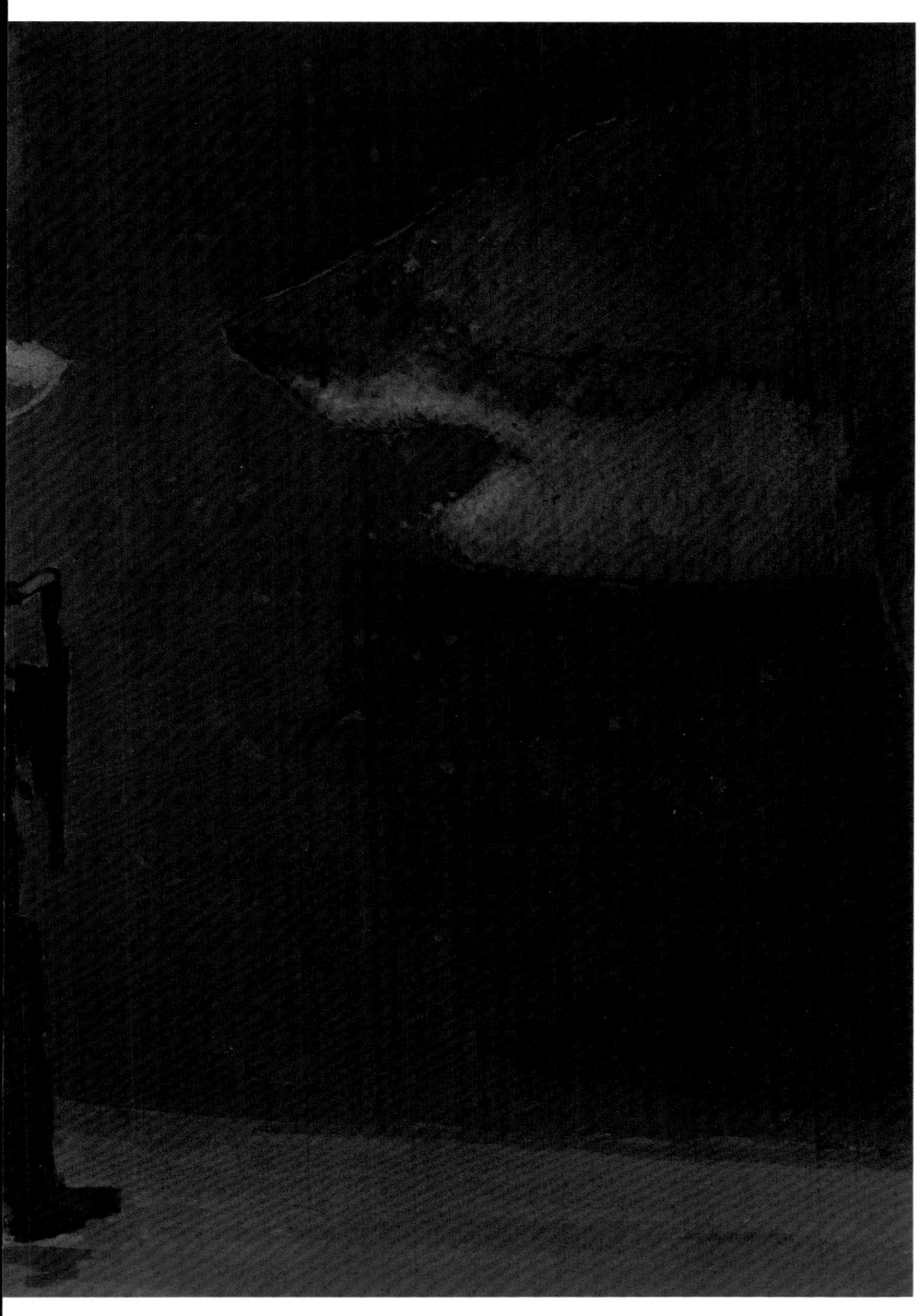

Scream For Freedom (study) | 4" x 10" | gouache on paper | 2023

You Seem Nearer To Me | 13″ x 14.5″ | gouache on paper | 2023

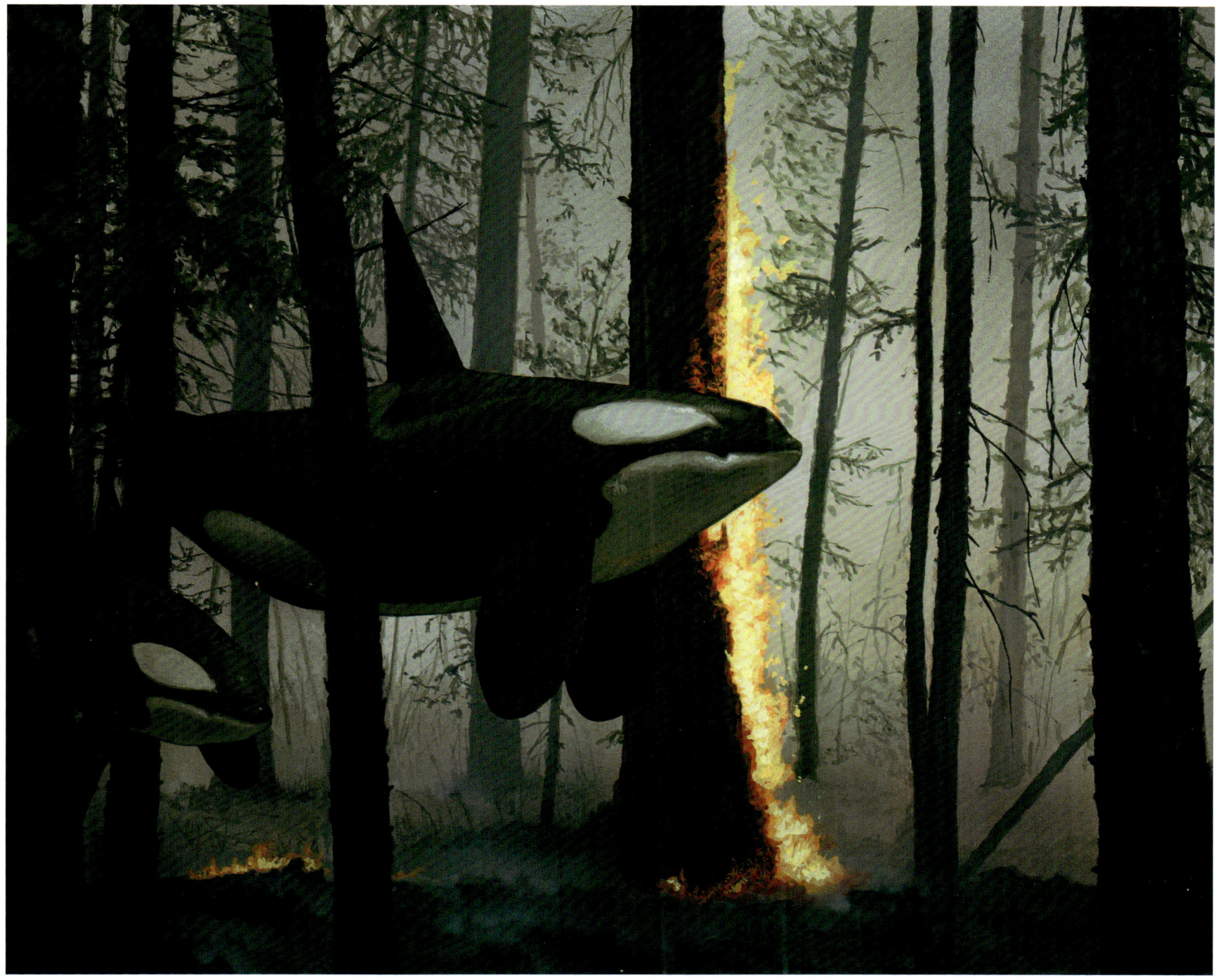

If We're Lost, We're Lost Together | 11" x 7" | gouache on paper | 2024

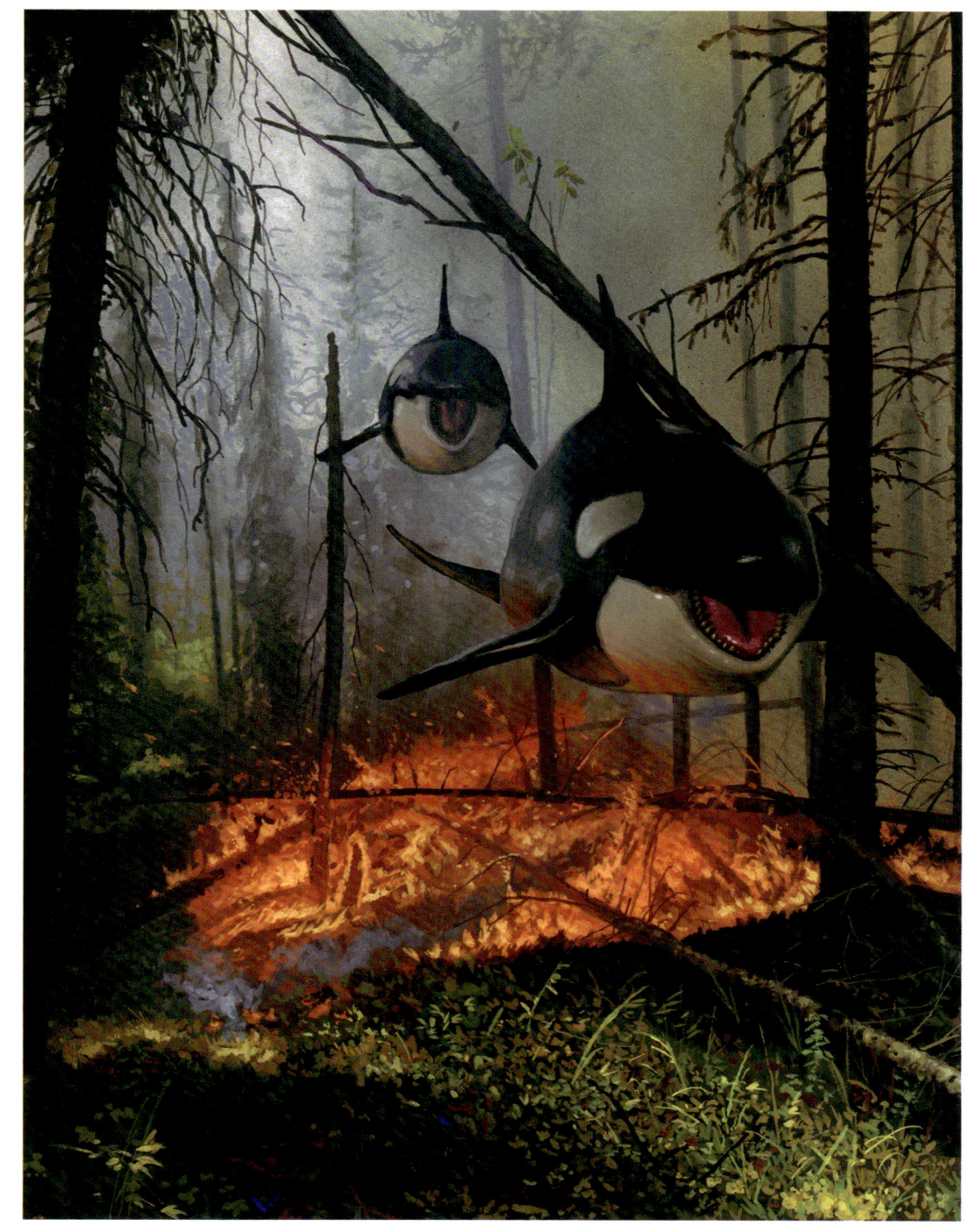

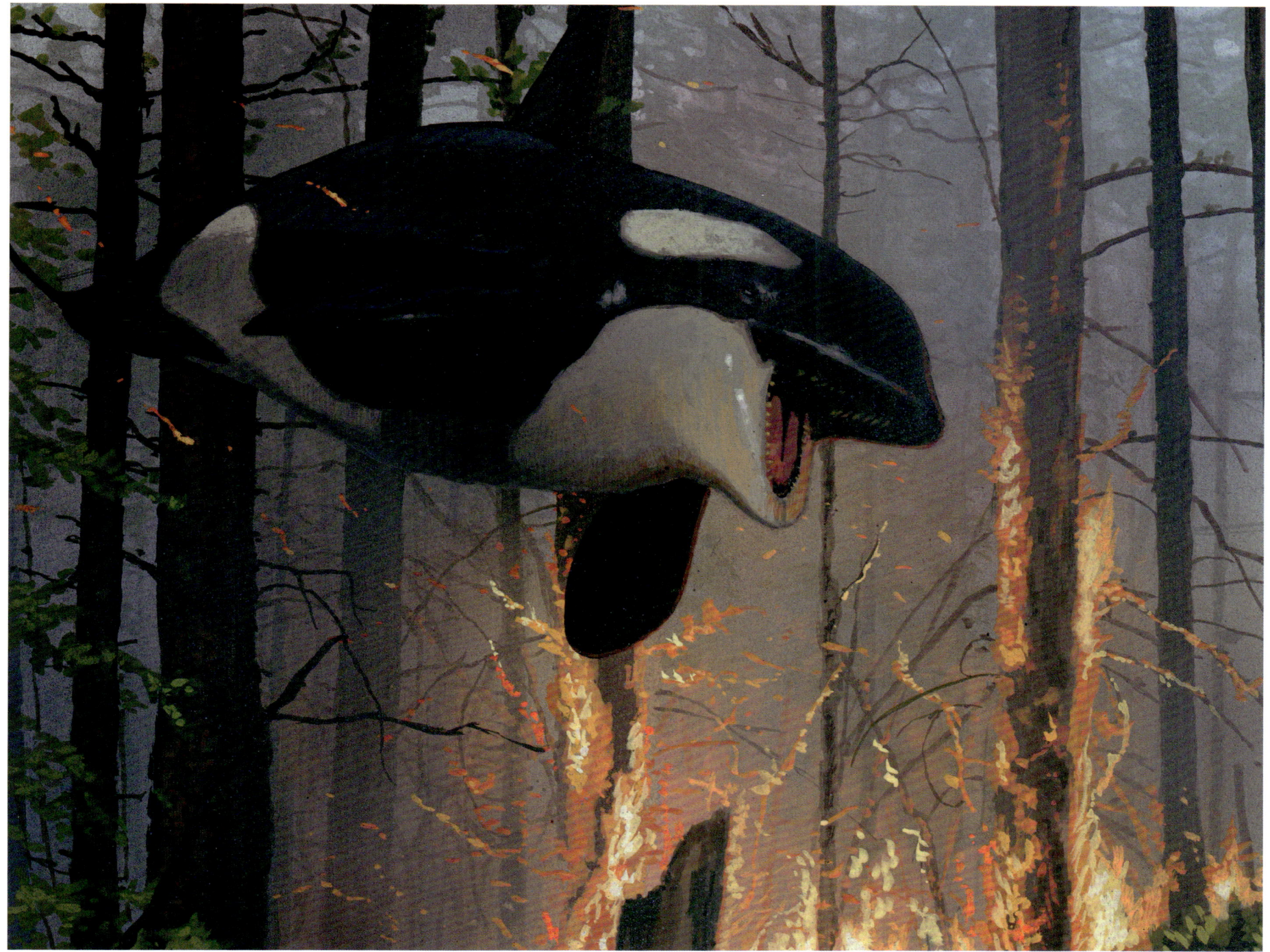

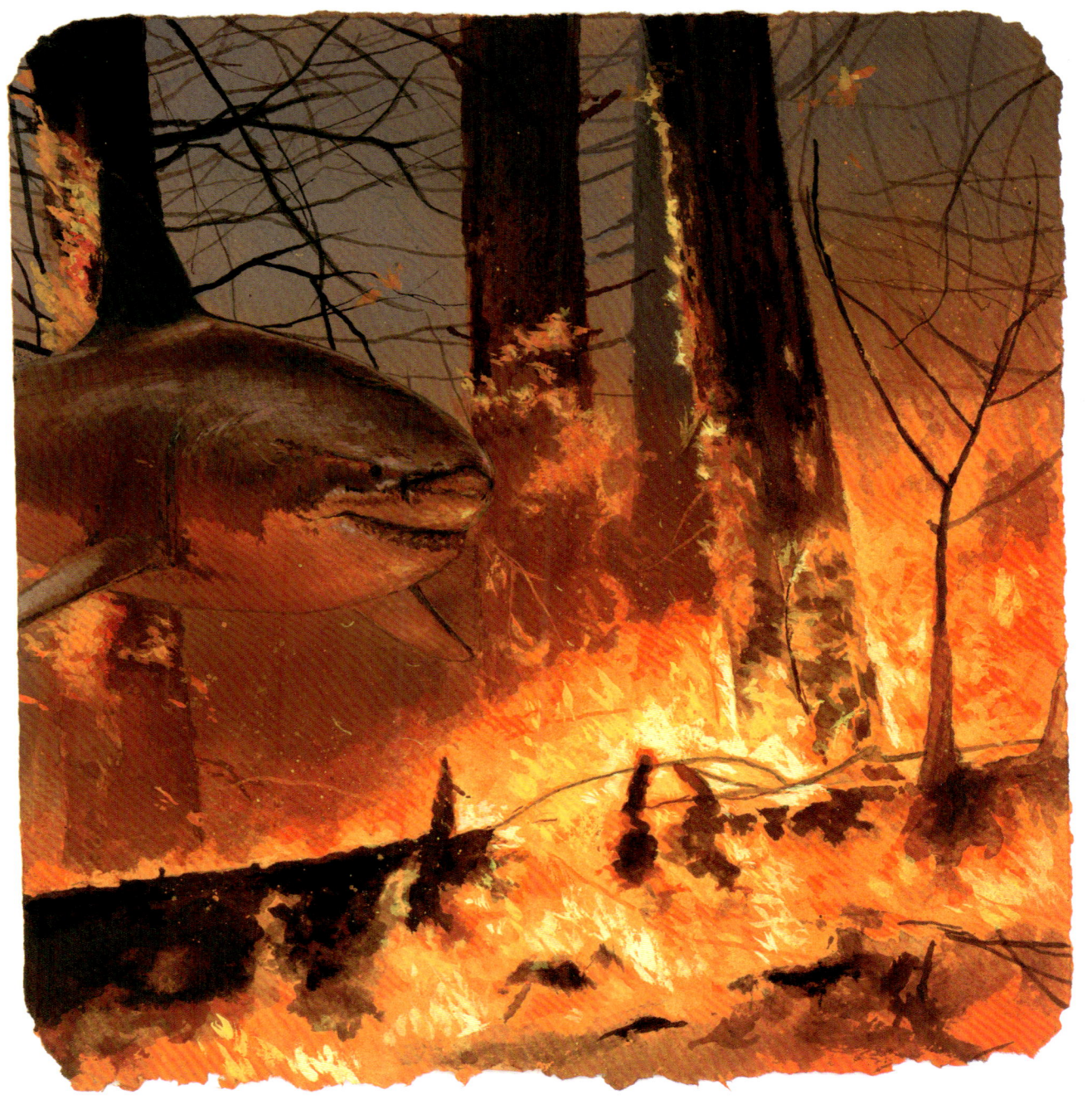

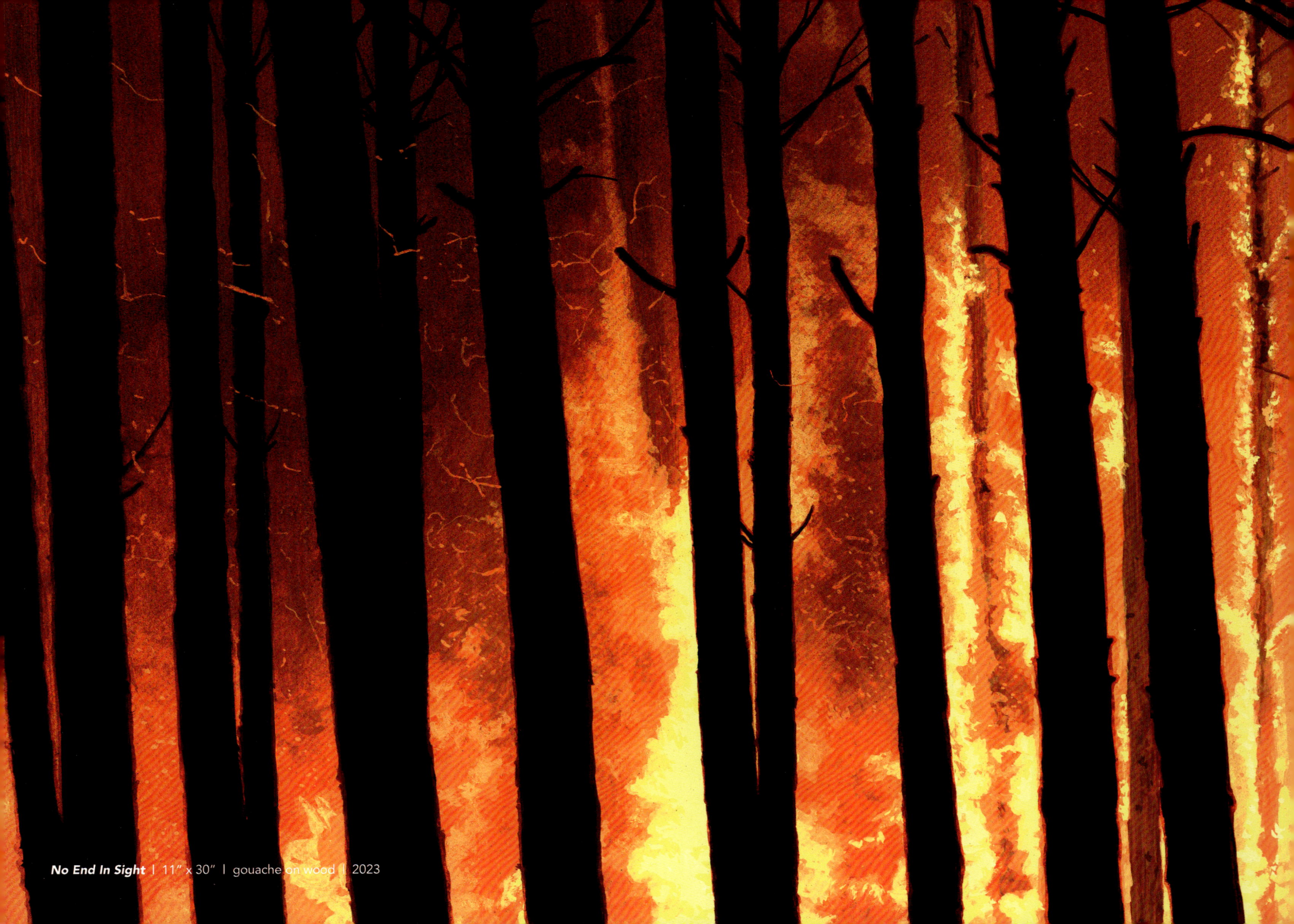

No End In Sight | 11" x 30" | gouache on wood | 2023

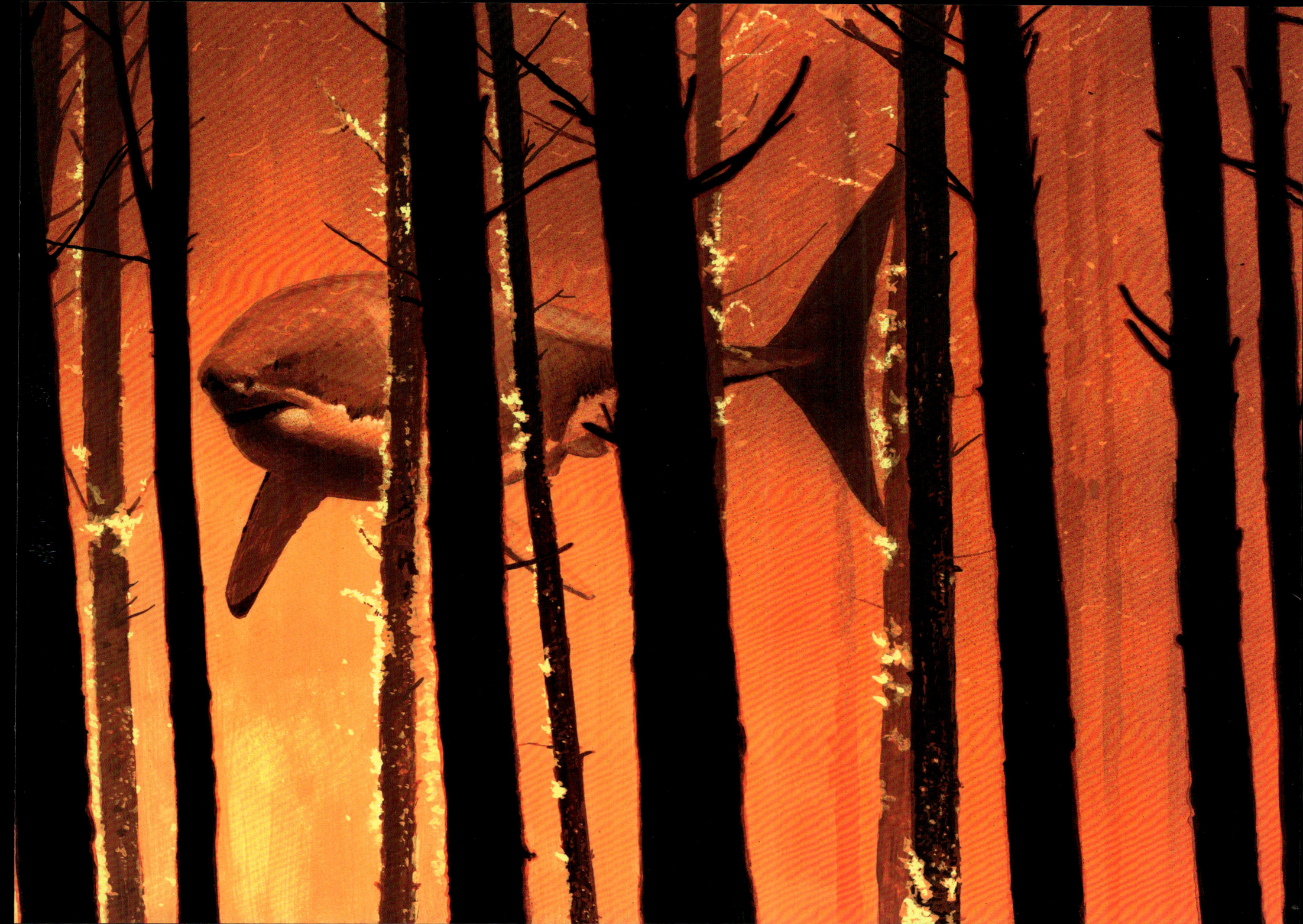

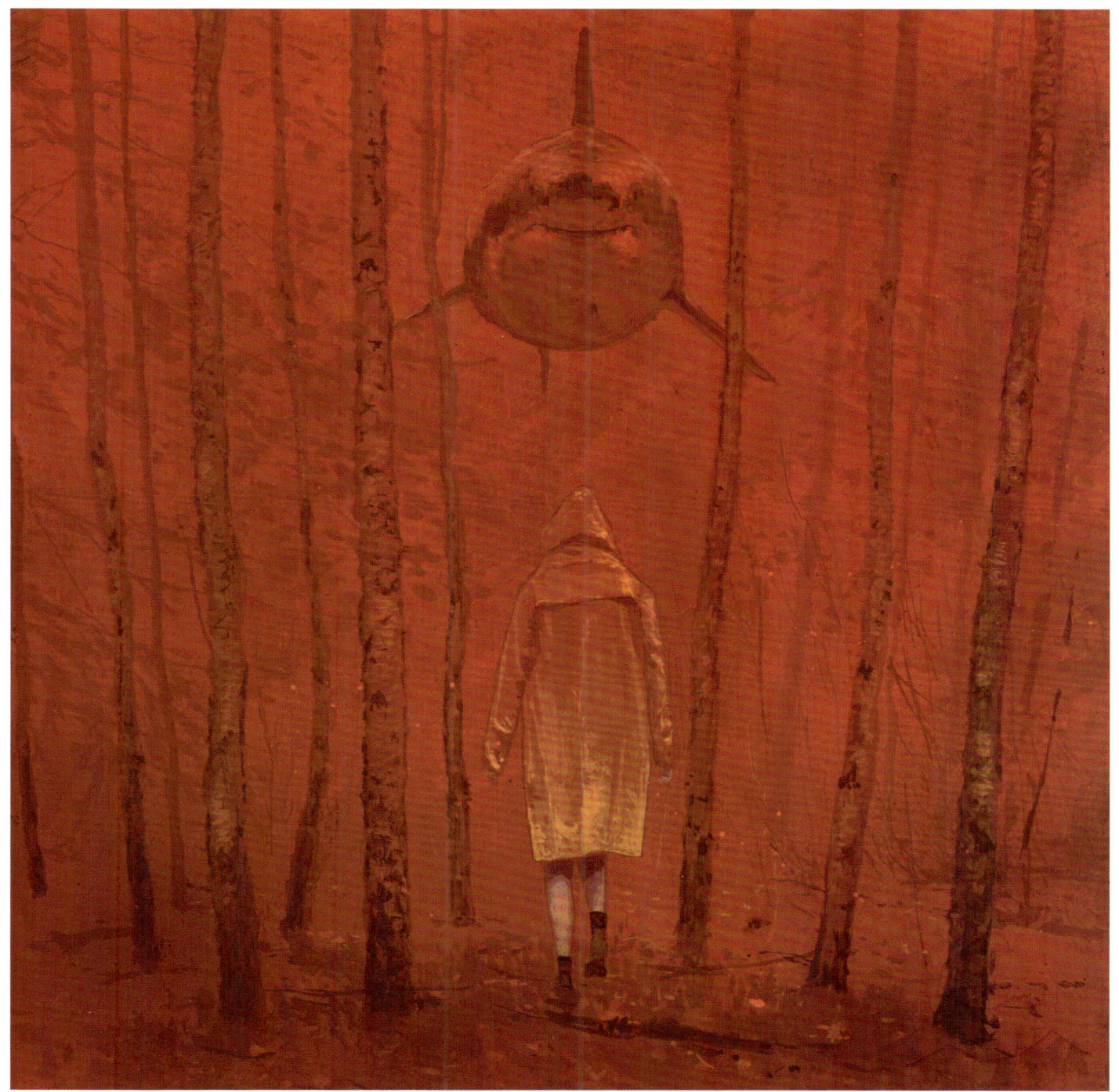

Let's Go Home (study) | 9" x 7" | gouache on paper | 2024

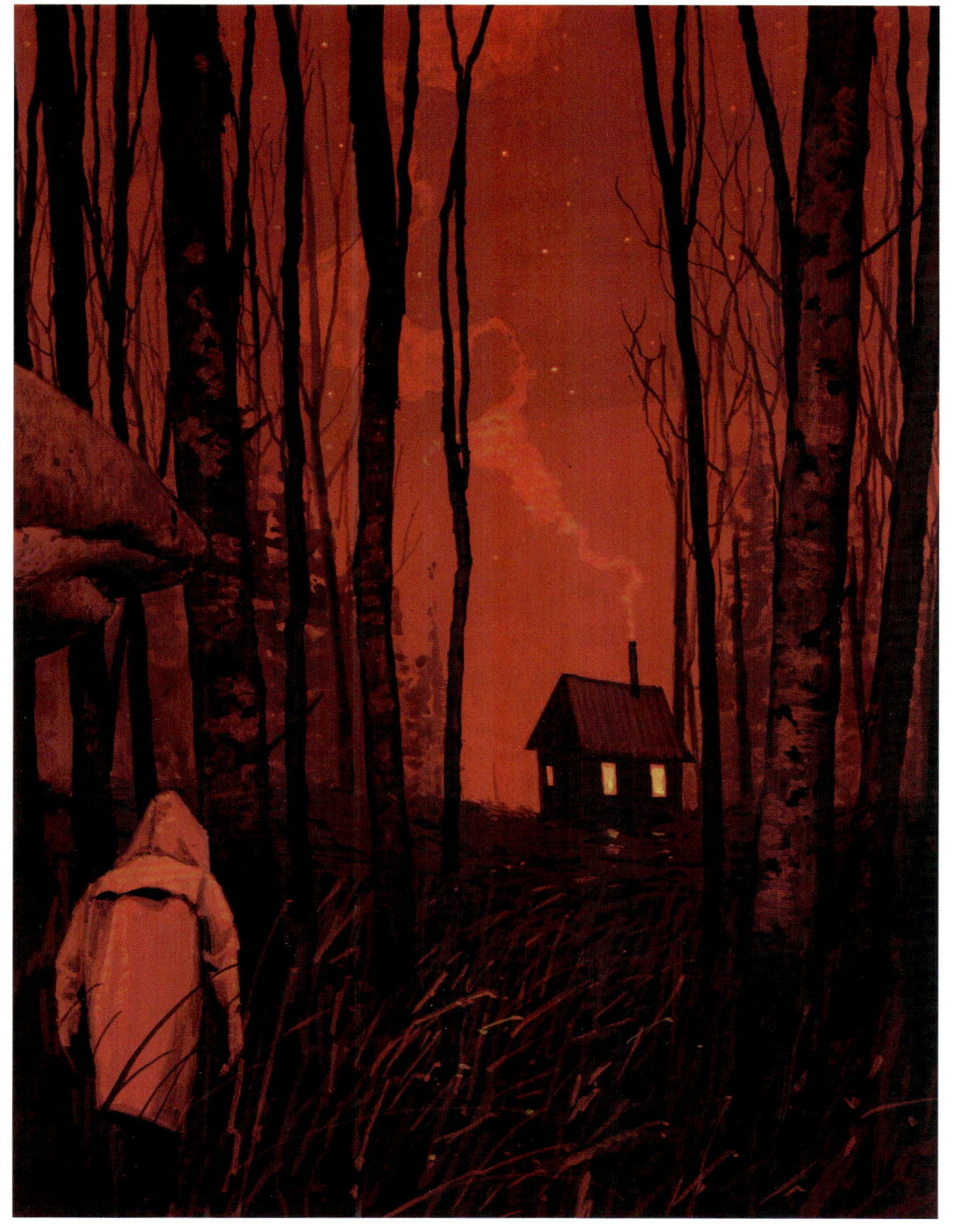

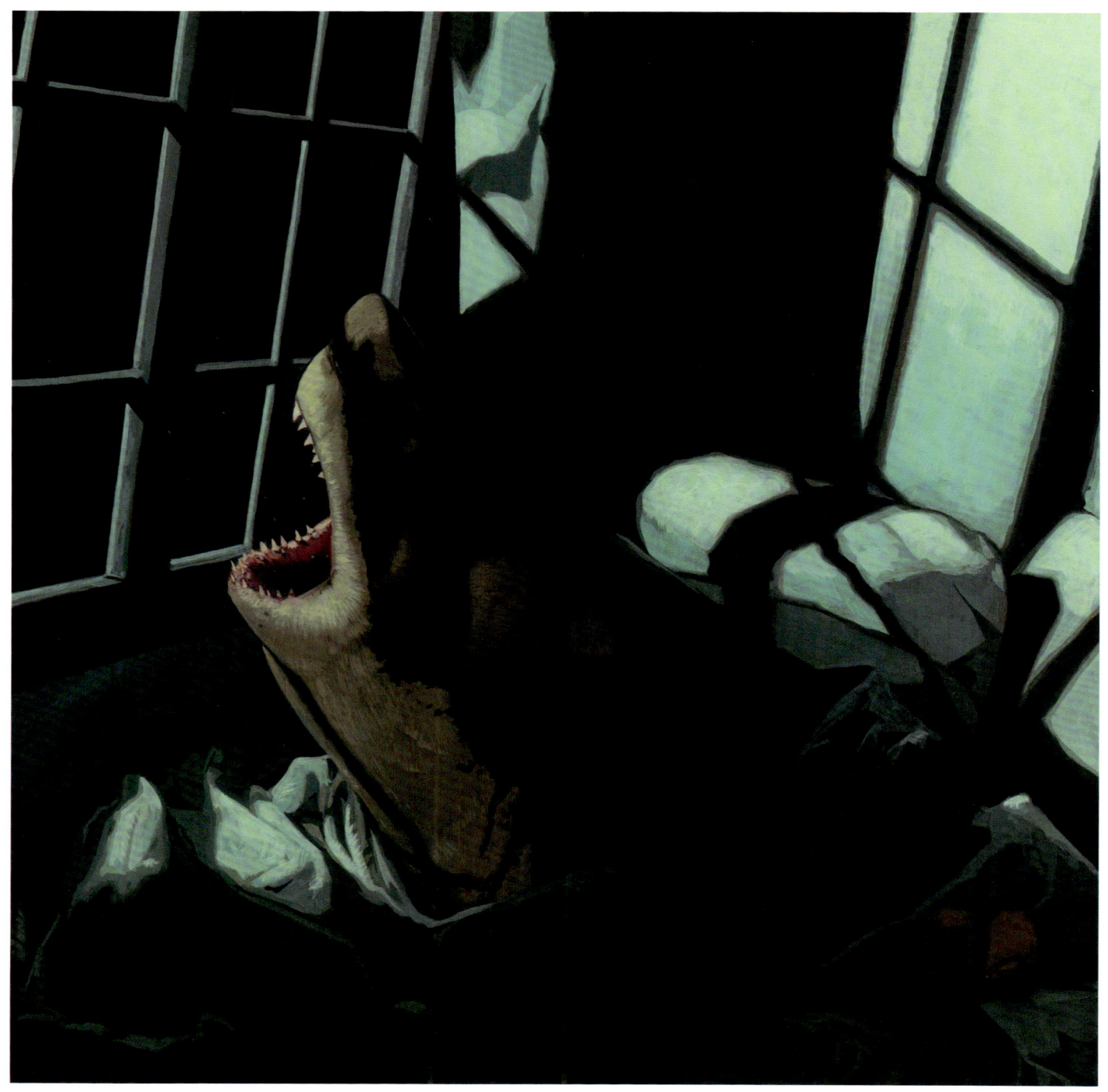

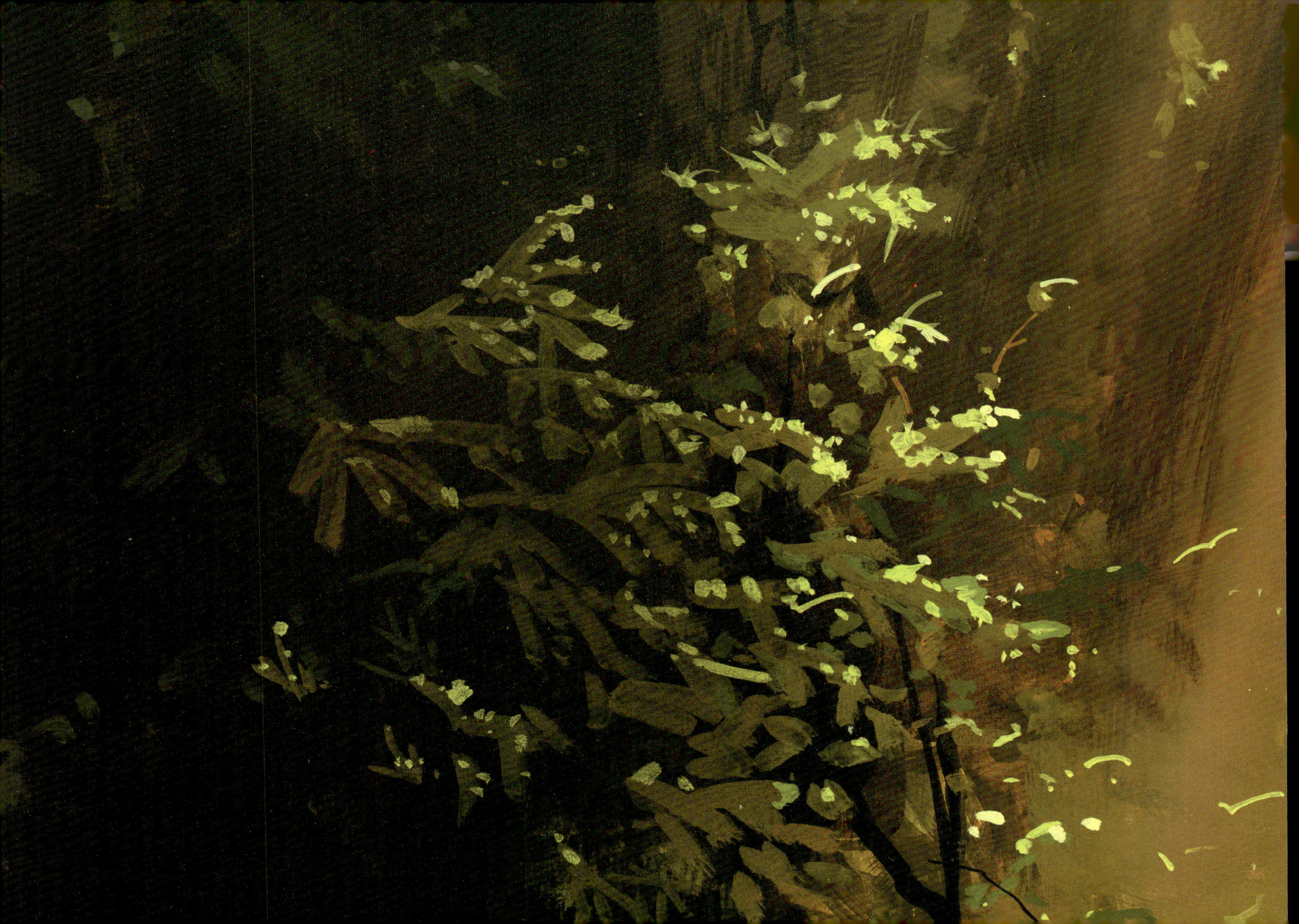

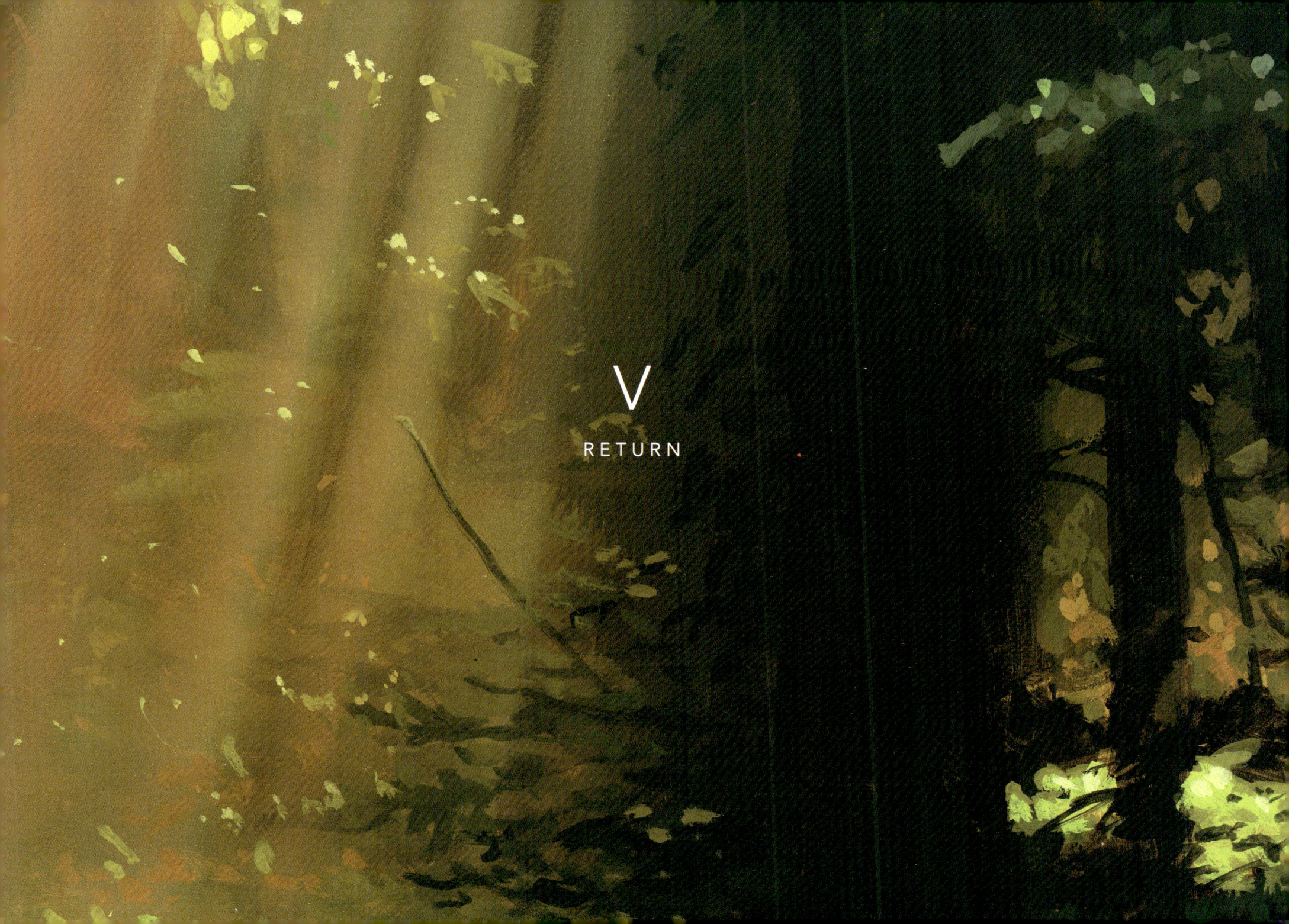

V

RETURN

Courage To Continue | 9" x 9" | gouache on wood | 2020

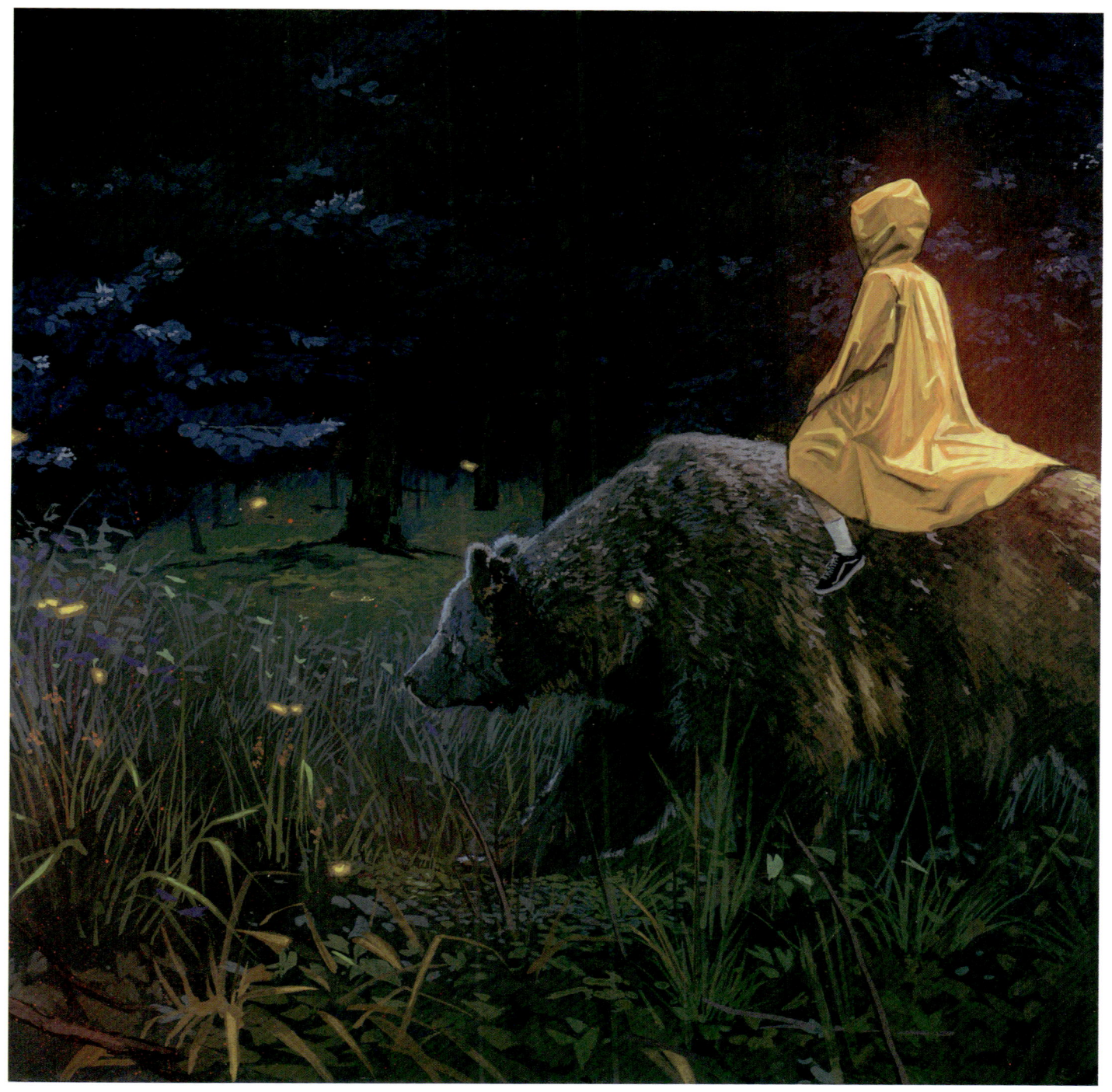

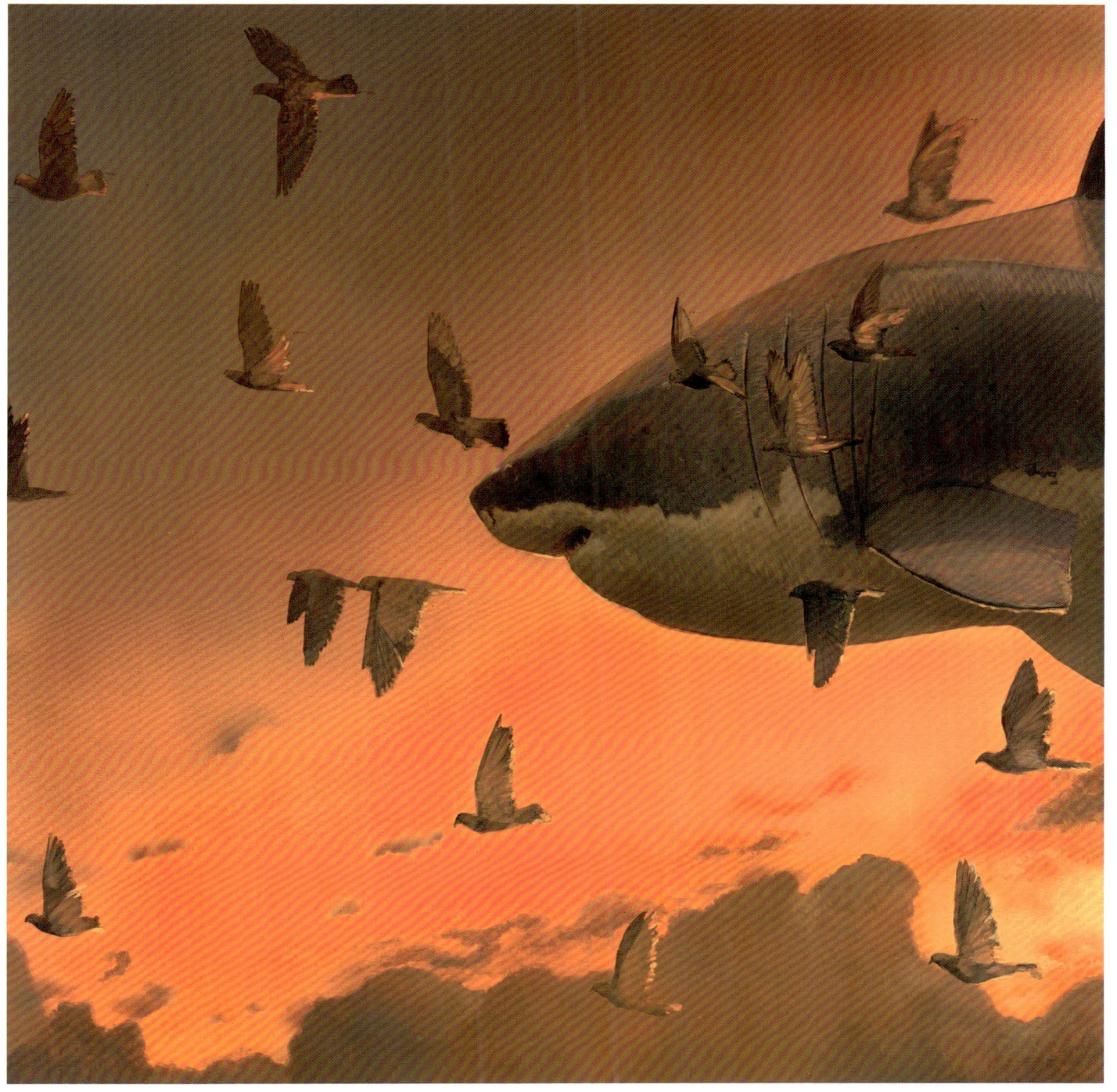

Brumbles Befriend The Bold | 24" x 24" | gouache on wood | 2021

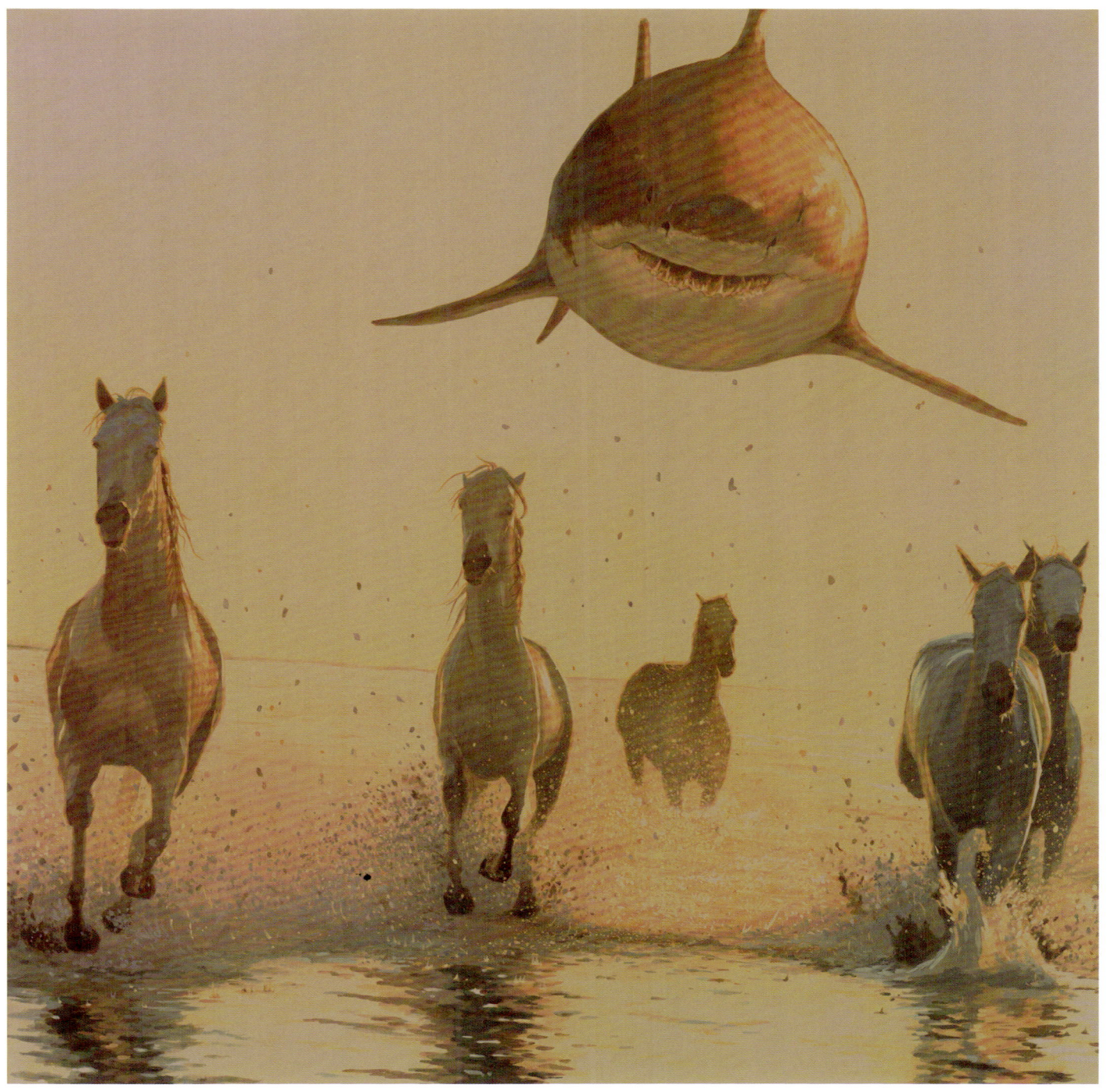

With Yourself For A While | 12″ x 18″ | gouache on wood | 2024

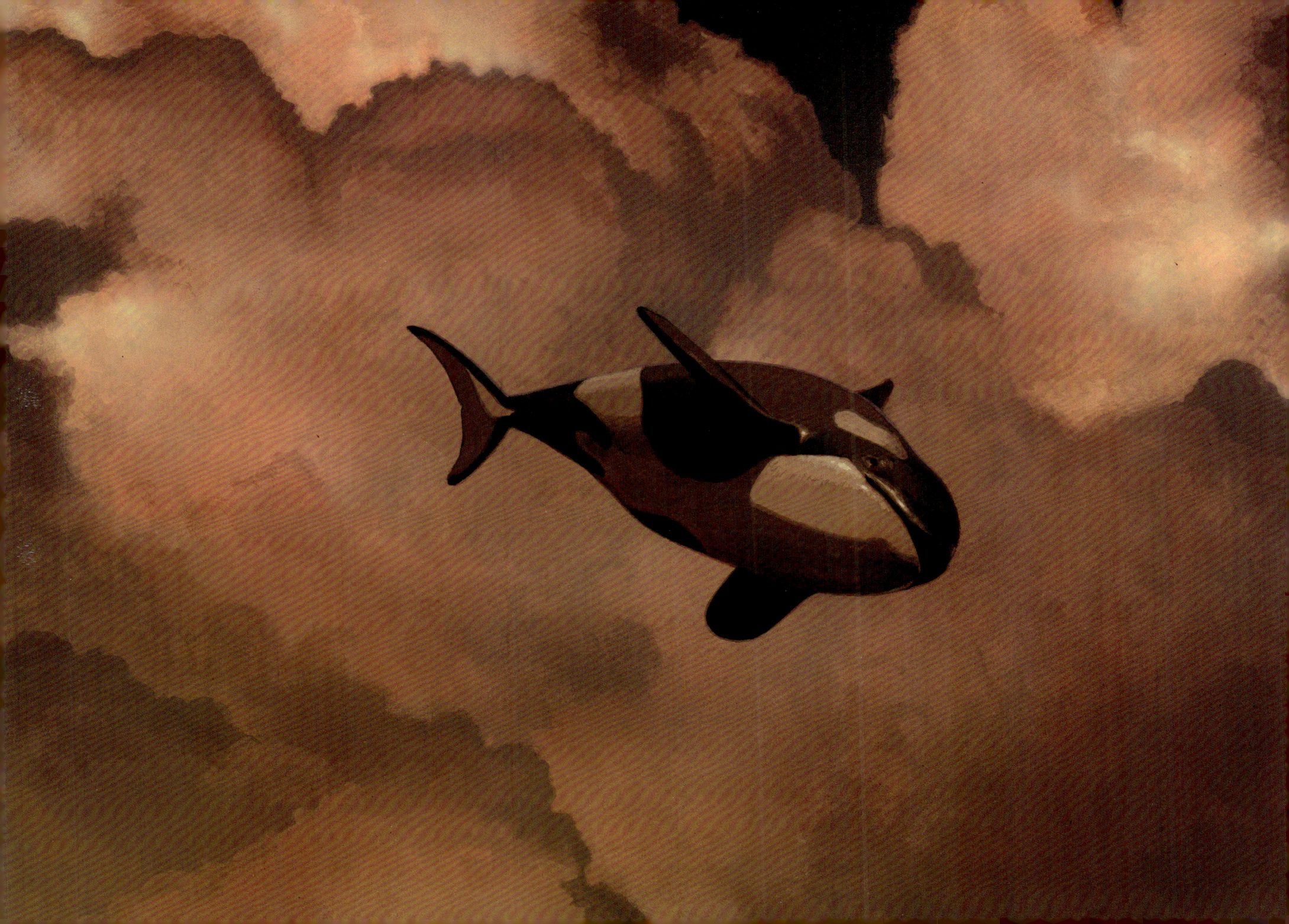

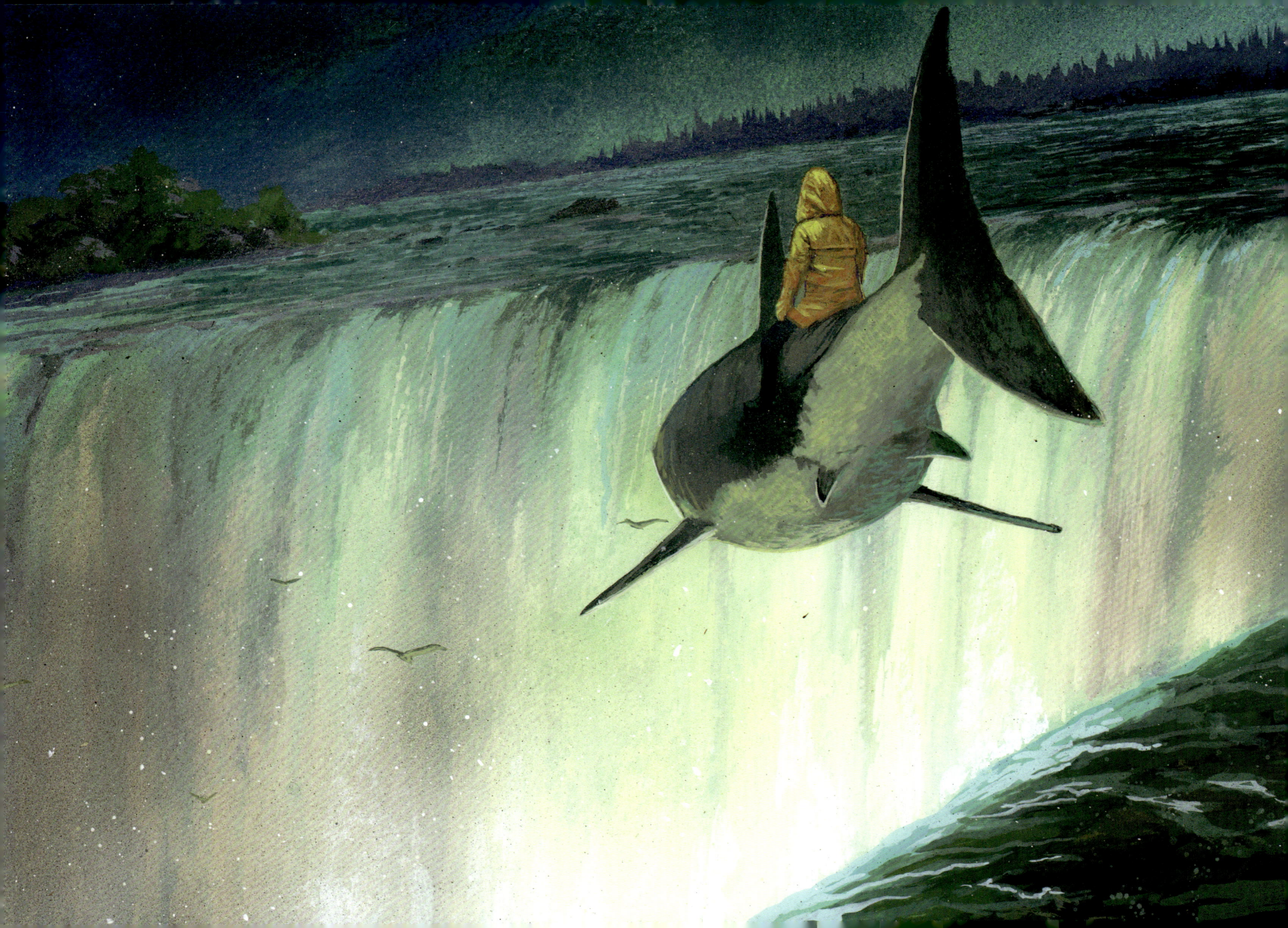

Where The Sky Touches The Sea | 11" x 10" | gouache on paper | 2020

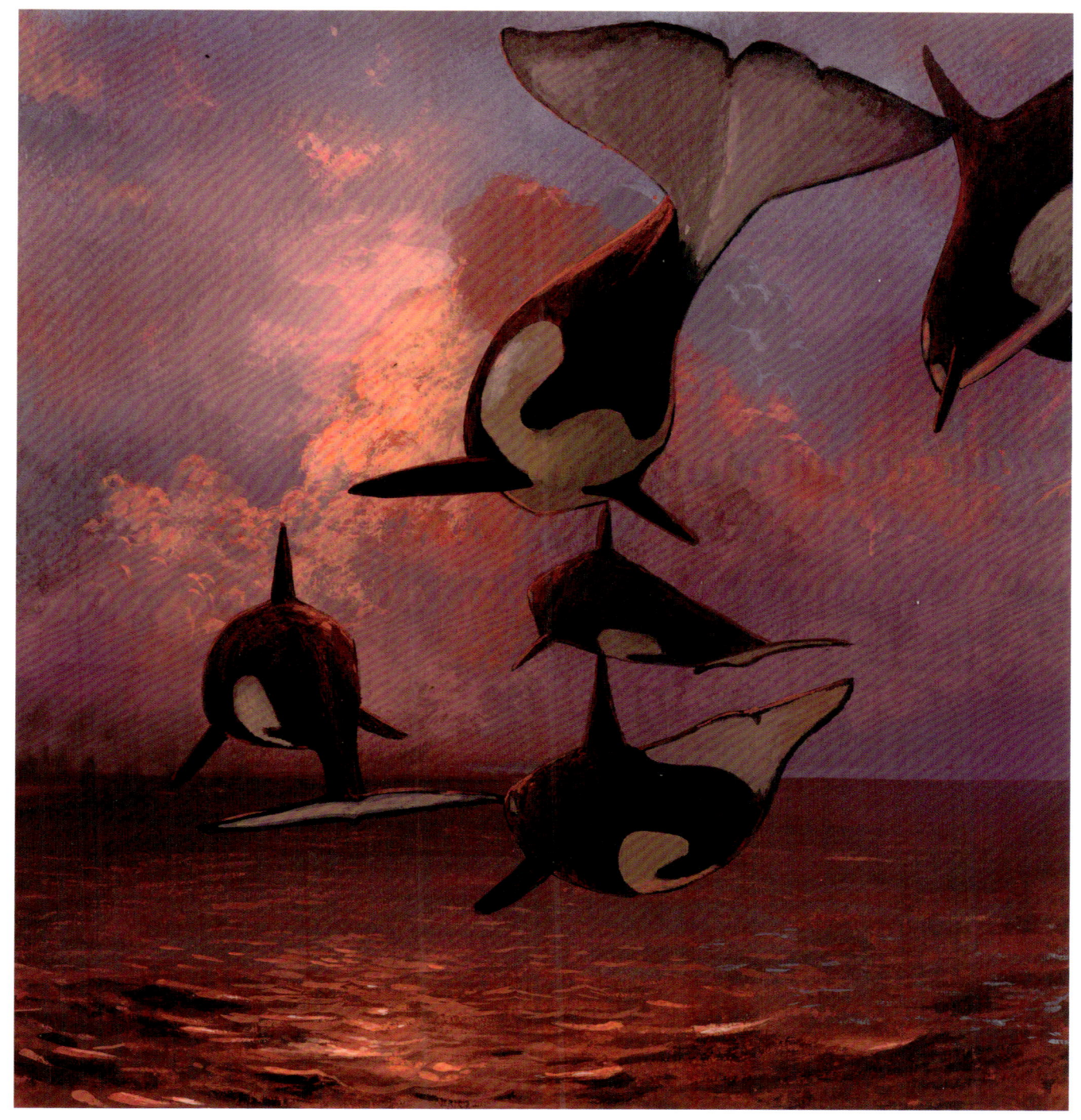

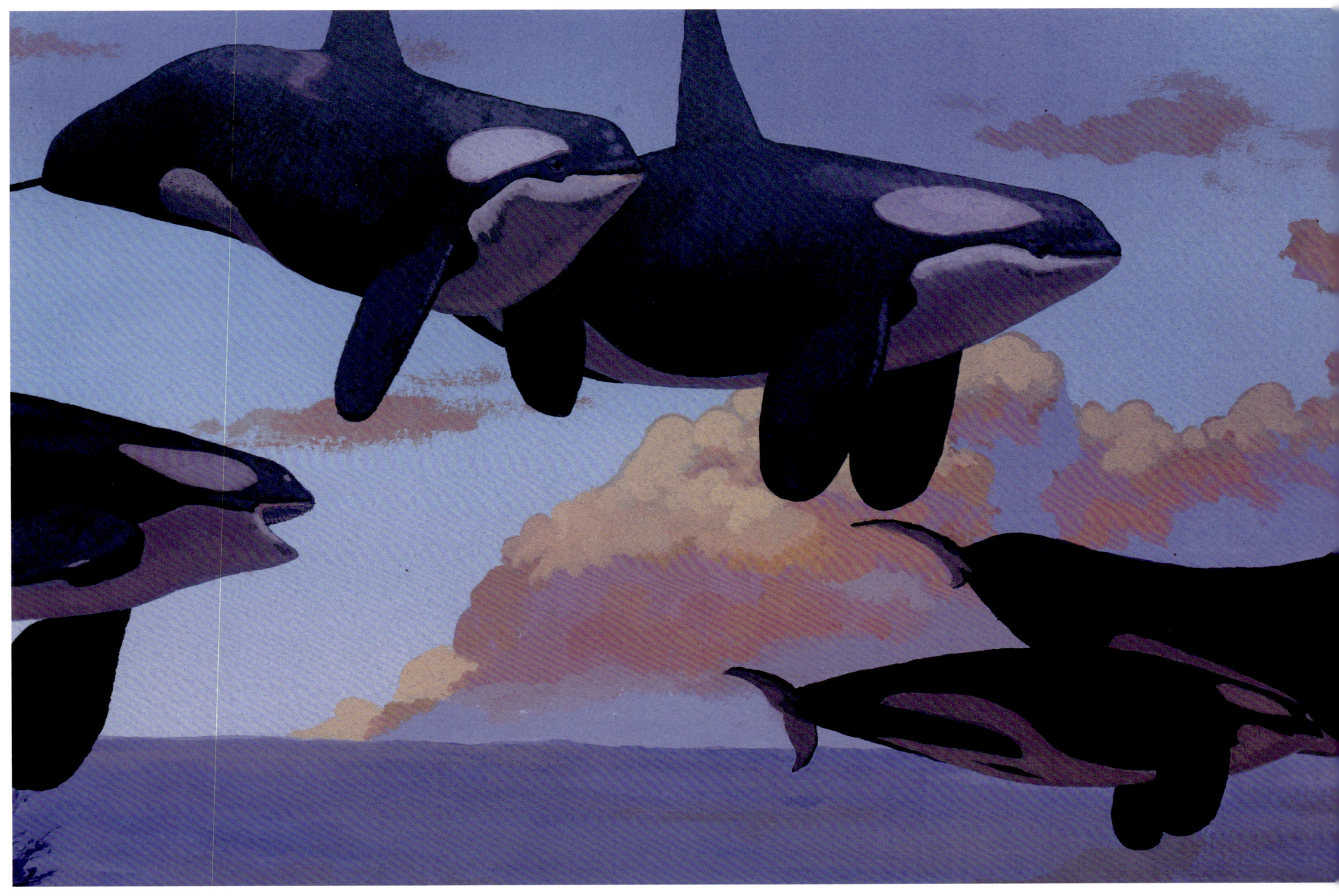

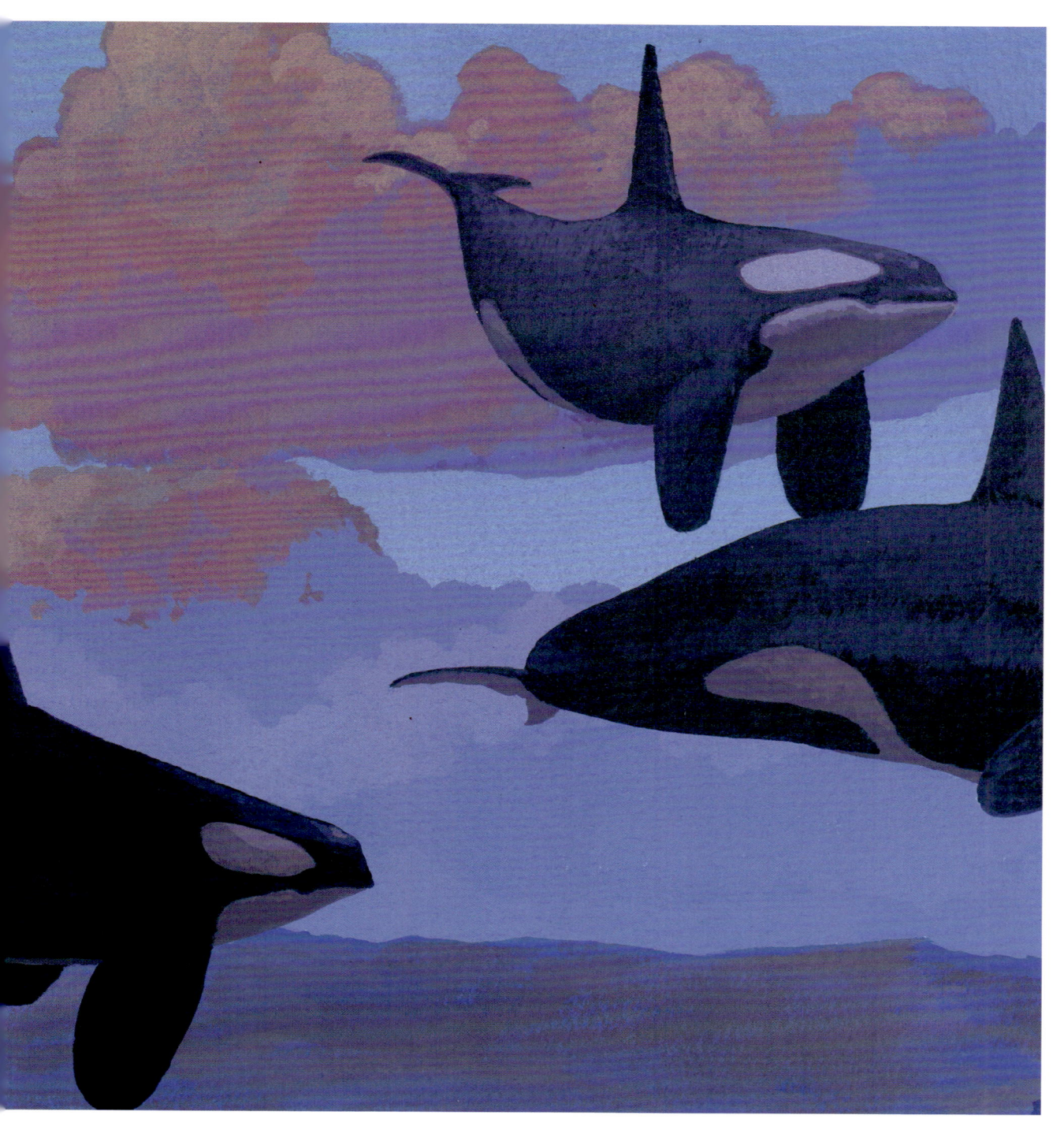

Who Was Wrong Remains Unclear
8" x 20"
gouache on paper mounted to wood
2023

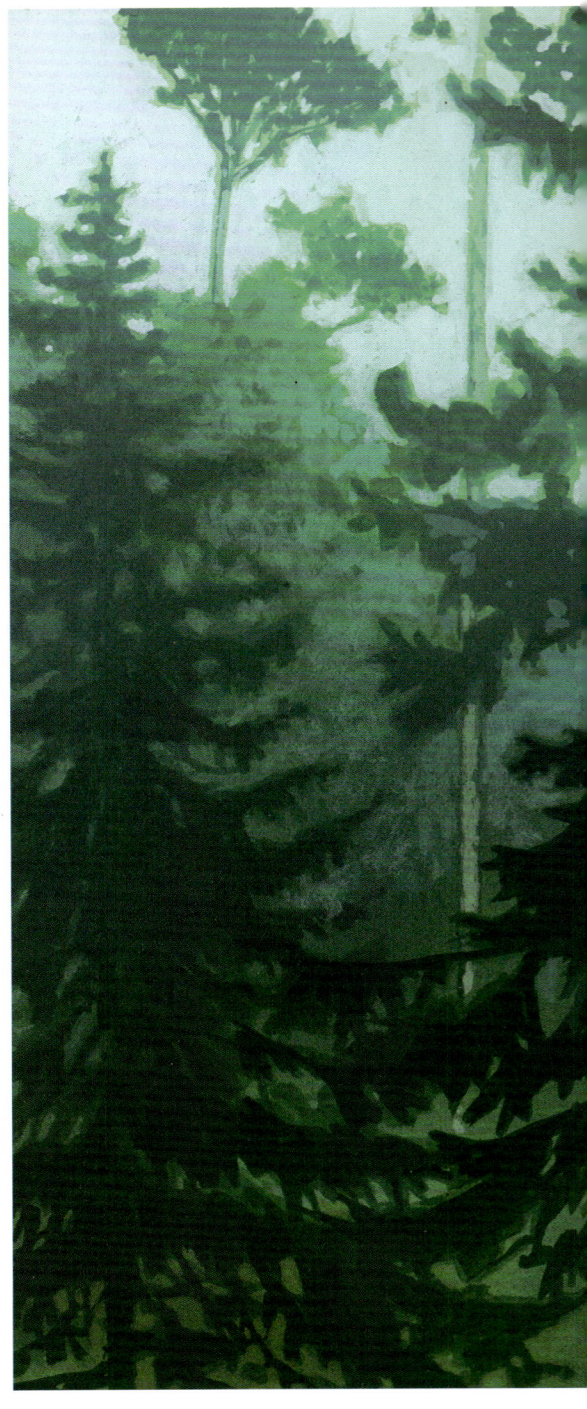

Fear Keeps You Honest | 12" x 24" | gouache on wood | 2023

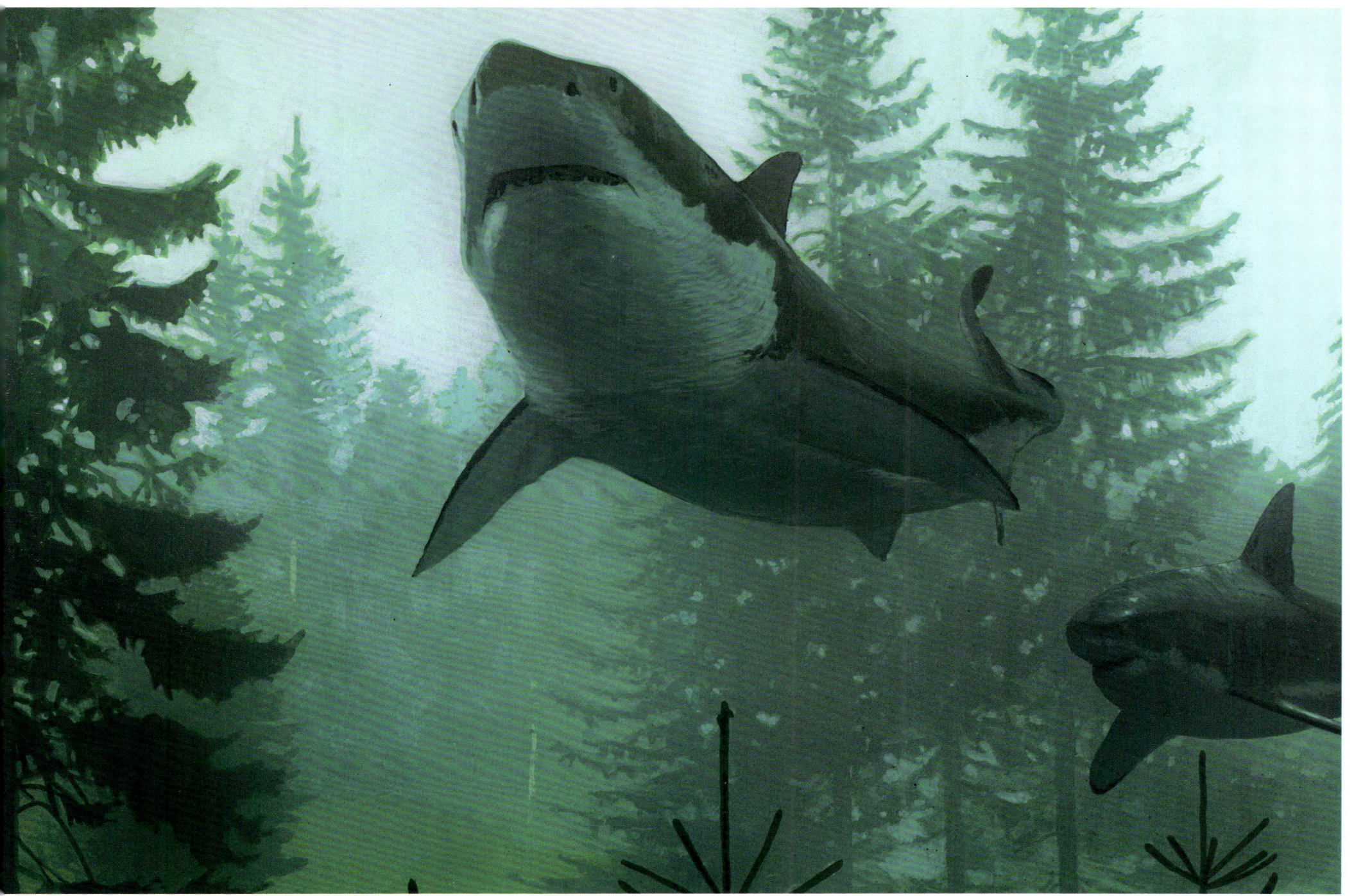

I Woke Up To Find You | 10" x 10" | gouache on wood | 2020

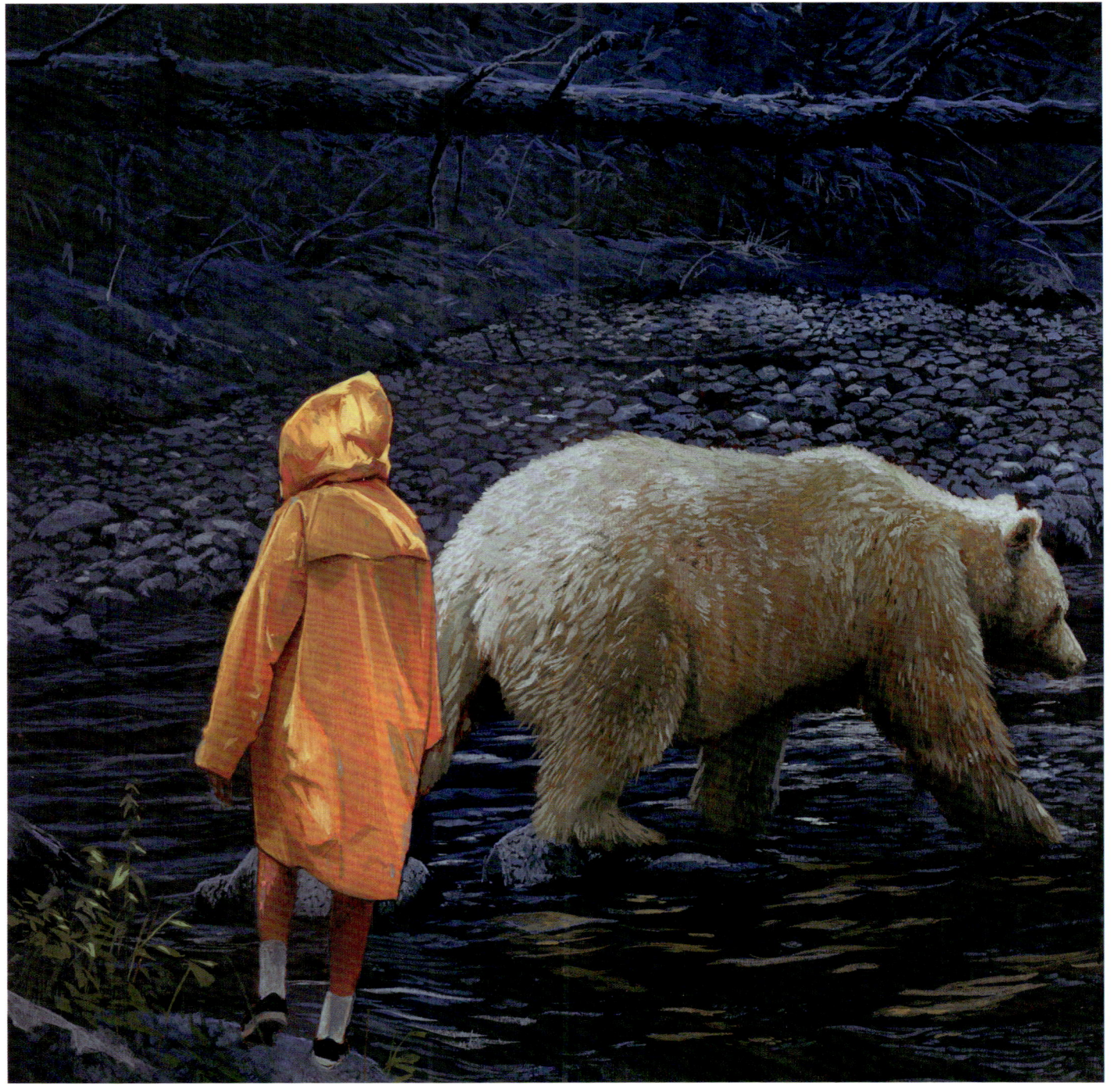

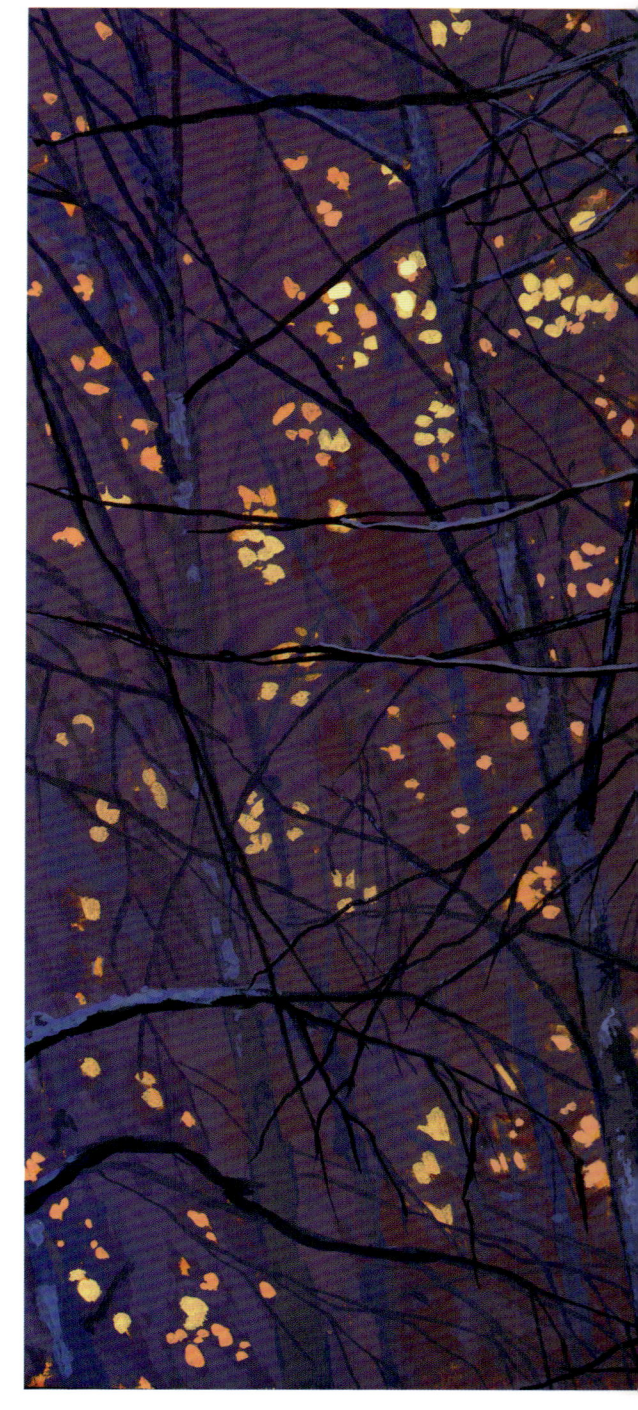

Tell Me Where We Are Going So Fast | 10" x 20" | gouache on wood | 2020

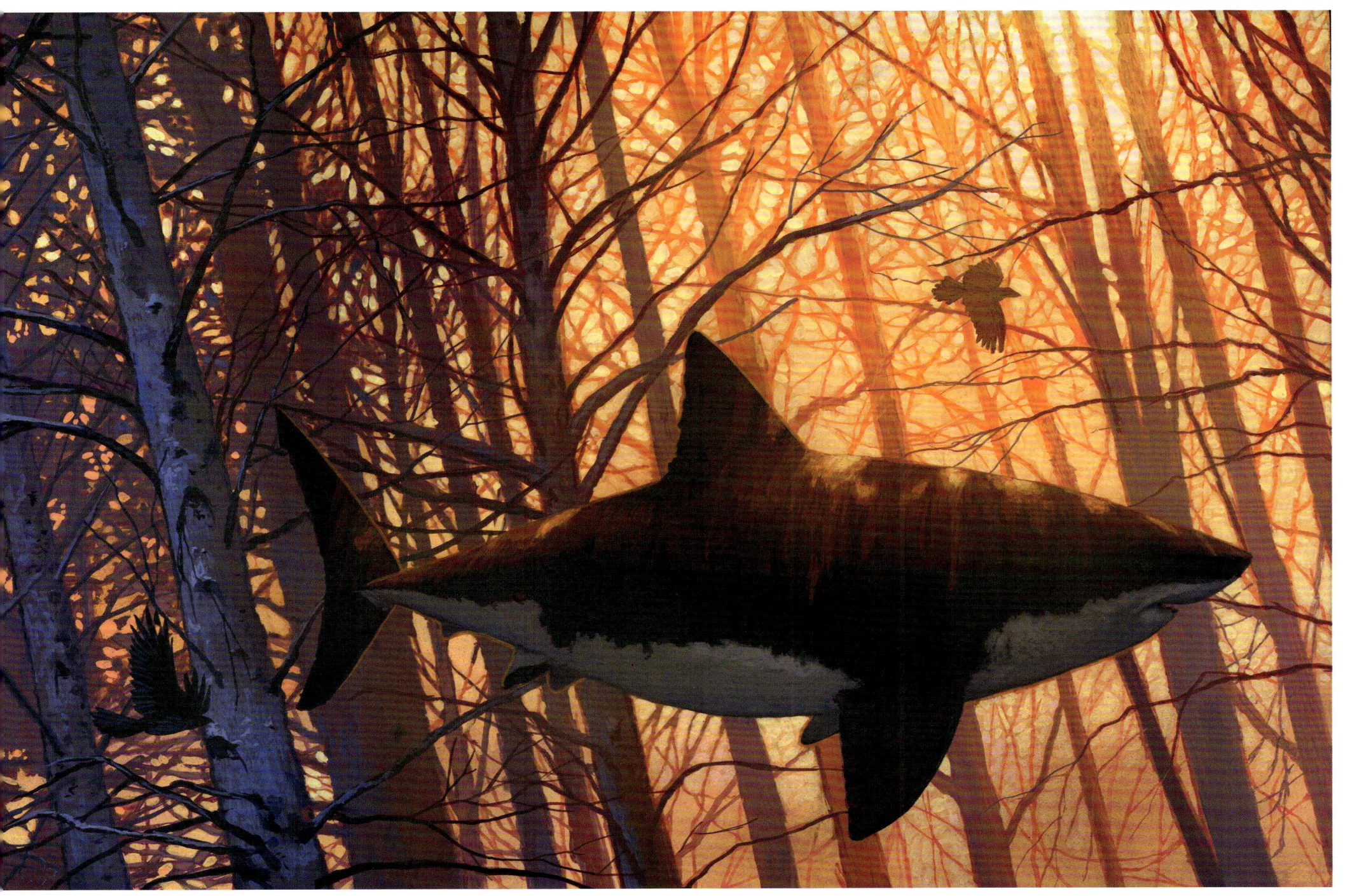

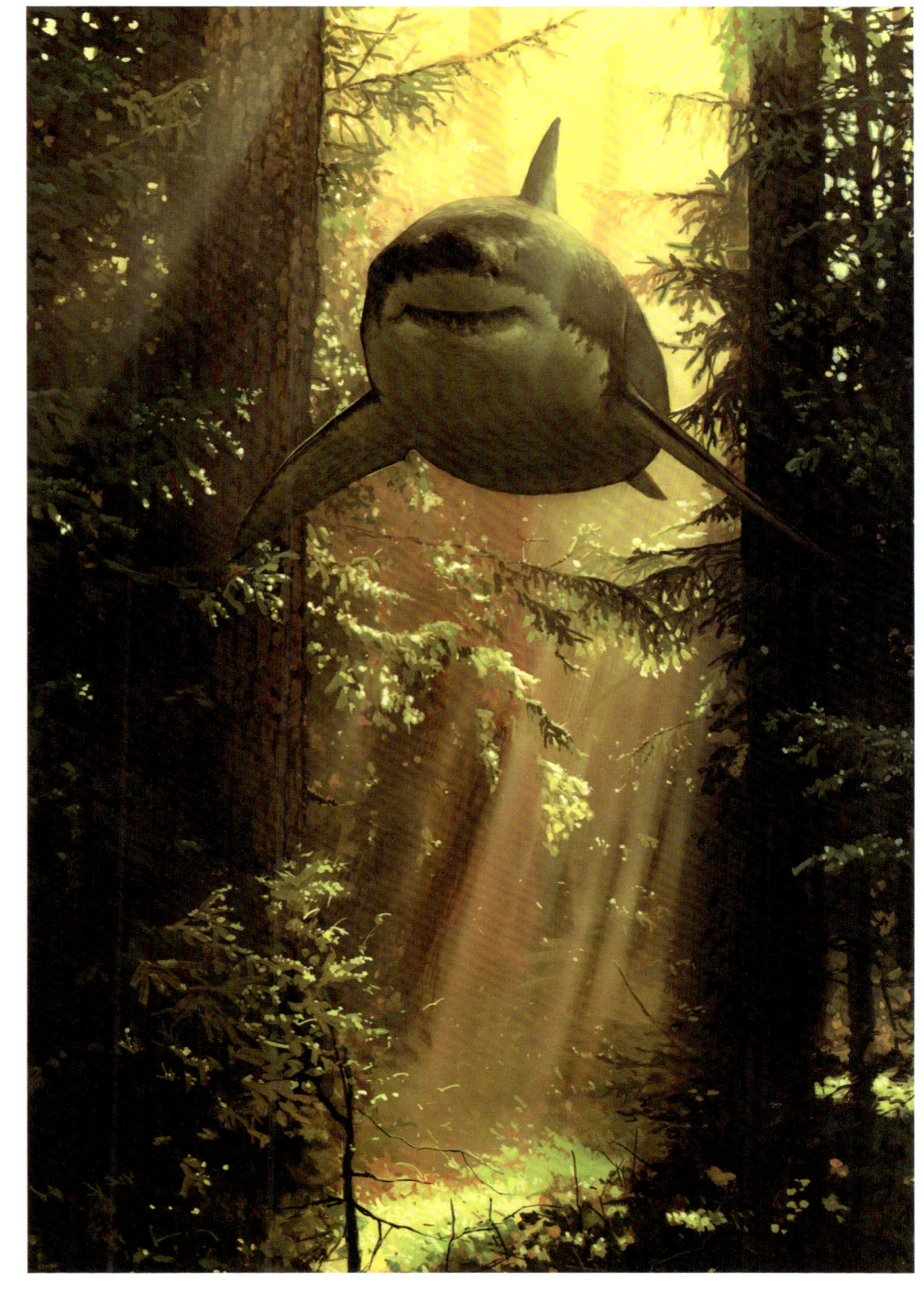

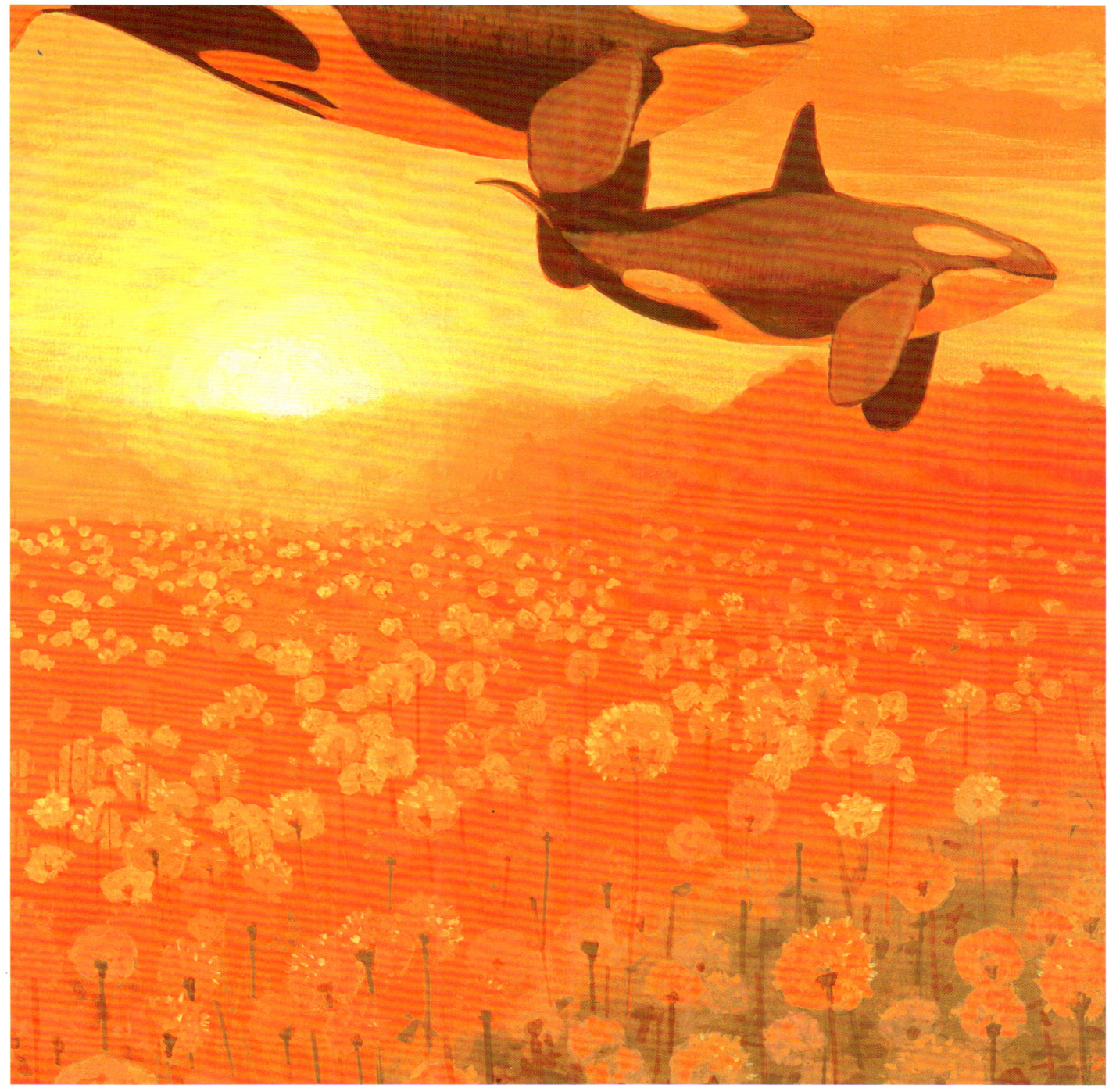

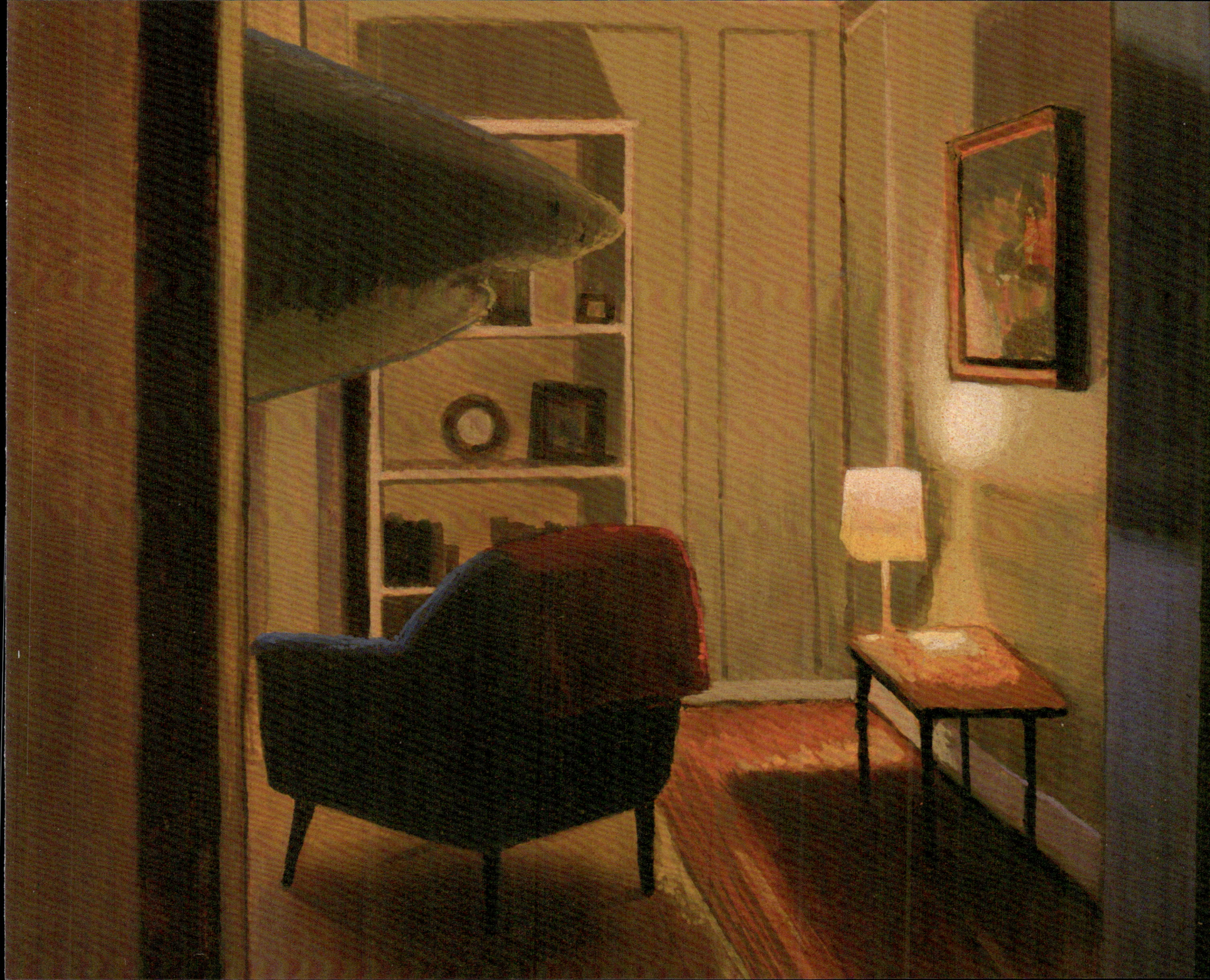

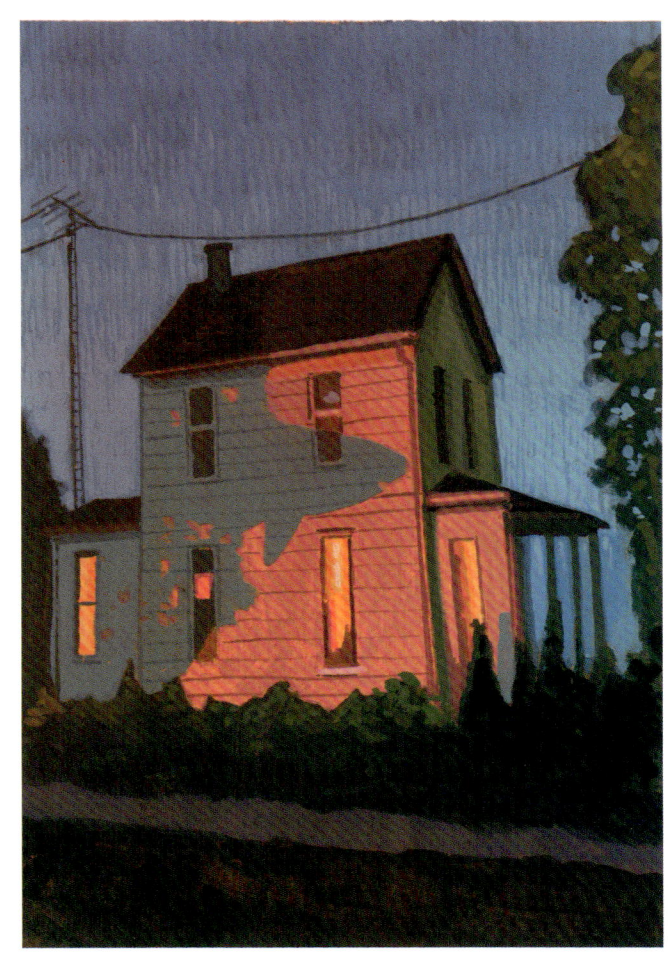

BIOGRAPHY

Chris Austin is a self-taught artist from Kitchener, Ontario, known for his surreal wildlife-inspired artwork that blends contrasting environments and species to explore themes of interconnectedness, adaptability, and personal growth. Influenced by bold colors, pop culture, skateboarding culture, and his love of the outdoors, Austin's art reflects the dualities he experienced in his own life, from moments of chaos to clarity. His work is both playful and introspective, using animals and nature as metaphors for his internal struggles and journey toward self-discovery. Austin's deep connection to his friendships and personal experiences serves as a driving force in his art, where each piece becomes a visual representation of resilience, transformation, and the unexpected connections that shape us.

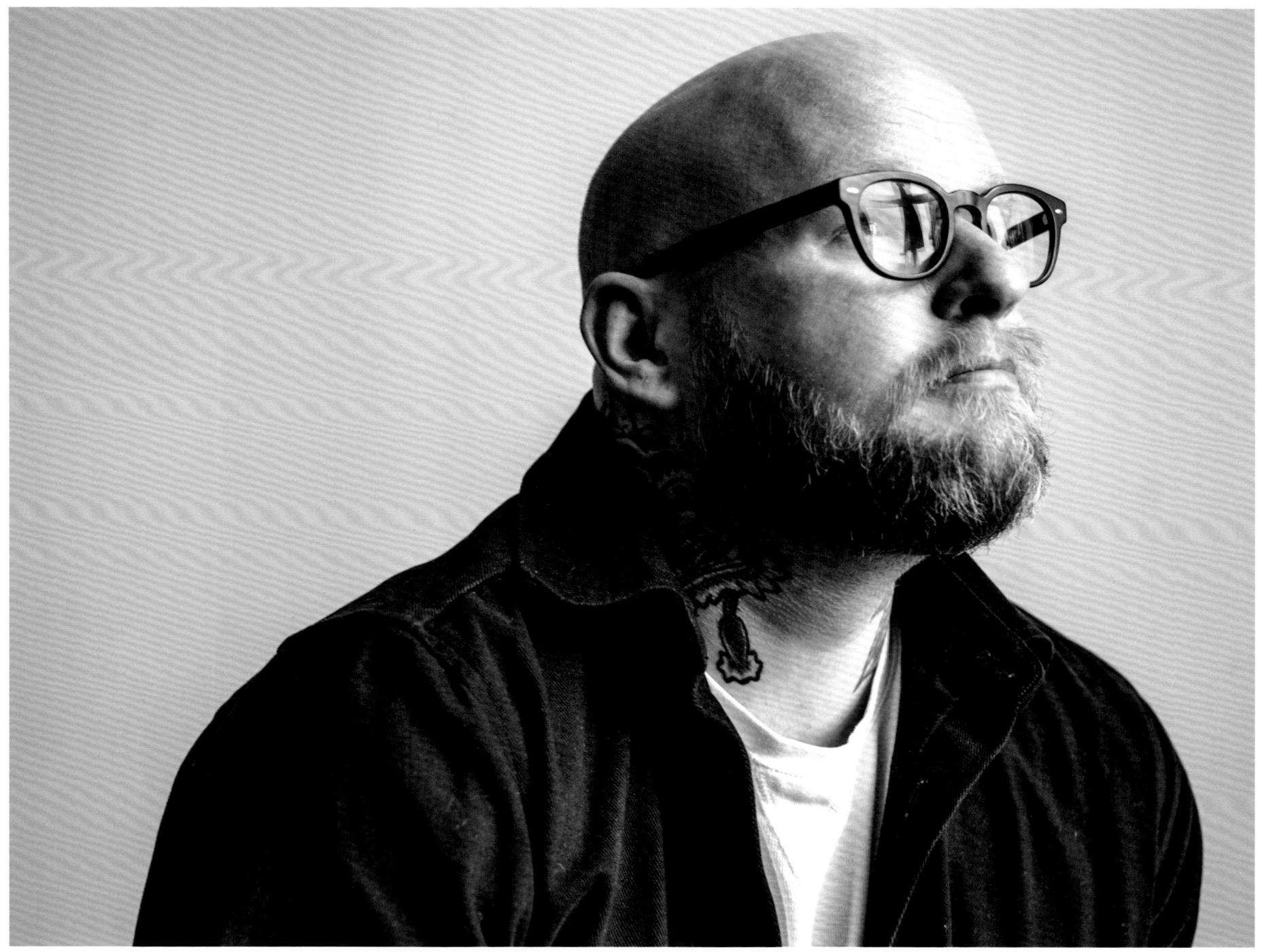

COLOPHON

CONTRASTS
The Art of Chris Austin

First Printing
June 2025
2000 copies
ISBN: 978-1-952251-40-5

Paragon Books
929 Camelia Street
Berkeley, CA 94710-1419
paragon-books.com

Publisher: Ken Hashimoto Harman

Design & Layout: Shaun Roberts

The text was composed using Avenir designed by Herb Lubalin, Tom Carnase, and Ed Benguiat.

Designed in Oakland, California
Printed in China

$50.00
ISBN 978-1-952251-40-5
55000>

9 781952 251405